I am impressionable enough to be flattered by the intimacy of this stranger on the Nile train, and to be entrusted with a secret by a holy man. The Coptic Bishop is wise enough to play me like a fiddle. In return for his intimacy, he exacts a promise.

"On your journey, you would like to see the future, then?" he asks, pulling gently on the thread he's created between us.

Of course I do. Secretly, don't we all? I pause, for I sense a sly conundrum, and nod out of curiosity of where the game is going.

"Then you must make this dying man a promise," he advances.

A pact with the devil? Have I been completely charmed by this old trickster in black robes?

I nod.

"Promise me you will return one day," he says slowly, staring me in the eyes. "Then will you see the future."

I'm slightly mystified by the extra care he's taking with his words.

"Why not today?" I ask. I'm not so sure about the future. If it looks good, however, I might stick around.

He thinks about it.

"When you return," he says. "But not today."

"Sure," I say. But I don't expect to survive the desert oasis.

"Good," is all he says, but with the finality of a deal struck. I've made a promise to a dying man, and damn, he is going to keep me to it.

men in Black Dresses

A Quest for the Future Among Wisdom-Makers of the Middle East

Yvonne Seng, Ph.D.

paraview pocket Books

New York London Toronto Sydney Singapore

An *Original* Publication of PARAVIEW POCKET BOOKS

PARAVIEW
191 Seventh Avenue, New York, NY 10011

POCKET BOOKS, a division of Simon & Schuster, Inc.
1230 Avenue of the Americas, New York, NY 10020

Copyright © 2003 by Yvonne J. Seng

ISBN: 0-7434-7726-X

First Paraview Pocket Books trade paperback edition November 2003

10   9   8   7   6   5   4   3   2   1

POCKET and colophon are registered trademarks of
Simon & Schuster, Inc.

Manufactured in the United States of America

For information regarding special discounts for bulk purchases,
please contact Simon & Schuster Special Sales at 1-800-456-6798
or business@simonandschuster.com

For my nieces, Kylie, Alissa, and Renee

contents

egypt

turkey

introduction

Men in black dresses used to scare the bloody hell out of me. The first time I saw one, a priest, in the Australian tropics where I was born and raised, I knew something was up. Even as a child it took a lot to throw me off stride—snakes, spiders, sharks, ballet teacher—but those holy guys got a bead on me.

I'd never seen a man in a dress before, let alone anyone in black, except the immigrant widows. They didn't speak English, so they didn't count back then. No one wore black in the tropics, where we wore as little as possible, except for dress-up occasions when we did The Full Colonial with the white gloves and all the rest.

Strange people, we were, but this man was even stranger. He wore jewelry, a gold cross, when the only man I knew who wore jewelry was Nick the Greek, the local grocer who also wore a lot of aftershave, which this fellow didn't. Nick also wore his shirt wide open over his obscene beer gut, while this guy auto-asphyxiated with a white cloth collar.

Something about the way this stranger addressed my mother, the only redheaded divorcée in shouting distance, made me stand close to her. My mother is not the kind to encourage clinging, nor I to cling, but he aroused a primitive bond against danger. I followed the frigid conversation about attending church, and my mother's rebuff that she saw his face enough at the pub (where she worked part-time as a barmaid) to want to see it one more day, thank you very much, sir. For all my precocious vocabulary it took years to understand that his parting phrase, which sounded something like child-a-sin, was not a Celtic blessing.

Nuns confused me even further. Were they also men? They behaved like them, stern and harsh, wielding the cane like demented Crusaders. They wore heavy black shoes. Some had chin hairs. If they were not men, then why were they so unhappy? Being a Bride of Christ looked a bitch—but don't get me started on marriage. They added the words feral and pagan to my vocabulary.

My first religious vision knocked me dizzy. I was five. A heat wave sizzled the mangoes that fell on the hot, tin roofs and drove our land-loving cattle dogs into the sea. Floundering around in the surf, an apparition staggered up onto the beach, hitching his swimsuit (black) over his belly: the priest, arms outstretched toward me.

I was dumbstruck. Except for the stark whiteness of flesh, the man under the black robe was human just like the rest of us. He was just, well, ordinary.

In punishment for my childish thoughts, however, God sent me my own personal plague of religious men and women to shadow me through life. For my twenty-first birthday in Italy, I got locked in a tomb with skulls and various body parts of medieval monks in some mountaintop cathedral. But fascination overrode repulsion, and my fate was set. Mostly I've met up with them in the Middle East, where I've spent much of my adult life mucking about; in remote oases in Egypt, up minarets, down tombs. Some dead, most alive, a few difficult to tell. God's big laugh came when I ended up doing my doctoral dissertation in the religious archives of Istanbul, surrounded by still more men in black dresses. Some turned out to be wise men in bad drag.

I no longer flinch when I run into one and have come to look forward to their company. They are, like me under my black cocktail dress, imperfect and human. Some of these wise men and women no longer bother with the black robes (just as

Queenslanders have finally given up their oppressive white gloves), and take many forms. They turn up as old storytellers in Syria willing to exchange ancient wisdom for a shared moment or a cigarette. Or desert monks in Egypt joyriding in the back of a pickup truck. Or a Muslim mystic who is a psychiatrist by day and a television commentator by night.

One holy man in particular got under my skin.

I'd met him years ago on the Nile train into Upper Egypt and, with the confidence of strangers who never expect to see each other again, we talked about life and death, and the future. I had been in a slightly suicidal frame of mind—combining a Ph.D. and divorce at the University of Chicago will do that to you—and was stubbornly challenging the whole damn universe as well as my own will to survive. Return to Egypt, he had said, and you will see the future. Promise me, he said, and I promised.

Instead, I tried to climb the greased ladder of academia and pretended to forget the promise. Thirteen years later in Turkey, I clung to that threadbare promise for dear life. In the middle of a hellacious inferno, a mountain and its ancient olive groves roaring around me, burning wild horses screaming through the ravines, life drained to numbness, I remembered the promise, the challenge to return to Egypt. In the face of death, I swore I would live to see the future.

As the ashes cooled around me, a small cinder flared within. The fire had been purposely set to drive the residents out. Land developers. Speculators. Mafia. Nobody knows for sure. The short of it is that someone tried to kill me and every living thing on the mountain. For what? A holiday resort for naked Germans?

No one died in the fire. A miracle, the villagers whispered. God had intervened.

All right, then, I decided. I'll go knock on God's door and ask why this had happened. And if he was busy, I'd talk to his representatives, the men in black dresses.

And I'd seek out the old holy man from the Nile train and show him I was still alive.

It was one of those inexplicably weird events when seemingly unrelated wires burned loose, melded, and reconnected into a new combination.

Return to Egypt, the holy man had challenged, and you will see the future. His words formed a conundrum, a word game that mystics like to play: Return to the land of the past and you'll find the future.

The renewed promise again evaporated once I was back in Washington, caught up in my academic career and the think tank circuit. For a year after the inferno, however, I struggled silently with the words of the old man. The past and the future had melted our flesh together and he could not be shaken off.

Then God did a kick-butt. I woke suddenly in the middle of the night and sat straight up. It was as clear as day. The Light. The Voice. The whole Vision Thing.

Men in Black Dresses, the Voice said.

Yes, of course. The holy men. The mystics.

I got out of bed and started taking dictation.

I'm not good with irrationalities, an expensive education has taken care of that. Chasing the ghost of a holy man wouldn't cut it, so God was smart enough to frame the quest as an intellectual project and present it in memo form, which made it easier for this argumentative committee of one to sign off on. There was no messy discussion of why this was an answer, or even to what: to that unpinnable sense of loss that pervaded my days, the emptiness that dogged my Manolo Blahnick heels.

The project appeared as a whole. Return to Egypt and ask wise and holy men where the hell they think humanity is going. Surely, with their timeless perspective, surviving generations of man-made and natural disaster, they have wisdom to share about our future. Surely, in their isolated desert monasteries and ancient cities, they can explain why someone would set fire to a village and sacrifice life in order to build high-rise tourist villas. Why we—as a planet—value life so little and laugh at murder.

I was sure it had to do with this New World we've entered,

where progress and ancient ways, science and faith, the old and the new, battle for ground. I wanted to hear what wise and holy men had to say about the state of the human soul in this new age of technology.

I also longed for a voice other than the Roman Catholic pope's. I had listened to his mediagenic pronouncements, followed his moratoriums on technology, and knew there had to be other perspectives out there. Perhaps I could help redress the imbalance by seeking out equally inspired spiritual leaders from the ancient cradle of civilization, Syria and Egypt, that gave us the early Church and Sufi mysticism. These fresh voices may even agree with Rome, but I wanted to hear for myself.

These were just peripheral thoughts as I brewed my morning coffee; nothing was written in stone.

Since I was already scheduled to leave for Turkey in a couple of weeks to return to the fire-scarred village for the summer, a side trip was neither unwelcome nor impossible. I checked the calendar and could squeeze three weeks out of it. Twenty-one days. If it worked, it worked. The details were up to God, whose bright idea this seemed, anyway.

Twenty-one days in 1998 to find the future. Twenty-one days to find the old man.

I called a close friend in Cairo to let her know I was coming. She was rarely there this time of year, but this year she was. The first step.

The next morning, I caught my boss at the university, a dashing Syrian scholar, between grading exams. With only five minutes to talk, I went straight to the vision. He smiled, held his calls, shouted to his assistant in the next room to bring the name of a contact in Cairo, another in Damascus, in case I got there, and gave his blessings on this quest, which we both knew was not driven by the mind.

I was out the door.

I had a name, a scrap of worn paper with an address, and a memory. I hoped it was enough.

PART ONE

Egypt

CHAPTER 1

The Nile Train

his is Cairo, Mother of the World, as Egyptians fondly call her. It's 1984. And I'm having trouble with my eyes.

In the Middle East, as in the Mediterranean in general, eyes have a secret language that my university professors never explained. Entire codes hide in the raising of an eyebrow, in the batting of lashes, and in full-frontal eye contact, that stirs up a slurry of self-consciousness and anger inside me. Throughout my life I've always felt different, but that was my internal landscape. Here, I am visibly different; tall and sandy blond, I stand out like a stevedore at a tea party.

Over the past months, I've found myself lowering my own eyes. I haven't seen the sky in weeks. And now that I have for a few short minutes, I'll be damned if I'm going to lower them again.

The old man's eyes on the Nile train, however, are more probing and direct than any I've yet experienced. Rheumy with cataracts, red-rimmed and swollen from decades of desert sand no longer brushed away, they are at once cold and hot, enforcing a distance yet drawing me toward the fire. They take no interest in my hair, my skin, even my own eyes. These are mere externalities.

His eyes drill beneath my damp white shirt, down to somewhere deep inside me. Like a skilled archaeologist, the old man takes a sounding of my soul.

I can't move, but neither do I lower my eyes.

While he fingers my inner depths, I study the smacks of history recorded on his own skin. I meet him inch for inch. His face is distended with gravity like the wax of a molten candle through which God has pushed and pulled his fingers. The once-soft ground of this man's forehead is now graven with the prints of pain and sorrow. Sweat seeps from his sunken cheeks like moisture from the walls of an underground cave and trickles into a long growth of beard that separates head from body, person from person. This gray, barbed hedge says barricade. No small bird would dare mistake it for the cottony nest of Father Christmas.

In the background, a primitive air conditioner cranks into action and the train prepares to move forward. Still we continue our probes. Passengers in the last stages of settling in stuff their luggage overhead and into every available crevice around us, but we don't move. The tea maker rattles his kettle on a butane stove at the end of the corridor and stacks his mountain of small glass cups for when the brew is ready. The family across from us is tucking into their picnic breakfasts, unfurling leaves of fresh bread, unwrapping homemade sandwiches. Pungent smells of white cheese, cucumbers and boiled eggs, fresh tomatoes and olives are being quietly salted into my memory.

I dig for a clue to the old man's identity, his reason for being on the train and bothering me. A thick silver chain with an ornate medallion of the Virgin Mary pulls at his neck. The train lurches forward, thumps the metal sharply against his chest and I imagine that under that dusty black robe, his heart is callused from the weight of his profession.

So this is a holy man, I rationalize, but not a Muslim. A man of God. A Copt, an old monk, perhaps. The Egyptian deserts are riddled with monasteries, some of the world's earliest. Today's descendants of the ancient Copts, Egypt's first Christians, consider themselves the Sons of the Pharaohs, a living and vital link to the past. Predominantly Orthodox, they include a subminority of Catholics and Protestants. I'm not sure and don't care which he is. I just resent his intrusion.

God, I hunger for silence.

The inspection over, he speaks, first in French, then English.

"You will be pleased to sit with me," he says.

Not an invitation or an order, it is a statement of fact. The clucking of passengers, who have been observing us closely, warns me that any protest will be useless and, more than that, unwise. They've determined that I should give up my coveted window seat and sit with the holy man. By the communication of eyes, eyebrows, and a secret garrison of small, loaded gestures, they've taken charge of the next several hours of my life and, given a chance, will gladly take over the rest of it.

The train shuffles south along the Nile, and I gradually relax into the surrender of the journey and the company of my enforced companion. I crane past the holy man's full beard to see the desert villages but he blocks my view. For the first hour or so he is an enraptured etymologist, giving derivations of the village names in Greek, Italian, Coptic and Arabic interspersed with a similar excursion into terms used in the Church.

We pass inland and beyond time, and I become pupil to his teacher. He nods when I correctly answer the questions he poses about the history of the region and pauses to take mental note where I fail.

"Beni-Suweyf," he recites as the train passes through a village south of Cairo. "Do you know the meaning of this name?"

I'm a captive, therefore a wary, audience. He's leading me back to the safety of grade school, which I at first resist as I sense I'm being set up.

The spider at his trap, he pulls information from me about myself and gives none in return. Save that his name is Nuweiba.

My perverse colonial respect for old-timers eventually wins out. Do I know the meaning of Beni-Suweyf, he asks me again.

"Sons of the Sword," I reply, anxious to prove I have learned something during all that bloody self-flagellation in preparation for grad school at the University of Chicago.

"Yes, but do you know why they are called this?" he asks.

I shake my head out of respect. I'm learning that in Egypt, a question often serves as the introduction to a long story and that the richest moments come through listening. Some of the best storytellers, I'm also learning, are tricksters.

The old man doesn't bother to wait for a reply.

"They were given this title in the old days for their bravery in fighting," Nuweiba says and begins to pull me forward into the adventure of the past.

He rolls the coral of his rosary through his fingers as he recites the names of villages and towns like Hail Marys on that mystical string. From time to time he mops his face with the folded white handkerchief he pulls from the internal pocket of his dark robe. An unfortunate young man in an adjacent seat turns on a transistor radio but quickly shuts off the joyful crowing of a balladeer when met with the elder's scowl. The carriage moves forward in respectful hush commanded by the holy man's presence.

By midmorning the sun pierces the metal of the train carriage with no more resistance than a knife against a rusting can. Passengers lie slumped in their seats like deflatable dolls, their collars unbuttoned, moving one hand occasionally to fan themselves with wilted, humid newspapers.

We continue southward to the lulling motion of the train and the hypnotic click of the old man's prayer beads. His recitation of villages gradually slows.

Mallawi. . . .

Manfalut. . . .

The rest of the train is asleep, but we continue talking.

Nuweiba has assumed I am continuing on to that great tourist trek from Asyout to Luxor or Abu Simbel to see the monuments of the Pharaohs. I tell him, rather smugly, that the desert oasis is my destination.

He pauses.

We listen to the train track's hypnotic clack.

"On your own?" he finally asks. "Are you not afraid?"

One of the cardinal rules for women traveling alone is never—never—admit you're traveling alone. Always have someone meeting you at the station, an imaginary friend of a friend of the family. I can't be bothered with the lies anymore. I'm tired of manufacturing a happy nuclear family. I carry photos of my sister's children, selling them off as my own. I offer my wedding ring as false evidence of a glowing eight-year marriage.

The back of my shirt is stuck to the seat. Sweat trails down my calf.

"Afraid?" I reply. "Of what?"

He doesn't answer, but watches my steady flush. I've let my guard down and he's seen it.

Growing up in Australia, I didn't have to hop a train to find excitement. Our sprawling house in the tropics was built on stilts to catch the occasional breeze and the underhouse breezeway served as a cool place of banishment and solitude for an introspective child. In the long, rainy season, however, my refuge became a tribal meeting ground for a rite of passage.

When we siblings and cousins had exhausted the twenty-year supply of *National Geographic,* had grown tired of chasing each other around the sweeping, rain-soaked verandahs and disintegrated into warfare, my mother would appear in the doorway of the kitchen, where she had barricaded herself with her sister and a few gin fizzes. She would place one hand on her generous hip and point the other toward Hell.

"Go. Now," she would say with that calm authority she used with the cattle dogs, a couple of which were quartered below in the breezeway. "Go. Now. Go to Hell."

We were free.

For hours, as the drumming rain formed red-clay islands under the house, we were masters of our own antipodes. Occasionally a snake would float by in the runoff. If it were dead, it would become another prop in our games of *Robinson Crusoe, Swiss Family Robinson,* or the abridged version of *Lord of the Flies.* If alive, we'd step back with respect.

In this netherworld of restless children, our favorite game by far was "Spider," the Australian version of "Chicken." We'd hold our young sunburned hands above the nests of the venomous funnel-web and trap-door spiders to test our reflexes. If bitten, you had minutes before a particularly nasty death, and with no casualties so far, the odds rose with the water level. That was only the beginning. That's where boys became useful.

There were always older cousins or neighbors in some corner under the house gawking at a purloined copy of *Playboy* or attempting to smoke cigarettes made from rolled up newspaper or sugarcane leaves. At the peak of concentration, just before the spiders were wagered to leap at you, one of the boys would sneak up behind you and place a hand on your shoulder. You knew he was going to do it, but just not when.

You were never to scream.

Go bug-eyed, yes, but never scream.

That was part of the game, the fear of the half-known, the half-anticipated—the spider's leap versus the hand on the shoulder—as was the betting on the side. From upstairs, we could hear the laughter of our mothers and knew they were telling those grown-up stories that we never quite understood. Life was pretty good when you lived on the edge of a small world.

I'm now heading to a dot on the map you need a magnifying glass to read. I'm going to test the spider. I want that surge of adrenaline I felt as a child just to prove I'm still alive. My world is now larger, but the horizon is smaller.

My pretext for going to the oasis is to retrace the steps of a turn-of-the-century archaeologist, whose field notes I stumbled on while doing research at the Smithsonian. Buy me another drink and I'll tell you the truth. I'm going because I've been told I shouldn't. It's dangerous for a girl. Perfect. I'm going there to check my ability to survive alone again and to test my will to live.

At this point in my life, it's divorce or suicide. Perhaps I exaggerate, but not much.

I'm not going to explain to the holy man on the Nile train about my childhood game of challenging the spiders. Neither am I going to tell him about the promise I made last year to the archaeologist's ghost after finding his yellowed field notes. About his fears of a disappearing world. Nuweiba is part of that world, and I am suddenly ashamed.

"Not particularly," I finally reply to his silence. "Why? Should I be afraid?"

The isolated oasis has its own laws, he explains, and can even be dangerous for a woman traveling alone.

In the days of the Pharaohs, it was a magical holding cell for their souls, halfway to the next world, before they became gods. Under Persian and Greek rule and well into the Christian era it was a bloody prison outpost, and until recent history, African slaves were castrated there and cauterized in the broiling sands. It sounds just fine.

I shrug. I appear impudent, I know, but the last thing I want is someone trying to interfere with my life. The next to last thing is another bloody lecture.

Instead of a lecture, however, the old man hits his fingertips together for emphasis, forms them into a tent, a pyramid, and begins to drive the wedge into the barrier I am quickly throwing up between us.

"So. That explains it. So you are going on a journey. A pilgrimage," he says like a bad fortune-teller. "Or are you planning to test fate?"

I don't reply. Save me. Surely I'm not that transparent.

"Then we should talk," he answers my silence.

He raises the palm of his hand toward me, whether in blessing or to stem my resistance, isn't important. Again, it is not a command, but a statement of fact. He turns immediately to the subject of religion, or rather, the soul I'm about to expose to fate like some bare-breasted pagan to the sun. Again, I guard my answers.

There is a story in my family, apocryphal, I'm sure. Once, as a child, when I'd been thrown out of school, I hurried home to my mother.

"Mum, am I a bloody little pagan?" I asked.

"Why, dear?" she responded.

"Because that's what the headmistress says I am," I replied.

I am told my mother didn't miss a beat but replied, straight-faced.

"No, child," she said. "You're not a pagan. You're just feral."

This I don't relate to the old man, but the memory makes me laugh and I begin to relax. Once we settle that I'm Christian, but not Catholic, the subject of my soul is no longer a pressing concern. That is, I'm within the fold and that's all that matters. There is no lecture.

To be an agnostic or an atheist, not to believe in a Greater Being outside (or carried inside) one's self, is for most in the Middle East an unnatural act. It means that you are alone and do not belong to a group, that you are without guidance from the wise ones, and therefore you suffer. The concept of a moral compass is strong here, an ancient compass that's calibrated with the poles of the community, its elders, and the wisdom of history they pass down.

On his part, the old man reveals that he is a humble member of the Catholic Coptic Church, from the diocese of Asyout. Nothing more. Nuweiba is insisting on his mysteries.

We resettle into our grudging companionship and solitary thoughts. We drift off into sleep, woken hours later by the tea-maker rattling through the carriage with his tray of hot tea.

Gray and ill-tempered, ripped from unsatisfying sleep, Nuweiba dips the end of a sugar cube into his glass of tea and watches it dissolve.

His black eyes latch onto mine as he sips the scalding tea.

"I have a secret," he finally says.

I don't answer. We all have secrets.

"A secret," he repeats, and concentrates his gaze on my face. "I am going to die."

He drops the remainder of the sugar cube into his tea and stirs it.

Why is he telling me this? We are all going to die; it's inevitable. In the last flush of extended youth, I'm more willing to lock horns in a challenge with death than to undergo the slow degradation of aging.

He looks past me, and quietly repeats: "I'm going home to die. This is my secret."

He isn't speaking to me; he's saying the words out loud to a stranger so he can hear them himself, perhaps for the first time. He's savoring them. The words, like the intimacies and addresses exchanged between strangers, are meant to fade at journey's end.

He has diabetes and the doctors say there is nothing they can do. He's just been to Cairo for prayers, twenty-two days in Cairo, and is returning home to die. Nobody else knows yet.

We both turn away and sink back into our own thoughts. He doesn't expect a reply and there is nothing I know how to say.

I am impressionable enough, however, to be flattered by the intimacy of this stranger, and to be entrusted with a secret by a holy man. He is wise enough to play me like a fiddle. In return for his intimacy, he exacts a promise.

"On your journey, you would like to see the future, then?" he asks, pulling gently on the thread he's created between us.

Of course I do. Secretly, don't we all? I pause, for I sense a sly conundrum, and nod out of curiosity of where the game is going.

"Then you must make this dying man a promise," he advances.

A pact with the devil? Have I been completely charmed by this old trickster in black robes?

I nod.

"Promise me you will return one day," he says slowly, staring me in the eyes. "Then will you see the future."

I'm slightly mystified by the extra care he's taking with his words.

"Why not today?" I ask. I'm not so sure about the future. If it looks good, however, I might stick around.

He thinks about it.

"When you return," he says. "But not today."

"Sure," I say. But I don't expect to survive the desert oasis.

"Good," is all he says, but with the finality of a deal struck. I've made a promise to a dying man, and damn, he is going to keep me to it.

I admit that I feel slightly manipulated, for he must know he's planted the seed of a dare, or challenge, I'd rise to. He knows, after all, about the game of spiders.

I add that promise to the one I made the previous year after reading the archaeologist's journal in the basement of the museum. That promise has led me to the train ride with the old man. I'm fast becoming an irretrievable link in a chain of good intentions.

As the Nile train approaches Asyout, a black-robed priest, who has been sitting nearby, comes forward to attend the elder. He hands the holy man a towering black hat and arranges its long veil as he helps him stand. From under the seat the attendant retrieves an ornate stave, its head decorated with silver, and places it in the elder's hand, which he then kisses.

The transformation complete, my traveling companion steps past me, without acknowledging my presence. He has become a magician. I no longer exist.

As the priest leads him down the aisle, strangers press forward to kiss the old man's hand. Their eyes are fixed on his, pleading for answers to their unspoken troubles. Some bow and try to touch or kiss the hem of his long dusty gown, others begin to cry, but he dismisses them, telling them coldly to stand. To have dignity. I catch the anger that flashes in his eyes and I'm chilled by the change in the holy man.

He walks past them toward a crowd of black-robed monks and priests who are waiting to claim him with unrestrained affection. He, in turn, is detached. He no longer belongs here. Like the ancients of the desert oasis to which I am going, he has already begun his journey to another world.

The dying old man is the venerable Bishop Nuweiba, the Catholic Coptic Bishop of Asyout and Upper Egypt. This is the beginning of Egypt's own Time of Troubles in which Islamic extremists are targeting Copts, Egypt's Christians, as agents of the West. This is part of the fallout of the Iranian Revolution. The responsibility for his community and the political interests of the Egyptian government are only two of the furrows engraved into his brow.

On the platform Bishop Nuweiba stops and glances over his shoulder. I'm standing near the train with my duffel and camera bags, watching the crowd disperse. He nods with some annoyance that he has to tell me to follow. Not an invitation or command, but a statement of fact. I am to have lunch with him and the monks at the cathedral before I head by bus into the desert.

Like a forgotten child, I am oddly pleased. Perhaps I'll keep my promise after all.

CHAPTER 2

naked in cairo

Leyla* whips me through customs at Cairo International Airport with an efficiency that makes my ears hum. I'm also spinning from time warp. Fourteen years ago I left Egypt, a disheveled graduate student in faded jeans, as sick as a dog with summer flu. Now look at me, groomed and buffed. And a private car and driver awaiting. Yeah, I look good on paper.

Leyla's office floats high above the Nile, a magic carpet of subsidized glass and steel. A hundred years ago, the land below belonged to her grandfather, a distinguished scholar of the old ruling class. As a child, she fed her grandfather's cats and took her lessons in the gardens the government confiscated in the fifties to build the skyscraper in which she, a top executive, now commands a view from the top, a view suspended above a young girl's dream.

We gaze at the expanding universe below like shell-shocked angels. Somewhere in all that sand is the answer to the holy man's challenge: Return to Egypt and you will see the future. And somewhere out there, between the Sphinx and the towering skyscrapers, are wise men who could tell us the lessons of history to guide us into that future.

When the first Arab general came to Egypt fourteen hundred years ago to conquer it in the name of Islam, he ran into a few problems. Not the Egyptians. The remnant sons and daughters of the Pharaohs, accustomed to invaders, accepted the passage of rulers as they did the inundation of the Nile. The problem was geography: There were no signposts to tell the new conqueror exactly where the shifting sands of the desert ended and the ethereal land of Egypt began.

From my vantage, treading in new territory, searching for mystics, I'm suffering a similar disorientation. I'm chasing an invisible path on a nonexistent map.

While I puzzle what the bloody hell I'm doing here, a vivid sunset feeds on the industrial pollution and outdoes the flaming jacarandas that line the wide boulevards into the city. On the far outskirts of Cairo, planned cities stretch into the desert, some already established, others just grids of roads and water pipes being laid in preparation for the expanding population. The population has almost doubled since my visit fourteen years ago.

"Your list, dear," Leyla interrupts my reverie. "Do you have your list?"

The question is unnecessary, but it is Leyla's way of zeroing in on my plans and reminding me that time is wasting, a very un-Egyptian concept. In the West, time is money. Here, amortized over eternity, time means nothing.

Right. I'm tracking. I have my list. I doodled it as the plane landed just over an hour ago, partly because I knew Leyla would expect one. Mostly because I have no idea what I'm doing, and writing a list gives me a semblance of control over the jackass scheme I'm off on.

So far, everything has fallen into place, including being bumped to first class, a miracle in itself. But my leads are thin: I have a name and a memory. Professor Abdul Aziz Said, my boss at the university, has given me a contact, a leading Sufi mystic in Egypt, and on a slip of worn paper tucked into my satchel is the address of the old bishop in Upper Egypt.

And here in Cairo I also have Leyla, a friend from Washington, who is tapping her well-shod foot.

"My list?" I say, turning to the Egyptian dynamo beside me. "Right. Got it."

I rattle it off.

Priority. Find the Catholic Coptic Bishop of Asyout, that is, the bishop on the Nile train from fourteen years ago. I'll not accept Bishop Nuweiba is dead until I can buy his relics in the marketplace.

Contact my boss's mystery friend, the Sufi mystic, and see if he will introduce me to some mystics willing to talk to a Western scholar.

Arrange to stay with the monks in the Sinai. Or one of the monasteries in the Eastern Desert. They've been around a couple of thousand years, minus a century or two, and should have it right by now.

Check out some young Copts, sons and daughters of the Pharaohs and Egypt's first Christians, and see how they're dealing with the future. . . .

Finally, give Leyla the slip. Only, this one I don't tell her. I have little chance of getting the kind of open interviews I want if there's any suspicion that a government official is helping me, even informally and even with the best intentions.

A side glance at my friend confirms that this will be a friendly struggle of wills. She has already waived aside my attempt to stay at a hotel, thus stanching my independence with the gauze of hospitality.

Leyla's driver waits below, the motor running.

From the new winding flyovers and highways, Cairo is almost unrecognizable from the memories of my last encounter. Only the heat remains the same. It's 42 degrees Celsius, that's approximately 120 degrees Fahrenheit, and the greatest contribution of the West to the East, the car air conditioner, is having a hard time of it.

At this time of day the traffic moves relatively smoothly. Cars are no longer of a vintage held together by a prayer and a rubber band, the streets are cleaned by uniformed workers, the shops filled with consumer goods and imports. Subways and railways now connect the outer limits with the city, so that a trip, which, little more than a decade ago, took hours by overcrowded bus, is greatly reduced. Light industry and businesses are moving to the desert towns. The mountain is finally coming to Muhammad.

The street culture has also changed but I can't quite put my finger on it. People look taller and healthier. Younger, that is, more youthful. Not only has the population almost doubled since I was last here, but sixty percent is under thirty years of age. I pose myself useful questions I will be expected to answer when I return to the Washington cocktail circuit after the summer.

I ask myself if the street optimism I perceive is a result of internationalization, of foreign aid and development, of outside investment, of growing identification of Egypt as marketplace, as both commodity and consumer? Or is youthfulness alone enough to explain the unusual energy in what even the Cairenes admit is a heat wave? I make a mental note to get some stats before I leave, but meanwhile I rely on my own observations.

Downtown, for example, the Hilton is now dwarfed by more, taller and glitzier hotels and buildings that buzz with international chic and cater to upscale tourism. Even the Egyptian Museum, the grande dame of archaeological intrigue that dominated Tahrir Square, is now wrapped by raised highways like a work by Christo. This is now a modern city that caters to the past. Mother Egypt's had a face job, but I suspect the old body under the robe is still sagging.

I see my first of many McDonald's, then Pizza Hut, Wimpy's and KFC. The Marlboro Man stares down at me from every corner and the only camels I see are in cigarette ads. Coca-Cola signs begin to glow on the skyline, replacing the sunset but so, too, do trademarks for computer companies and air conditioners, evidence of a different kind of opening to the world. Among this skyline of Babel, a few distinctive Arabic signs for locally owned industries shine proudly. Directly across the river a curvaceous neon sign in Arabic proudly advertises the success of Bim-Bim, an Egyptian owned company whose cookie ads bombard you from every television, radio, bus and billboard.

As we near the upper-middle-class enclave where I will be staying, display is ostentatious. I know better than to take what I see as the norm: The disparity between rich and poor is a well-known and widening gap in Egypt. The other side of the Nile, where I rented a room as a graduate student, was never like this, but the comparison is moot, for neither Cairo nor I am the same. I smooth the creases from the legs of my designer safari suit and remind myself that fourteen years was a lifetime ago.

Still, I am impressed. This is Cairo, Mother of the World, and she welcomes me home. For an old lady, she's got one hell of a grip.

Hussein,* Leyla's husband, also welcomes me with exuberance and warmth. At ten o'clock, they give me a refresher course on the Mediterranean concept of time. I'm ready for bed. My hosts are ready to go out for dinner in celebration of my return.

A cool breeze floats off the Nile and lifts the white tablecloths at the private club. The patrons are lively yet restrained, sporting understated dress, an indicator of class, picked up on their assignments in Europe. They laugh openly, as Egyptians do, and kiss and hug each new arrival, male or female. Charming old men kiss my hand as Leyla and Hussein introduce me and toast my welcome across a sea of fluttering white tablecloths.

Hospitality in Egypt is an engulfing experience.

"Welcome in Egypt," the locals say, from taxi driver to greengrocer. Here in the club, however, an invisible cordon keeps those kinds of locals at a distance.

Outside the cordon, families and friends walk hand in hand on the twinkle-lit bridges and concourse, taking the summer air. Flower sellers are hawking jasmine braids. Taxis honk. The voices of Lebanese pop stars ululate from mobile stands doing a brisk business in pirated tapes. River traffic skits maniacally across the water. Curious boatloads of tourists with coarse American laughs edge too close to the club, trying to see how the Other Half lives, and are shushed away by waiters brandishing white cloth napkins. They leave us in a jolly fart of diesel fumes and raucous belly dancing music, which we all try to ignore.

I'm just taking it all in, smiling deliriously, hanging on to the tail of a daydream. Fourteen years ago, this club was not part of my world. I was one of the curious, looking in, wondering who all those Powerful People were drinking cocktails by the Nile. From any perspective, the Nile on a midsummer's night is intoxicating.

Hussein orders plateloads of fish and grilled vegetables, which we devour between stories and reminiscences. Our conversation flows from technology to mystics. He is the reflective side of his wife. Returning to Egypt after several years in the United States, he made a vow that if God would help him find his first engineering project that would use his training to benefit the community, he would relinquish the profit from it. This would be his gift of thanks to Egypt.

He tells me about an old Coptic mystic, Matta al-Maskin, or Matthew the Poor, who's using the technology of the Pharaohs to make a desert monastery self-sustaining. I'd read a brief article about him a few months earlier, was intrigued, but tucked the information away behind a billion, more urgent, pieces. My new ATM password, for example, or the code to the department copying machine.

The hovering waiter brings dessert.

"What are your plans?" Hussein asks, catching me with a mouth stuffed with pastry.

"She has her list," Leyla answers on my behalf as I chew and swallow, and stall for time.

Hussein grins. He knows Leyla's lists well. And that I pad mine, as does he.

"Yes, I have a list," I reply, sheepishly. I recite it for him. He remains silent.

"What about your wish list. You will have a wish list," he says. "If you could have a conversation with anyone, who would it be?"

I hate this type of question and draw crosses in the condensation of my water glass while I consider my answer.

"Your man in the desert, for one," I reply, extending the crosses in the condensation until my glass begins to look like a chalice.

He nods. Leyla nods, but less enthusiastically.

"Matta the Poor?" she asks. She explains that this may not be possible, that the Desert Father is elderly and ill, and could die tomorrow. And that the monastery is too far away and under high security because of the threats of Islamist extremists.

I snort quietly.

Hussein chuckles.

"More reason she will want to go."

Enchantment is Egypt's snare and I succumb. Spend your days trying to conform Egypt to your reality, and you'll end up wasted. But make a wish, or spin a daydream, and watch it unfold.

"Okay, then," I say. "The Grand Sheikh of Islam."

The look on Leyla's face is enough to tell me I'm insane. I'm honestly not sure why he sprang to mind. The Grand Sheikh at Al-Azhar is a spiritual and intellectual guide of the world's billion Sunni Muslims. He doesn't do interviews.

Hussein takes my answer in stride.

"Your plan?" he prompts.

I roll my eyes, suggesting I'm not serious, but he doesn't buy it.

"How do you plan to get these interviews?" he asks. "With the Grand Sheikh, with the Master of the Desert?"

I'm now silent. A rowboat passes close by and the Nile laps against the concourse. Leyla is making fond *tccching* sounds to discourage our foolishness.

"Okay. Look," I say. With Leyla and Hussein there is no need for me to be a defensive academic. "I don't know what the hell I'm supposed to be doing. But I know I'm supposed to be here. I know I can't get to them directly, but there's a way. A path. I have to step onto that path."

Hussein and I exchange glances. I've already stepped onto the path. I close my eyes.

"There's someone along the path," I continue, "who will take me to the next person, who will lead me to the next person. I have only to find that first person, or they find me, I don't know. But one step then another, I'll move closer, and I'll reach the door. Eventually."

"You believe this?" he asks, softly.

Leyla is holding her breath, and in the silence, inside her head, I hear the whirring of schedules and timetables, plans and orders.

"There is no other way," I reply.

Two weeks, I have two weeks. Broken by a week in Syria for which I booked a ticket. Twenty-one days total. The hubris of my quest overshadows its enormity. By trying to force it to happen, I'll be lucky if I get to talk to a choirboy, let alone the Grand Sheikh or a famed Desert Father.

If this is to happen, there can be no other way. I have to let it happen.

"And then?" Hussein asks, drawing me back into the game. I open my eyes.

"And then?" I repeat. I'm slightly pissed with his insistence. "And then it's up to me to knock, isn't it?"

"Good girl," Hussein says. From anyone else I would take this affection as condescension and bloody his nose. But this is Hussein and it's no fun punching out a pacifist.

At two, my hosts are ready to sleep, but sleep is now far from my mind. Excitement and talk have revived me. I have entered another world.

I dial directory assistance—hoping the lines are free at this time—and ask for the number of the Catholic cathedral in Asyout. Asyout is way out of the assistant's directory and she can't connect me, but after the participation of several other assistants, she comes up with the numbers of two of the five Catholic churches in Cairo. We all repeat the numbers back and forth in Arabic until I'm thoroughly confused.

In the apartment, Leyla pads about in her insomnia, opening and closing doors, talking with ghosts.

I reach for the phone again to dial the Catholic churches, but realize it's the middle of the night. Even in the house of God. Damn. I'll have to contain myself until morning.

CHAPTER 3

sufi shrink

I've never had to search for holy men before. I just sat still and they appeared. But unlike now, I wasn't looking. The room remains empty.

Leyla has sequestered me in the corner of her glass tower while she's in strategy meetings down the hall. I have a phone in one hand and an endless supply of hot tea in the other. My list stares back at me, a blank slate.

My felt-tip gives out mid-doodle. I remove my glasses and squeeze the ache from the bridge of my nose. During the last two hours, my list has grown sideways without moving forward, a fat lady snoring on a park bench.

Scrounging around in my satchel for a fresh pen, my fingers nudge a small, forgotten package I shoved in with my university mail to read on the flight. A thank-you present from a doctoral student who'd just won a grant. Inside the box is a small glass paperweight with floating orange-red dots. I put on my glasses and take it over to the plate glass windows where I turn it over and around in the light.

The orange dots have black dots on them. And wings and feet. A score of ladybugs hang suspended among the frozen air bubbles. What warped mind conceived this? I turn it over. Made in China.

"Ladybug, Ladybug fly away home," I whisper, reflexively, at this macabre still life.

The rhyme carries the mixed signals of childhood, of a good deed, of pending disaster.

"Your house is on fire, your children . . . alone."

I flash on the fire in Turkey, on the scorched calf bursting out of the flaming mountains screaming for its mother, the herds of wild horses, the wild boar, pheasant, turtles, all destroyed. And the ongoing miles of ancient olive groves, trees twisting for days as the fire continued to consume them inside out.

Who set the bloody fire?

Why did someone try to kill me?

Where is the old holy man?

My chest constricts and I swallow back a surge of sadness. I roll the paperweight across my notepad as I drink another tea and consider a professional dilemma.

A few years ago, when I visited my mother in Sydney, where she's moved, she took me to the newly opened Museum of Australian History. Museums, artifacts, culture, these are my business. I've put a few people behind glass in my time, but even I wasn't prepared for what I saw.

My own childhood stood on display in a museum, with humidity sensors guarding it. My life, or a reasonable facsimile of it, raw and naked, its skinny little sunburned limbs frozen stark in black-and-white, were exposed in a glass showcase for all the bloody world to see. I felt both invaded and repulsed.

There was the writing slate like the one on which I etched my first sentence—a weighty sentence, I'm sure, which would have changed the world if preserved. Ladybug, Ladybug. . . . The Victorian embroidery sampler of the standard rose-covered cottage into which I jabbed a needle like some voodoo doll. The god-awful tea towels that initiated the quickly abandoned hope chest I was supposed to offer to Prince Charming in return for living happily ever after, as if tea towels could buy happiness. And the *National Geographic*s with their schizophrenic covers that summarized the strange era in which we lived: the spacewalk on one; newly discovered, bare-breasted natives on the other.

In those glass cases a curator had reduced my scrawny little life—which is not that long, mind you—to a series of collector's items, museum pieces, artifacts for strangers to gawk at. How could a tourist paying a five-dollar entrance fee understand that my life was never that quaint? Absent were the lost afternoons climbing trees, the smell of earth after first rain, daydreams of the Amazon....

I toss the embedded ladybugs into the air and catch them.

"Okay guys," I say to the air around me. "I promise not to stick you behind glass like dead insects. But first, you have to come out so I can see you."

I begin dialing the Catholic churches again. One finally answers on first try, knocking me speechless. The janitor, who is of limited vocabulary, tells me to try later when the office opens. I sit in silence and contemplate the glass of hot tea.

Fourteen years ago, in 1984, I was drinking hot tea from a similar glass on the Nile train when the Bishop of Asyout told me he was going to die and extracted his promise. I will not believe the old trickster is dead until I see it. Until then, I could dismiss his challenge as a harmless joke—return to Egypt and you will see the future—but the promise, rising from the Turkish fire like some ancient phoenix, has taken on its own life.

I call the Asyout number the telephone directory also gave me last night, but the phone I'm using will not accept an outgoing long distance call.

Dammit, I will not be deterred.

I am Western Woman.

I have my list. Unlike Cleopatra, I can conquer the world without Marc Antony or an army.

On cue, Leyla breezes into the office, a battalion of sharp assistants in her wake. She glances at my list and sharpens an eyebrow on me.

I retreat with my precious list back to her apartment to catch a nap and continue my calls.

Late afternoon brings the clarion call of success. Notch one up to brute persistence. Or so I think.

I've been in Cairo less than twenty-four hours and my first appointment buzzes the door to the apartment building. Abdul Aziz's friend, the Sufi mystic. I fumble the intercom entrance release and end up running down the stairs to let him in.

At the bottom of the stairs in the foyer, a tall, thin man rests his long hands on a cane, supporting his weight. He's fifty, perhaps seventy, and wears a dove gray business suit, the color of his hair. I pause in my flight down.

His eyes are closed. His face is expressionless. I've never seen him before, but somehow I know him.

I'm conscious of the swirls of my long, black linen skirt as they settle in slow motion around me. A few seconds earlier, they had floated behind, almost holding me aloft. I stand very still, midstep, sensing this man may fly away, he is so ethereal. Conversely, the force of his transparency has brought me to a full stop.

He opens his eyes, catches me with points of raw pain, and pins my wings.

The world slows and I can almost see each word as I think it.

I think, this man has a power, without understanding what I've thought. This is a man to whom I cannot lie.

My hand remains extended midair, interrupted in its journey to shake his. I allow him to look into my face, my own eyes, without looking away, just as the holy man on the Nile train had done fourteen years earlier.

He immediately peels aside the armor of my life: my degrees, the awards and accomplishments, like an old dressing gown. There's nothing left to hide behind, I realize. I am exposed.

And then he slips into my soul.

My breath catches with shock as I'm plunged into freezing water, and my brain struggles to make sense.

He's looking inside me and I'm completely naked. His eyes

trickle across my black-and-blue soul. I flinch. I don't want him looking there, down deep into my secret life. They rest on the dark thoughts and harmful, stupid, things I've done, the petty hatreds, the fumbling ego, the pain I've caused, or wish to cause, others. . . .

He smiles. These mean nothing to him. And his eyes keep going, searching for something else.

Love, warm as butter, melts through me, from head to toe.

What a strange and wonderful thought, I think, and I relax. This is not a rational response, I tell myself. But, this is where I want to be. I'm completely at peace. He has seen everything. And something else.

It seems a long time, I'm not sure, before I move forward.

His handshake is magnetic and I stand waiting to be released, but enjoying the pleasure of captivation. I'm watching those eyes.

We haven't spoken yet.

Dr. Mohammed's face suddenly becomes devilish and playful. His voice, when it comes, is low and gravelly.

"Welcome, my sister," he says. "And peace be upon you."

"And upon you," I reply to the traditional Islamic greeting.

His breathing, like his step, is so slow and measured that, as he moves forward, he glides. He takes my arm for balance and we walk across the marble entrance hall as if on water.

His heart is not good, he tells me as we begin to climb the stairs together. There is no elevator in this small building. I pace myself according to his breath and his step and fall into a rhythm of calm. Step. Breath. Step. The universe has cadence. Dr. Mohammed has just given me my first lesson on how to walk slowly.

Mohammed Shaalan is the man at the end of the name given by my friend Abdul Aziz back in Washington. He is Director of the Department of Psychiatry at Al-Azhar University, where he is a physician and a psychiatrist. He is also a Sufi, that is, a mystic from the predominantly, but not exclusively, Islamic tradition. He appears on television regularly, and has just come from taping a special program for the holy month of Ramadhan in which he debated a conservative religious sheikh.

His learned opponent, he claims, understands the words of the Qur'an but not the meaning of the words.

"One can hide behind words . . . ," he says as we mount the steps to the apartment on the second floor, pausing after each one.

"Yes . . . ," I reply. I understand this to be the beginning of a negotiation. Our sentences appear unfinished to the listening, but we have no need to complete them for each other. To those accustomed to drawing straight lines, the trace of the butterfly appears enigmatic.

I sigh with deep relief. What freedom to be released from the defensive academic jargon that's become my second skin, my straitjacket.

Inside my friend's apartment, I offer the Sufi master the formal chair of honor, an upright affair of red brocade and silk cushions. He declines, and takes a corner of the well-used sofa, balancing his cane against the edge.

"Our good friend, Abdul Aziz . . . ," he says when settled.

We both smile at the mention of our good friend's name.

"Our good friend has sent me a fax with your vitae. He asked me to set up interviews for you in advance. Like in America. But, our friend, he knows better. This is not America."

I nod. Slowly.

"Of course."

"And your list," he says. "You live in America, you will have your lists."

I pour cool water from the jug I've prepared beforehand, and place a glass in front of him with a bowl of fresh apricots.

I throw away my mental list. The list I prepared for Leyla was just doodling time until whatever was supposed to happen caught my attention. Mohammed Shaalan has my attention.

"I have no list," I reply.

The Sufi doctor narrows his eyes, keeping them on me as I sit.

"Only you," I add.

He chuckles, tapping his cane on the floor, and settles back, ready to continue negotiating.

I wait in silence. He sips the water, takes a tissue from the decorative box on the side table, folds it and slowly pats the beads of sweat from his face.

"From your vitae I see you have been in our world many times," he finally says.

"Many times," I reply. "But in Egypt only once."

"In Egypt," he continues, "first we meet face-to-face. Then we decide if we can help."

I hold this thought.

I am asking him to lead me to mystical leaders, to trust me. There may be some danger in it for them. Few mystics bear the government seal of approval. He's checking if I'm a risk. A possible agitator. Or a flake.

"Some foreigners," he says, "Americans? Europeans? It is no difference. Not so long ago, a few months, they try to perform a pagan sacrifice on the Nile. There is a riot, the crowd tried to kill them. The police, the government tried to keep it quiet, but it is in the newspapers, and everybody talks. An outrage."

"Outrage against the foreigners?" I ask. "Or that the Egyptian crowd attacked them?" I can envisage Islamic extremists attacking tourists, but not the easygoing majority of Egyptians you meet in the street.

"Both," he replies. "You see, the people of Egypt, ordinary people, are not ready for this . . . openness. We are too nervous with our own problems."

"Egypt claims she is the Mother of Civilization, of the World," I say. "It is difficult to keep the World from coming home."

"Aah, but yes, my dear sister," he replies. "But the Egyptian people are not pagan. Or primitive. We are not even radical."

I nod.

"So you understand?" he asks. "Yes?"

He lapses into silence and grins at me. I'm ready to grin him down. My mind's still clinging like a rat terrier to his earlier comment, and not ready to be shaken loose.

"I have a question," I say. "Something you said."

He nods for me to proceed.

"You can?" I ask. "Or you will?"

It is his turn to look quizzical.

"You said you will decide if you *can* help me," I say. "Or if you *will* help me."

We grin each other down, eye to eye. Now that he has seen inside me, seen me naked, I have nothing to lose. I'm not backing down.

He laughs, an unexpected chortle of delight, and searches the room with his eyes.

"Where is the phone?" he asks.

I pass him the heavy black receiver.

He has decided to help.

CHAPTER 4

god's gatekeepers

We move in air-conditioned torpor past the City of the Dead. A million or so squatters have taken over the elaborate stone tombs and earth-colored mausoleums where, until recently, wealthy Egyptians gave their ancestors a Pharaonic farewell, complete with dinner service for the next world. Ragpickers have swept aside the ancestral dust, carted off the family crystal to the bazaar, jerry-rigged the vaults with electricity, and plugged in their soap operas. The streets, overcrowded, impoverished, nevertheless remain eerily silent.

"When you are wanting solitude," Dr. Mohammed says, "we will bring you here for the night."

I raise my eyebrows. A small, ancient mosque in the City of the Dead still offers overnight lodging for mystics with insomnia, he tells me. I recall the unguarded pain in his eyes when I first met him yesterday, and wonder who feeds his demon.

"Papa sleeps here often," his daughter adds, and squeezes her father's arm.

The dark-eyed beauty of Dr. Mohammed's nineteen-year-old daughter leaves me feeling as faded as a sheet hung too long in the sun. She's studying jazz guitar in addition to voice and opera, and is along for the ride. She sits in the front beside a surly driver in a Hawaiian print shirt.

A mystic with a Don Ho-driver. Okay.

Our driver's job is not an easy one. We've spent the best part of the morning on Cairo's flyovers, stuck in honking, shouting, music-blaring, pollution-belching traffic jams, moving from one corner of the city to the next searching for mystics. The driver waits outside each building in the desiccating heat as we search the stifling corridors and offices inside, only to find that the mystics are all in meetings.

After passing a heroic statue for the third time, I'm beginning to believe this is a forty-year trek in the desert. Dr. Mohammed's face is locked in an intense inner conversation. In the middle of the crowded highway, he suddenly leans forward and commands the driver to turn the car around.

"We are taking your daughter to her lesson?" I ask, fishing for some kind of direction in our wanderings. We have not discussed our schedule and are drifting in a perpetual float around the city.

"We are taking you to the Grand Sheikh," Dr. Mohammed says.

I try not to choke, and although sitting, my knees go weak.

Yesterday afternoon, after he agreed to help me, I asked Dr. Mohammed if he knew the Sheikh, the Grand Sheikh of Islam.

"A good man, and a holy man," he replied obtusely. "He understands the spiritual life. Not just a scholar."

I pressed him further on how well he knows the Sheikh. Well enough to get us a private audience?

"Yes, of course, you will want to talk to the Sheikh," he replied, and for a few seconds I wasn't sure if he was mocking me. "But an interview with the Sheikh is not usual."

Dr. Mohammed didn't have to fill in the blanks. The Grand Sheikh is a seriously busy man. In the Islamic world, his status is similar to the pope's and I stand as much chance of an interview as I would knocking on the front door of St. Peter's. My request is especially absurd since I am neither a head of state, nor a Muslim. I'm not even a bothersome journalist, just another foreign woman dropping in for a chat about the state of the world.

"Is it possible, though?" I pressed.

"It is possible, yes," he says, and I light up prematurely. "Everything is possible. But I have not accomplished this possibility before." Many times he's tried to help friends and colleagues, and as many times failed. Even he has not had a private audience with this revered teacher.

The driver finesses a slow U-turn through a crowded intersection outside our destination, his fender nuzzling the butts of slow pedestrians who, along with the policeman directing traffic, largely ignore him. We're only doing five miles an hour tops, but he manages to squeal the brakes as we pull up outside Al-Azhar. A few pigeons murmur and move aside.

A thousand years ago, when the Islamic Empire sported between the Atlantic and Indian Oceans, a rebel Shi'ite dynasty overpowered the local Sunni rulers of Egypt. In their exuberance they founded a new city on the ruins of ancient Memphis and built a fabulous university in its center. The Fatimids named their city Cairo, The Victorious. With similar modesty they called the university Al-Azhar, The Spectacular.

Al-Azhar is a madrasa, a mosque-university, the same concept of church-university that later shaped Oxford. At its founding, a thousand years ago, it was the center of learning for the Islamic Empire, then the world's most extensive and advanced civilization. Europe was still the land of the mindless barbarian, who thought with his mouth open.

Here, students sat in a circle around their professors' feet to absorb their wisdom. They translated the texts of the ancient Greeks that had been lost to a Western Christianity bent on purging the influence of pagans. At the madrasa they discussed the new advances in ophthalmology and psychology, debated metaphysics and philosophy, played with the latest equivalent of software—algorithms and algebra. Some, it was rumored, under the influence first of hashish (and later coffee), listened to the poetry of mystics late into the night.

Circassians took over the palace, then Turks again. Napoleon, the French and British colonialists came, saw and conquered— and left. At present America skirts the horizon. The eclectic tradition of Al-Azhar continues.

Today Al-Azhar is considered the center of moderate Islamic thought for the planet's billion Sunni Muslims. In a dense city of 17 million, its distinctive minarets stretch their throats above a choking stream of cars, noise and humanity and compete with skyscrapers for air. Outside, the madrasa's pollution-stained walls are girded by beams as masons, artists and engineers undertake the renovation of the world's oldest standing university. Inside, in the Office of the Grand Sheikh, a renewal is also taking place.

In a few minutes I will meet the Grand Sheikh. Holy Hell. I'm overwhelmed with thanks when Dr. Mohammed leans forward and whispers.

"We have no appointment," he says.

He shakes his head, and like a foolish mirror, I mimic him.

"No appointment," I repeat.

"I am following your lead and bringing you as far as I can," he says. Yesterday afternoon I also told him my plan. "Let us see if we can get you to your door. Then it is up to you."

If I were not in shock, I'd be nervous. Knocking over a bank would be easier.

And so we turn up, unannounced, on the worn front steps of the Office of the Grand Sheikh of Islam where countless petitioners over a thousand years have tried to enter before me. But they were not accompanied by Dr. Mohammed.

The entrance guard claps the frail doctor in a firm and affectionate embrace. Men and women, employees and passers-through, who recognize Dr. Mohammed from his television program, press forward to kiss or shake his hand and offer blessings for his good health. They accord me status by association. Like his reedy, beautiful daughter on whose arm he leans, my hair is uncovered, and passes without comment. I'm wearing a simple linen trouser suit, the color of midnight, and all my appendages are hidden. My scarf is in my camera bag, but I'm following the cues of his daughter and the other women in the building who wear fashionable combinations of Western and Middle Eastern dress. Not all their heads are covered. This is my first surprise.

The stone entrance hall resounds with cool activity and we walk slowly up the branching curved stairs, pacing ourselves to the good doctor's steps, to the first floor. From this grand height we can see that the building unfolds into four arched wings around a sun-filtered courtyard. The pillars curve energetically and undulate with a lack of restraint not associated with contemporary Islam. Along the balconies, potted plants in tin containers twist toward the light and add an unexpected touch of homeyness.

An assistant escorts us down a carpeted hall to the administrative office of the religious leader, where again we are greeted with warmth and enthusiasm. Assorted male secretaries and personal administrators are in various stages of shouting over the telephones, drinking tea, and assigning tasks to underlings, all of which immediately stops as we enter. Two stern, gray-bearded religious men in black robes almost leap over their desks to embrace Dr. Mohammed and kiss his hand with respect.

The communal office is dark and expansive, with ceilings, as tall as the room is wide, from a bygone age when one bore the heat with a stiff upper lip. Large, dusty windows that look out on the restoration of the madrasa, are closed, and even if they could be opened, they seal out the dust, noise and pollution and would remain shut. Weathered venetian blinds try to keep the midday sun from heating the room to a medium roast and the clacking fans only serve to further baste us.

Scattered around the room are a half-dozen desks, each with a vintage manual typewriter and a telephone so old and heavy it could double in a weight-lifting room. A yacht-size power desk is docked outside a closed door to another office, or antechamber.

This is the safe harbor of the Grand Sheikh and the man behind the desk is the personal secretary whose sharp eye guards the inner sanctum and the appointment calendar. Like his underlings, he wears long black robes, but with a full, white turban. He'd be formidable but that he has Dr. Mohammed in an affectionate bear hug.

We drink tea around the power desk and the men swap stories. I've been introduced but temporarily backgrounded. Over the third glass, Dr. Mohammed quietly satisfies their curiosity.

"Aaah," they say. "Doktora. Amrika."

"Yes," I reply in Arabic. "From America."

Dr. Mohammed signals me to zip it. This is his gig for now and he begins to present my case.

A short, perspiring man juts his head over a glass barrier to the side of the communal office and narrows his eyes on me. He's been on the phone during our arrival, but doesn't come forward to join the familiar chatter. Unlike the others in the office, he's not in mufti, but wears a short-sleeved gray safari suit, the camouflage preferred by Egyptian bureaucrats. I nod respectfully, dismiss him as the accountant, and he goes back to his paperwork.

Return at noon, the personal secretary tells us after the third round of tea. The Grand Sheikh is not only intellectual advisor to a billion Sunni Muslims, he is also president of the university. Today is the first day of final exams, so he is doing the rounds, urging the students on to their best. The staff check their watches and agree that he should be back in two hours, by noon, when they will arrange for me to present my request for a private interview. Not an interview, but a request for an interview.

"Inshallah, God willing," we mumble back and forth to each other.

We leave with my identity established in the outer chamber and at the front door. The driver has found shade under a handkerchief and waits impatiently to turn on the air conditioner. We set out to circle the highways again, depositing his daughter at the conservatory.

In contrast to the downtown madrasa, the new campus of Al-Azhar University sprawls self-consciously modern at the north end of the city. The students, male and female, in a variety of dress but predominantly blue jeans, walk as if they have somewhere to go. Young women wear brightly colored headscarves with their tight blue jeans, others long fashionable skirts, with or without scarves. They appear as intent as students all over the world in the week of final exams.

When I later ask Dr. Mohammed's daughter why, judging from the streets, there appear to be so many more men than women at the university, she replies, with a smile, that while the boys are outside strutting their machismo, the girls are inside, studying to become doctors and engineers. She speaks without guile.

Dr. Mohammed drops me back on the sidewalk outside the Office of the Grand Sheikh. That is, in lieu of a convenient parking space, the driver parks the car on the sidewalk while the good doctor and I talk. Pedestrians move around us.

"I have brought you to the door," Dr. Mohammed says as I gather my belongings and tie the silk scarf under my chin. "Now you are on your own."

He laughs. I want to pinch him, but instead kiss him on the cheek.

"Thanks, pardner," I say.

The guard waves me through—he's been watching us from the door. Upstairs in the antechamber, my entrance is not so assured.

The muftis are silent when I return, surprised that I've actually turned up. I stake a seat facing the mystery door and away from the two other women in the room, a young, fashionable student and an older, worn-out woman, who both nod at me with their eyes. I don't want to be mistaken for an Egyptian woman. They are accompanied by men, relatives who leave and return at intervals smelling of cigarettes. Assistants walk in and out delivering envelopes and correspondence. My stomach growls loudly as smells of cafeteria lunches drift into the room. One by one, a staff member disappears to return shortly, the odor of rice and lamb stew trailing in his black robes.

Working with religious officials, men in black, is nothing new to me. Two years among the religious men in the legal archives of Istanbul taught me more than how to read sixteenth-century documents. They taught me patience, perseverance, and the value of having a rich inner—or fantasy—life. As my men in black dresses rocked back and forth chanting the Qur'an, I joined in silently with a compatible jazz riff, Ella of the Archives, and rocked with them as I puzzled through my documents. We accommodated our different tunes and by the end of two years they were trying to marry me off to their cousins.

I also learned that, having seen humanity's flaws in close detail, these guys usually have a startling sense of humor, quickly apparent upon Dr. Mohammed's arrival, but hidden upon my return. Still, they banter back and forth between making and taking calls on the heavy telephones, and signing pieces of paper and moving them to the next desk. There is affection here as well as hierarchy.

Right now I'm under surveillance. The closest Western approximation to the Grand Sheikh would be the pope, and a private interview with this man is a rare honor. These men will decide whether I get to see him, let alone whether I get to talk to him. In Istanbul, I watched their cohorts hide documents from researchers they didn't like, and eased the way of others. Their power is subtle, but it is power, nonetheless. They are gatekeepers.

The gatekeepers of the Grand Sheikh have placed my résumé on the desk of the safari-suited man who is at lunch, and leave me alone to contemplate the historical wallpaper.

The little safari-suited man returns. He sits behind me in his booth and I watch his reflection in a framed calligraphy on the wall opposite as he turns the pages of my résumé. He stands and clears his throat, which is his signal he is ready to see me. An assistant in black robes tells me that Ahmed Abdel-Khalik, the personal translator to the Grand Sheikh, is ready to see me now. It is all very theatrical.

We circle each other politely as he rehashes my résumé and reasons for wanting to see the Sheikh. Our conversation is unnaturally strained and formal, especially as we are both sweating like animals and fanning ourselves with wilted pieces of paper. He asks to see my list of questions, which, in anticipation, I have prepared. As he reads each word, I watch the hands of the prewar wall clock jump and stall in fits and starts.

I want to turn the clock forward and get past this awkward first kiss, but this is not my game. I'm being put through the test of time.

A young assistant in a sharp, brown business suit strides into the office and changes the balance. He has a clipped mustache, fashionable buzzed hair and a general air of confidence more at home in an international house of finance than the central office of Islam. He sits down brusquely and just as quickly stands up. His low place in the pecking order means his desk swelters in the direct sunlight.

He struggles with one of the heavy ancient metal fans, positioning it carefully on top of an equally ancient filing cabinet, and turns it on. The fan shudders, then takes off with the ferocity of an airplane engine, sending newspapers, correspondence, typing paper airborne. The holy men shout at him in one loud chorus to turn it off. They burst out laughing, and so do I.

The spell has been broken.

"The traffic," Abdel-Khalik attempts to explain. He looks a little guilty as he tries to straighten his persona. "We cannot open the window because of the traffic. The noise."

"I know," I commiserate. "Traffic. Terrible."

"Yes, terrible," he repeats, unsure how to pick up his inquisition.

"Teaches you patience, though," I say.

"Yes," he replies. "Patience is good."

"Yes, especially waiting for an appointment," I say. I raise my eyebrows and wait for his reply.

Abdel-Khalik pauses to check what I have just said, then splutters untidily. He wipes the spittle off his jacket as he translates my comment to the Sheikh's personal secretary, who watches our interaction. The room begins to laugh.

"Yes. You are very patient," the secretary says and assures me that another hour, two o'clock, and the Grand Sheikh will be here. Inshallah. God willing. I don't mind, I'm thoroughly enjoying myself with the minor sheikhs. Besides, I am about to be primed to meet a saint.

When not pretending to be a gruff bureaucrat, Ahmed Abdel-Khalik, personal translator to the Sheikh, is a garrulous, middle-aged Cairene. He takes me under his gray safari-suited wing and equally vets and prepares me with background on the madrasa and its leader. He speaks with excitement and pauses mid-patter only to wipe his brow.

Across the room, the personal secretary plays straight man to the translator's routine. Good-natured banter shifts back and forth between them. They are graduates of rival universities, the personal secretary in religious studies from Al-Azhar (he is a religious sheikh), and the personal translator in English literature from the more secular Ain-Shams University. Although entitled to wear the turban, as is an Oxford don his cap and gown, Abdel-Khalik prefers the secular safari suit.

Other attendants move in and out of the conversation as their work and deference to their seniors permit. The serious young latecomer in the brown suit has a question for me. He is in his late twenties and has a university degree and a software business. He wants to know how, if you have capital and are educated, can you start a business in the States? He has his own money and a good family, does not need any support, will work hard and is ready go.

I suggest he try the American consulate, and he rolls his eyes as if I should know better.

"Why doesn't America like us?" he says.

The men in black cluck their tongues. I nod that it's all right. Each day young Egyptians will ask me this question or a form of it and I'm already becoming used to it. The question flows from confusion, not belligerence, the confusion when someone you admire rejects you.

"We need opportunity," he says. "There is no opportunity in Egypt. I am educated, but there is no opportunity."

I bite my lip. I have no answer.

Abdel-Khalik steers the conversation away from potential conflict and back to the man I am about to meet. He is soft-spoken and gentle, a good example for young people, he adds for the benefit of the young man.

The Grand Sheikh of Al-Azhar, Sheikh Tantawi, is a scholar, the translator tells me as if talking about his own son, and different from his predecessor Al-Hak, for whom he also worked. He speaks with obvious affection of Tantawi being more moderate. Whereas Al-Hak was interested in the meaning of the word as written, Tantawi is interested in contemporary application for unwritten situations, he tells me. (If the situation is recorded in the law books or any of its sources, however, he carefully stresses, it must be observed.)

Sheikh Tantawi is often compared favorably with one of the most respected leaders of the institution, Muhammad Abduh, Sheikh of Al-Azhar at the turn of the twentieth century. Abduh was both a spiritual man and a thinker, and credited with modernizing Islam. "In Europe," he is reported to have said, "I found Christians who practiced Islam as it is meant to be practiced. When I returned to the East, I found Muslims without Islam." The comparison with Abduh is timely. Abduh was concerned with the beginning of a new century; Tantawi is interested in directing the course of both Islam and Egypt, not always compatible partners, into the new millennium.

I sigh with relief to learn that the Grand Sheikh has not escaped that famed national characteristic of Egyptians, humor, which he uses in counsel. The men tell me the story of a Pakistani delegation who had come to discuss his controversial views on birth control. The Pakistanis considered the Egyptian's lenient stance to be against the Qur'an and Hadith, which guide sharia, Islamic law. Tantawi explained that there is nowhere that con-

demns it. Moreover, he told them, in Egypt we encourage absti-
nence, and recommend the husband withdraw from their wives
(that is, from intercourse) for a month or longer.

The Pakistanis were shocked.

"How can a man stay away from his wife for an entire month?"
one asked. "It is not possible!"

Tantawi replied, "For you, yes. You may think it difficult. You
are young and your wife, maybe she is beautiful. But for others
not so fortunate, they welcome my words!"

Abdel-Khalik takes my stunned silence for a go-ahead. Now
off on his own riff, he cannot resist an audience. I am the best
kind of audience: I am captive and have a vested interest—getting
to the other side of the door. The others, including the women
petitioners, chuckle as much at the enthusiasm of the storyteller
as the stories, which they will repeat tonight.

Wait. Wait. I have to take a reality check. I'm sitting in the
outer office of the Office of the Grand Sheikh, listening to a
stand-up comedian doing a religious floor show. And what's
more, the jokes involve sex.

And I'm thoroughly at home.

I try to remember my position, my training, and attempt a
show of disapproval. But Abdel-Khalik's humor is infectious and I
begin to laugh again. He begins a joke concerning the nature of
marriage and I give up all pretense of Christian priggishness.

"Three Egyptian friends die and go to the gates of Heaven,"
Abdel-Khalik begins. "Gabriel, the Gatekeeper, checks the Book of
Life for their deeds, nods, then asks the first if he has ever been
unfaithful to his wife.

" 'Why, no,' the man replies. 'I have always resisted temptation
and never, ever touched another woman.'

" 'You may enter Paradise,' the Gatekeeper replies, 'and here
are the keys to a gold Mercedes to use while you're here.'

"Music sounds and the gates open to let him in.

"The Gatekeeper asks the second friend: 'And you, have you
ever been unfaithful?'

"The second bows his head: 'Well, only every now and again . . . my old girlfriend back in the village, but only after her husband died . . . and never to hurt my wife. I fall upon the mercy of God and ask him to forgive me.'

"The Gatekeeper clucks his tongue and says: 'Very well, in you go. And here are the keys to a broken-down Renault to use.'

"The gates to Paradise open and in passes a very thankful man.

"The third doesn't even wait for the Gatekeeper to question him. He falls upon the ground, weeping and beating his head.

" 'Woe unto me, woe unto me,' he wails. 'I was always unfaithful. I tried but . . . Oh woe. Please God, forgive me, for I am truly sorry.'

"The Gatekeeper shakes his head and thinks for a minute.

" 'Okay,' he says, 'You may enter Paradise.'

"He points to a rusted old bicycle .

" '. . . and this is for you to use.'

"A week or so later, the three friends meet in the village square of Paradise and are greeting each other. They hug, they kiss cheek to cheek. The first man is quite miserable.

" 'Brother, brother,' the other two say, 'Why the long face? Here we all are in Paradise. And you have this gold Mercedes. Why so sad?'

" 'Yes, I have this gold Mercedes,' he replies. 'But I just saw my wife. She's here, too.'

" 'And? So why are you not happy?' they ask.

" 'Aiie, aiie, aiie,' he replies. 'She was riding a bicycle.' "

CHAPTER 5

we, the petitioners

At 2:00 P.M. a flurry of activity ripples down the hall of the Office of the Grand Sheikh and into the anteroom. Conversation stops midsentence. An assistant in black robes and clerical cap gives the signal to stand and ushers us, a ragtag band of petitioners, down the long marble corridor and through security into a large reception hall. After hours of waiting, this is happening too quickly.

Governments, heads of state, leaders, all have access to Sheikh Tantawi, as does the common petitioner, the man and woman in the street, the honest seeker. I've seen this process in action before, but this time I am about to become part of it.

One miserable Istanbul winter, when I was reading documents by the potbellied stove in the office of the Grand Mufti, a petitioner came in with a question for the legal expert. I eavesdropped, fascinated. He was going in for open-heart surgery at the American Hospital and his surgeon was a Christian. Was it permitted for the hands of a non-Muslim to handle the heart of a Muslim, he asked. He glanced at me. Don't worry, the legal expert replied, she doesn't understand, which was legally a fib. The petitioner continued: Could he place his heart in the hands of a non-believer? The legal expert sighed, then responded: If it is the will of God that he use the hands of a Christian to save your life, so be it.

Now, I am putting my own heart in the hands of a stranger. I swallow hard and concentrate on my surroundings, waiting for the stranger to appear.

Despite its lofty function, the office of the Grand Sheikh is spare. High ceilings and book-lined. A large circle of leather chairs hyphenated by coffee tables dominates the center. Simple, framed calligraphic verses from the Qur'an, an electric incense burner, and a few plaques of honor barely make their presence known. Blinds are drawn in vertical and horizontal layers in an attempt to batten out the desert sun. The resulting half-light transports us into a black-and-white art film of the fifties where every mote of dust hangs suspended in the light of the projector. This is a refuge without air-conditioning, where silence is the preferred luxury.

An assistant lays the Sheikh's black attaché case in the center of an expansive but organized clutter of a desk any intellectual would relish. I imagine the case contains the most pressing worries of one of the world's most important Muslim thinkers and spiritual leaders. Close by the desk is a series of telephones, in a range of colors indicative of the decade in which they were acquired: heavy black, avocado, beige, and red, followed by a recent slimline black. I wonder if each of the phones is reserved for a specific emergency. If so, the closest would be for the latest Israeli occupation of Palestinian homes for which the Sheikh has just given a controversial *fatwa* or legal pronouncement in condemnation. The next would then be reserved for the human rights investigators who are probing Egypt's record on treatment of the Christian minority, the Copts. This line is likely shared with the international development agencies that protest the local practice of female circumcision.

In this scheme, the two busiest lines would be the competing interests of the people and the palace, which ring in tandem.

Reformists urge the Grand Sheikh to speak against government policies concerning poverty, overpopulation, and public corruption that have become fodder for militant Islamists. In turn, because Al-Azhar is now a state institution and the Sheikh is appointed by Egypt's president, he must negotiate between the wiles of government and the will of the conservative religious community. The government, if not the president, also has his direct number.

Sheikh Tantawi's grand passion is knowledge and, knowledge, according to a saying of the Prophet Muhammad, is meant to be used. His position as director of the thousand-year-old university involves him in knowledge transfer and education of Egypt's youth, the generation that will lead this ancient civilization into the future.

These religious men in front of me, the *ulama,* are basically holy lawyers. The holy law, or *sharia,* of Islam deals mostly with family and societal relations, that is, the guidelines for a good society, or *Umma,* Community, as Muslims refer to themselves. Like all human law, it is man-made. Its source, however is holy, based on the Qur'an or the Holy Word of Allah, which was transmitted through Muhammad, God's Messenger or Prophet, in the early seventh century. Sharia also draws upon the Hadith and Sunna, the traditions and examples from the life of Muhammad. These three sources are interpreted by a body of religious scholars, or the *ulama.*

Sheikh Tantawi, the man before me, now leads the *ulama.*

But for the jockeying around me, I might have missed his entrance. The Grand Sheikh is 'a small man. Shoulders slight. Hands elegantly slim. Features softly honed. A gray beard shaven close for the summer heat outlines his face. Tired black eyes swear, by God, they'd enjoy a good joke, as soon as they got some sleep. He wears the collarless, black robe of his profession, and the modified turban—a green felt cap swathed in white muslin—but he carries them almost absentmindedly as if someone has to remind him each morning to put them on.

I immediately like this unassuming man. He inhabits his body so economically, you could pass him in the hall of a university, a monastery perhaps, and return his quiet nod without knowing who he is.

Sheikh Tantawi settles himself in the open circle of chairs. The scholar's desk, the attaché case and telephones wait behind him. His black-robed assistants, qualified men of learning themselves, have clustered on either side of him. He indicates there is room on both sides for us to join him and we move closer.

He politely waves away the fuss his assistants make around him, and sips a sweating glass of water. He gives us, his petitioners, his full attention. We have already given him ours.

There are three women, including myself, among a half-dozen men, and the Sheikh takes our petitions first. Damn. This apparent nicety actually prevents us from hearing the concerns of the men and I'm slightly peeved, not knowing I'm about to receive insight into the strongheaded world of Egyptian women.

The university student leads off. She stands and steps forward. Her brother stands beside her and hangs his head, pretending he's not there. She's decorated herself in perfect magazine-inspired makeup, the very latest in long floral skirts and high heels. An imitation Chanel headscarf artfully covers her black hair. I'm feeling slightly dowdy in a simple navy trouser suit. I stick to my leather chair, and sweat rolls down my legs.

The university student is about to sit for her graduating exams, she explains, and asks for a personal letter of recommendation from the Sheikh, with whom she had once taken a class. Such a letter would influence the examiners in her favor.

Pardon?

The Grand Sheikh manages to restrain his incredulity, which the attendants beside him are less able to conceal.

Abdel-Khalik, the translator who has become my ally during the last two hours of waiting, nudges me with a sideward glance to check if I've understood her request. I raise my eyebrows in reply. He hides a smile.

"It is their right," he whispers. All Muslims have the right to approach the head religious leader and petition his advice and intervention in everyday matters.

Now, inside the Grand Sheikh's library, I am finding that the religious leader is a saint. Or at least has the patience of one. As he considers the university student's unorthodox request, I am just hoping that his patience survives long enough to hear my own.

He spreads his hands before him in the universal sign of frustration by professors at exam time.

"There can be no favoritism with students," he says. "If I give a letter to you, I must give one to all the students at the university. How will that be of benefit to you?"

The young woman persists. Her voice strains. She is not used to not getting her way. Those big brown eyes brim with frustration.

The Grand Sheikh restates that it is not possible. His hands rest firm on the arms of the chair, his prayer beads dangling from his palm. He flicks them once, the only slip of annoyance he reveals.

"Go home and study," he says and casts a look at her brother, who has stood quietly by, studying the carpet.

The next woman is a large, older village woman in a traditional long black gown and a white gauze scarf tied loosely around her head. She resembles the millions of women in Cairo's back-street markets about to drive a hard bargain for dinner. The dismissal of the college student means that she must rise to the challenge. This man may be humble but he is no pushover. She begins with hand-wringing and pleading and works her way up the emotional ladder.

Her petition is this: She is a cleaning woman who works for the Al-Azhar complex. Her daughter also wishes to work as a cleaning woman in a new building owned by the mosque. The building has not yet been opened, nor is the position yet available, but hundreds of cleaning women have applied for this job. The mother wishes to jump queue and would like the Grand Sheikh to intervene and reserve the job for her daughter.

She begins to wail. She is shameless. She looks up and tilts her head to one side to gauge her effect.

The Sheikh's assistants are clucking and protesting at the way his time is being wasted while trying to quiet the cleaning woman. Her voice continues to rise with each admonition. I watch my chances of an interview dribble away.

"Auntie," they say, "Auntie." They don't tell her how busy the Sheikh is, that doesn't interest her. Instead, they tell her simply that he cannot help her.

What?! You can almost hear her saying. Her eyes bulge in disbelief. This small, old man in front of her is the most important person in her religious universe. Why, he is as close as you can get to Allah, yet she understands her age-old right to petition him in person. To come here has taken a certain amount of balls. And pride, perhaps. She is determined not to return to her street, her apartment building, her family, without something. Dinner depends on it.

Sheikh Tantawi quietly raises his hand to the concert and both her wailing and the clucking of the assistants trails off into silence. He instructs the cleaning woman to go to the general office manager, whose duty is to oversee employment.

She lets out a last plea for his signature, his word, but quietens when she sees it is not to be. She leaves with a slip of paper with the name of the personnel director. No more.

The Grand Sheikh finally turns his attention to me.

"Come, come here, sister," he says, and sighs. I stand and move forward, unsure now of what to say. He speaks in soft, classical Arabic, a beautiful convoluted language which, unlike the more direct Egyptian dialect of the street, is reserved for formal occasions.

"What is it you want?" he asks.

I have waited more than two hours in the outer offices just to petition him for a private interview. I've endured bad jokes and fielded questions about my personal life and philosophy to get here. The religious scholars in the outer chamber have quietly vetted me and now I stand before the man. This is the moment.

He, on the other hand, has been walking around a thousand-year-old madrasa in the shadowless sun, encouraging students, checking on faculty. Today is the first day of final exams and, as is his custom, he has spent most of it urging the university's students on to greatness. He has not yet had lunch. He is only human and appears slightly impatient.

"What is it that you want?" the translator repeats in English and nudges me with his eyes.

Do I tell the Grand Sheikh that what I really want is to sit down beside him when he's rested and ask him what it's all about—all this, the world, what's going on. It would take hours, centuries, perhaps. All those books I've read, about history and religion, and all the words I've absorbed, tell me what was it *really* like? I would ask because I believe he's been there.

Instead I tell the translator, who stands beside me, "Please tell him . . . Please tell him I want to understand . . ."

I can sense that Adbel-Khalik wants the interview to take place as much as I do and is ready to elaborate.

Sheikh Tantawi studies me as the translator mentions my patron, Dr. Mohammed, and expands upon my request.

I fear suddenly that the Prussian-pink floral scarf was overkill, but then I relax. There is nothing I can do but to surrender to his questioning gaze.

This is a nakedness I am not prepared for, a nakedness from which my education, my diplomas, my clothes, even my friends cannot shield me. To this man, like Dr. Mohammed, these are mere externalities for which he has no time. The person he is trying to gauge is beneath the clothes, the skin, the thin veneer of protective gestures and social accretions. He is going for the core. And if I want this bloody interview . . .

My body tenses.

What if he sees the time I shoplifted the Mary Quant lipstick on a lark . . .

Or . . .

I close my eyes for a second.

What if he can see into the dark recesses of my soul?

Calm slides through me as if God has given me a spoonful of honey.

I smile.

None of it matters.

When I open my eyes, the Sheikh is looking into them. He seems amused.

"Yes," he says. "Our sister can return in the morning."

CHAPTER 6

The grand sheikh

Six-thirty in the morning is an ungodly hour for a conversation, let alone a conversation with the planet's foremost Muslim cleric about the state of the human soul. As the taxi drags my lumpen carcass across the Nile, I vaguely remember slugging down the thick Arabic coffee Leyla prepared before daybreak. Her attempts to wrest complete sentences from me were met with grunts. Now, a cheerful taxi driver attempts small talk about American music and plugs in a cassette of Arab hip-hop to make me feel at home. I'm trying bloody hard to be a morning person.

I pull the Prussian-pink scarf from my camera bag and adjust it in the rearview mirror. The driver does a double take at my covered head, my Disappearing-Blonde Trick and reciprocates with his version of Look-No-Hands, deftly fishing for a cassette under the car seat with both hands while steering with his knees, and changes the music for a melodious recitation of the Qur'an.

He glows with pride as we approach our destination.

"You are Muslim?" he says, uncertain.

"I am Christian," I reply. These words form awkwardly on my tongue.

"Aaaah," he says and adjusts the mirror again. After a pause, "We are all God's children."

"Thank you," I say.

"But you are visiting our mosque," he says, indicating Al-Azhar.

"No," I reply, nodding toward the building opposite. "I am meeting with your Sheikh."

His face changes from confusion, to disbelief, and back to confusion. This is not a joking matter. Egyptians hold the Grand Sheikh of Al-Azhar in high regard. When the cabbie sees I'm serious, he bows slightly. I bow in return. I also find it difficult to believe.

The security guard at the street entrance to the Office of the Grand Sheikh of Al-Azhar recognizes me from yesterday and checks me through. He adds a smile of encouragement. Or is it congratulations? The Grand Sheikh rarely gives private interviews.

Al-Azhar is our planet's oldest living university, and in the quiet of morning, before the chaos of city life has had time to wind its spring, its grandeur seeps through even my pique. Today, I join the Grand Sheikh of Islam, Sheikh Mohammed Tantawi, scholar, mystic, and a spiritual leader of the planet's billion Sunni Muslims. His decisions and pronouncements guide the lives of the planet's fastest growing religion.

I shake myself: How did I get here?

A uniformed guard escorts me through elaborate security into the Sheikh's library. Sheikh Tantawi looks up from his seat, trying to place me. Much has happened in the world since our encounter yesterday. He's in the middle of an earnest conversation, speaking slowly and quietly into the heavy retro black telephone on the coffee table beside him. My ears prick up at the mention of Jerusalem.

One of his dark-robed assistants taps his wristwatch to indicate that there are more important things to attend to than this foreign chick with lots of questions. The Sheikh signals over his conversation for me to sit. The assistant sighs and pins me with a warning: Time is valuable. Each minute is a gift.

Some men and women at life's end look as if they are floating along in a river of perfect temperature. It is a time of peace. Reflection. Perhaps self-congratulation. Others are possessed by an urgency not to sleep, as if they are aware of the finity of their hours and that every minute has meaning and is accountable. The Grand Sheikh is of the latter: At the biblical age of three-score-and-ten he is clearly weary from lack of sleep.

Beside me is the Sheikh's affable and articulate translator, Abdel-Khalik—he's nervous—and between us is our digital scribe, the tape recorder. In Egypt, technology of any level is still a Y-chromosome thing and he's trying to resist helping me set it up, but fails. Now is not the time to tell him that I don't need his help.

I'm now also nervous.

This is the first interview. And this is a new tape recorder.

"Let's begin," the Sheikh says and cuts into my setup. He's replaced the phone.

I'm fumbling with loose wires. Damn, I want to swear. But damn if I'm giving up now. I refocus myself and settle my breathing. I surrender to cadence.

My first question is natural, given the tangle of wires before us: Technology.

"Your Holiness, may I ask you your honest opinion of technology?" I ask, leaving out the expletives.

At that moment the tape recorder, the uncontested center of attention, kicks into gear.

His Holiness, the Grand Sheikh, smiles. Abdel-Khalik and the other assistants are visibly relieved. We have all faced the blinking clock on the VCR and for a moment we are all in this, whatever this is, together. Man has prevailed over Machine. The tension dissolves.

"From your perspective," I continue after a nod from the Sheikh, which doubles as both encouragement and a call for order, "what is our relationship with technology, its effect on our lives?"

He pauses before answering, as after each question I will ask, and considers his words. This is a man of history. His words bear weight.

He gestures toward the tape recorder that has both distracted and focused us and begins to speak so softly I lean forward to catch each word.

"Islam is on the side of progress and development," he says. "We welcome all machines invented in this age if they are for the progress and service of humanity."

The Grand Sheikh then tents his fine hands and taps them together.

"We should make it clear, however, that technology is to be used for the sake of humanity, not against it."

Technology is a subject surprisingly dear to his heart. Literally. He recently announced that his heart, as well as other organs, be donated upon accidental death.

Just before my visit, the Grand Sheikh took on other religious scholars in a very public debate on television and the newspapers. At issue were cloning, organ transplants and technology transfer, subjects that have met with caution from America's religious and science communities. I predicted an even more conservative conclusion to the Muslim debate. I was wrong.

The open and feisty exchange between these seemingly traditionalist and orthodox leaders shook my prepackaged, albeit informed, image of them. The views of the Grand Sheikh, more so. It was one of many wait-a-minute moments in the discussion with the men in black.

Around the time Al-Azhar was built, a thousand years ago, the focus of these learned men dwindled to such legalistic minutiae as whether the water into which a gnat fell could be used for ritual ablution (yes). Eventually, their interpretations became so painfully convoluted that only the limits of the imagination—or the state—could halt them. The prevailing belief, especially among Westerners, is that the so-called Gates of Interpretation (*Ijtihad*) rusted shut and Islamic law is the remnant of medieval society.

So when it comes to high-tech issues such as cloning, I assume their minds are also rusted shut. Al-Azhar, the bastion of conservative thinking, however, stands firmly behind Dolly, the cloned sheep. They have no problem with her. Religious scholars argue that since the cell used to create another being originates from the Creator, the end product is still of God. Man as Scientist is just an intermediary. Besides, they say, the process already is used widely in horticulture.

According to their argument, there is no difference in diddling with a palm tree, sheep, or human. They are all God's creation, with the special footnote that man is created in the image of God.

During the debate, the Grand Sheikh's opponent, the more conservative Sheikh Ashrawi, also came out on the side of cloning. Discussion then turned to organ transplants, another matter altogether. The debate that followed drew a larger viewing audience than *Baywatch*, Egypt's favorite import.

The reason? The f-word: Fate.

Some Muslims believe that God has written the Fate of each person on his or her forehead. For example, it may be someone's Fate that God gives her a particular disease. Since the genetic diseases of one person can be passed to another through donated organs, the argument goes, man is changing destiny by inserting one person's organs into another. Physical determinism.

Quite simply, the ultraconservative Ashrawi argued, the body is meant to finish when the soul is taken. The rest is tampering with God's Will. With Fate. For Tantawi, the "Fate" argument reeks of superstition, which preys upon ignorance.

In reality, these old guys were debating more than human innards. It was all about the place of education and knowledge. In the far corner was Fatalism, with its purported attendants, folk-belief, superstition and ignorance. Over here in the green Everlast trunks was metaphysics. The Nature of Man. It was all about leaving the planet a better place for future generations.

Thus came Tantawi's stunning move: The holy man donated his heart.

The Prophet Muhammad said, three things undermine a society: poverty, ignorance and oppression. In his trusted position, the Sheikh must wrestle with them all. Prophet Muhammad also said that Muslims should seek knowledge to the ends of the earth, to China, if necessary. By his own example, the Grand Sheikh has followed this directive and accepted at least one new technology for the "progress and service of humanity."

Other world spiritual leaders have not been so open. In his publication on the millennium, Pope John Paul II draws a link between the new technologies, scientific exploration, and the human soul. The pope warns that in this age of rapid change and discovery, we are in danger of worshiping our ability to create and our creations themselves. We no longer worship the Creator, but we worship ourselves as creators. Scientists have become gods. Technological advances lead to consumerism, a disease of un-Godly capitalism. Consumption, as Camille will tell you, is a damn deadly disease.

"Your Holiness," I say, after explaining the pope's warnings about technology, "may I ask your views on your colleague's pronouncements?"

Before the words are out of my mouth, I realize this is a stupid question, a tactical error, a serious breach of protocol to ask a world religious leader directly about another. I'm sure the interview's over.

The question proves moot, anyway. Sheikh Tantawi would prefer to talk about the planet than about the pope.

"These are his concerns," he says, and raises an eyebrow, "and he is allowed these concerns."

I turn to another of the Sheikh's own concerns: the intricate balance of the planet's resources and population, which continues to warp under stress.

"In the Qur'an," I say to the Grand Sheikh, "Adam is referred to in Arabic as the *kalifa*. The caretaker, or God's vice-regent, of the planet."

"Kalifa," he repeats and nods. "Yes, we are caretakers."

"How are we doing then as caretakers of our planet?" I ask. "How are we faring in our relationship with the environment and each other?"

"Almighty God has created us from the earth of this planet," the Sheikh begins. "And we shall return to it after death. Therefore we should do every good thing possible for the sake of the earth and to benefit future generations."

We are all settling into our chairs and into the heart of the discussion. The assistants are now engaged. I exhale.

"Our investment in the planet is not purely physical," the Sheikh continues. "It is also spiritual."

He quotes a verse in the Qur'an—"From the earth We have created you and We shall receive you back again in the Last Day"—and pauses to see if I understand what he is saying.

The Qur'an can be understood on many different levels, and an understanding suggests itself to me, then floats away. Spiritual men and women also speak in revealed meanings, what the Sufi mystic Pir Inayet Khan refers to as "the meaning of that which exists behind that which is revealed."

I watch the Sheikh's mouth in my intense desire to understand each word clearly, and then I realize that the words are not coming from his mouth, but somewhere deep inside. And I am no longer listening with my ears. The sensation is inexplicable, but I have no time to roll in it and Abdel-Khalik will help me resolve this later.

He says that this earth we are polluting and destroying comprises the spiritual and physical raw ingredients for the creation of future generations. To build stronger generations, we must therefore strengthen and replenish the earth. Quite simply, by our abuse or misuse of the planet, we poison the spiritual and physical life-stock, the basic building material, from which our children and future generations are formed. And since we return to the earth upon death, our lives, our selves, enrich or weaken that stock.

This is not an ashes-to-ashes, dust-to-dust homily. He is saying that our responsibility does not end with death. When it comes down to it, we are spiritual compost.

If we return to the earth as corrupted beings, we corrupt the future. However, if we fill the earth with goodness, both through treatment of it and betterment of ourselves, we contribute to a better future. Rumi, the fourteenth-century mystical poet, alluded to this when he spoke of himself as a seed beneath winter's cold clay, waiting for the life-giving spring of the Beloved. Somehow I can't imagine that the spring Rumi yearned for was polluted with toxic waste or effluence.

"On a practical level—" I begin to ask. The Sheikh holds his hand in a simple gesture, fingertips together, palm cupped toward heaven as if catching raindrops, that says have patience. He's already going in that direction.

Tantawi moves easily between the spiritual and the pragmatic. He may speak softly of spiritual legacy, but his immediate advice is down to earth. Saving lives is as important as saving souls. Clean water is as important as the spirit.

"Yes, we should plant beneficial plants and trees," he says as he begins a list in which he refers to the universal We of the much-hyped Global Village. "We should see there is water in the wells by preserving the rivers. We should try to preserve every good thing for the sake of the future generations and for the people living now. We should construct houses for the poor and build factories to give a hand in the progress and prosperity of humanity."

These are equally global and local responsibilities. The Sheikh encourages international collaboration, the exchange of commerce and ideas that benefit and advance humanity. I begin to wonder what Egypt has to exchange when it becomes clear that the Sheikh does not condone charity as a lifestyle.

Sheikh Tantawi is adamant about personal responsibility. Along with charity, which, as one of the Five Pillars, is part of the moral core of the religion, Islam also believes in the Day of Judgment when God will ascertain the actions and works of each person. Humanity must therefore do the best possible, collectively and individually. Each man must be productive by his own hands and mind, not sit and wait for the rain to make his fields grow for him. The rest is in the hands of God.

He clearly gives short shrift to laziness or self-indulgence and refers to a verse in the Qur'an: "God Almighty has created the earth for you and it is in your hands to do whatever you will. You should do whatever you can to have prosperity and good things for yourself."

The Sheikh's refusal to show favoritism to the university student who petitioned him yesterday is a case in point. She must advance through her own endeavor, not a holy handout. The mind-set of Inshallah—God willing—a common Arabic expression often used to circumvent responsibility or commitment, is not acceptable to this leader of Islam. Fatalism, like favoritism, just doesn't cut it.

"Where does religion fit in to our lives today?" I ask him.

"The role of the religion is to correct what people have spoiled in this world," he replies, "and to advise them, to lead them, toward what will make them live in safety and peace."

He returns to our theme of Earth as a garden. The Paradise given by God to be enriched by man has become a jungle, overgrown from neglect and man's injustice to man.

"We cannot deny," he says, "that all nations in this age, at the end of this century, are living in a type of jungle. The strong try to eat the weak who live with them. In this jungle there is no mercy and no justice."

In addition to knowledge, responsibility, commitment and hard work, the Sheikh also believes in the moral imperative of the strong to practice justice and protect the weak. Planting trees and providing clean water is not enough.

The assistants are leaning forward, nodding in somber agreement as they focus on middle space. Newspaper headlines are filled with the failing negotiations between Palestinians and Israeli settlers. Television images capture mosques set alight in Pakistan. Bosnia is still burning. Africa has become kindling.

"In building a global community," I ask him, "are there lessons we can learn from history?"

According to Tantawi, oppression is one of the negative lessons of history.

"To build a good nation, a good society," he says, "one must spread good morals and justice and mercy in all aspects of society. You should respect the freedom of others and do your best to spread the prospect of peace and safety to all who live with you. This is what history has told us in all the past ages and will continue to say for the future."

"From your perspective," I ask, referring back to our earlier discussion of spiritual compost, "the planet both benefits and suffers from the generations that go before. How, then, would you describe the present state of the human spirit?"

He glances at his watch. His assistants shift in their seats and try to signal the end of the interview. For me, the conversation has just begun. I see the interest in his eye, and with a gesture of his hand, he tells his assistants to hold tight.

"Spiritual life in today's world—East or West, North or South—has become distracted," he says, and the translator searches for another word. "Illegitimate."

How can the spiritual life be bound or legitimated through laws, I wonder, but as he continues I begin to understand that he is talking about a core characteristic of humanity: the state of virtue—or the belief in it.

The Grand Sheikh characterizes virtue as "mercy, kindness, the sincere love and respect for one another." He calls for a return to virtue, but believes that this will only come with a return to the spiritual side of life. One of the keys, he says, is that we must rid ourselves of selfishness.

"In this way," he says, "we will prevent man from being reduced to an animal."

The images he is offering are sobering. The garden as an overgrown jungle. Man, God's vice-regent, reduced to an animal.

"If the world remains as it is today," he continues, "it will

weaken in the next century. But if we increase the number of reasonable people—people who think and are educated, people who
are involved in their culture, good moral people—virtue will
increase."

Then, he says, the world will be characterized by peace and
fulfillment.

The Sheikh also argues for quality, not quantity. He argues for
balance and tolerance.

"We can learn from each other," the Sheikh says quietly, "from
our differences, as well as what we have in common."

According to his personal translator, who has been by his side
during the ten years since his inauguration, Tantawi believes there
are common beliefs in religions that provide room for cooperation and negotiation. For example, bringing man out of darkness
into light is a concept that most religions share. We all benefit
from this enlightenment.

The timekeeper taps his watch dramatically. We have gone way
over schedule, but neither the Sheikh nor I move.

He signals one last time to his assistants to be patient.

I smile at the use of this simple Egyptian hand signal for
patience by one of the most important men in the region. Cairo
has to be the only place in the world that has a hand sign urging
patience and they use it as often as New Yorkers give the finger in
insult. This may be the secret of their long existence.

That Egyptians are conservative and moderate is a recurrent
theme told by many different people during my stay. Extremes
and conflict are alien to their nature, I am told. Take, for example,
the traffic of Cairo, my friends tell me. In view of the deafening
multilane anarchy that alternately sweeps and nudges life along, I
find this a strange parallel.

It is not anarchy, but an elaborate process of negotiation and
compromise. How many times have you seen a traffic accident in
the city (the open roads are a different matter), or a violent argument? I admit, few and rarely, if at all.

How many cars are there, and yet how often have you seen an

argument? Insults? Yes. Defamation of bloodline? Sure. But not violent confrontation. Drivers ignore the rules, the One Way Only signs, with the tacit understanding that one of them may have to back up, and not necessarily the transgressor.

Drivers, like pedestrians, understand coexistence, I am told. Cars come within inches, touch hips as often as the general population. They say—no problem, no offense—and move on without argument. One is always able to back up along a one-way street.

I try not to test the Sheikh's patience with one last question, but he motions me to go ahead.

"As teacher and spiritual leader," I ask, "what advice would you give to children? And to the next generations?"

He knows I am a cultural historian, and I am suspicious at first that he has pulled out a stock answer tailored to my interests.

"I say to the following generations," he begins, "that you have to be careful to understand the lessons history gave to us."

These he has already spoken about, especially oppression.

Then he continues to lay out practicalities, which reinforce the restraints of society and the role of religion within it.

"You should respect religious realities and virtues," he says, "and keep those morals and virtues."

But then he leaves the official path and begins to add his personal advice. He is speaking not only to children of Egypt, or to Muslims throughout the world. He speaks almost wistfully to all children, perhaps the Universal Child, and from experience.

His voice is soft.

"I advise children to keep sight of those who set a good example and benefit humanity; to always seek to build good relations between individuals and others. I urge the young not to destroy or spoil the earth, nor to commit any act that could harm humanity. Look after other people, so that they may live in safety. Do not discriminate among them."

He pauses for a moment and looks down at his hands. We, too, look down at his hands.

"If you do these things," he says, "I assure you that you will live in goodness. You will live in prosperity, and peace. And you will live a better future than previous generations."

We sit in thick silence, digesting his advice. It is likely that his assistants have children and are thinking of them and the world they live in and inherit. I think of how these principles are universal. We each nod agreement from wherever our thoughts have taken us.

The Grand Sheikh of Islam stands and shakes my hand. With that, he shakes us out of the warm state into which he has led us. The vision of a perfect world.

He breaks his circle and begins to walk away, accompanied by his head assistant who is going over the day's schedule. My eyes follow, unwilling to let him go.

The Sheikh stops, midstep, places his hand on his assistant's arm and turns back toward me.

His face is now stern and he looks me straight in the eye. I am uncomfortable and swallow hard.

"The message which I send to all people in the world," he says, "is the saying of Almighty God in the Holy Qur'an: You should do your best to work together for the sake of piety and for the sake of good, and for the sake of peace. Not for the sake of aggression and oppression."

A small, tired man turns and leaves for another endless day of meetings.

CHAPTER 7

fire Bird

The alleys of the bazaar wrap back upon themselves, dead-end and twist much like the circuitry of a motherboard. At intersections they surge with code—eye contact, touch, gesture, shouts—communication limited yet enhanced by the slow-moving humans that carry it. I'm on overload.

Less than 24 hours ago, I was knocking on the outer doors of the Grand Sheikh of Islam. Now it's over. Or should be.

My feet and mind are frozen. Shock, I suppose. I'm searching for some reconnect with the mundane world, at the same time scanning the crowd for a signal. I spot him.

A pulse of energy, a young barefooted tea boy in a cotton gallabiya, threads between the thighs of pedestrians dispensing vials of hot brew and sweet chatter to the storekeepers who sit under shaded canvas overhangings waiting for the day's first customers to enter their stalls. We bump each other, the electric-eyed boy and I. I touch his shoulder to right his balance, and we exchange a beat of recognition.

I enter the stream.

Heraclitus said that you can't enter the same river twice for neither you nor the river are the same. Leaving the Grand Sheikh, stepping outside into the muddy deluge of humanity, I sense the shift inside me. If you were to excavate my soul and scrape its stratigraphy in the early morning light when the evening moisture still clings to the soil, before the noon heat sucks the detail from dimension, you would see the charred layer of an inferno displaced by a tremblor so gentle that children slept undisturbed by its subterranean movement. The straightforward line of my soul, like the lifeline in the palm of my hand, is now dislocated, broken, jarred, one point up, the other down, and the edges will never touch again.

The disjuncture is not quite clear, but I know it's there. And I'm not sure I signed off on the outpatient metaphysical surgery.

Abdel-Khalik and I have just spent hours in the Grand Sheikh's antechamber bent over the tape recorder, our digital scribe, playing and replaying, translating the words of Sheikh Tantawi. We'd pause, digress, wipe sweat and drink tea, write, cross out, rewrite. The translator and I took turns at pressing buttons, he to get the exact, precise and official translation, I to replay phrases for the sound I'd missed; the staccato background of rising traffic, doors opening and closing, the clink of tea glasses, of prayer beads. I'd rewind for the clarity of silence, the pauses that organize thoughts, the cadence of a language so old you downshift to an earlier life to catch its meaning. And to attach to the words their companion images of tone and nuance, gesture and expression, before they slide away. Finally we were sated. Tonight, after a visit with Dr. Mohammed's family, I plan to sit alone with the words and read them through in silence. God willing.

Right now in the bazaar not far from Al-Azhar, my head pounds, a combination of the piercing light and the expiation of focus. Right now, I could die of thirst. Right now. My throat is tight, but I have no small change to buy bottled water and need to cash some AmEx. I'm also famished. My body, now waking to its normal rhythm, finds it's already burned a million anxious calories. I slide the scarf from my head and shake my hair loose, and immediately regret it. Even in the shade, the sun sears my skull, and all that loose hair around my neck is stifling.

After hours of the cerebral, I seek the sensual familiar as antidote.

I find myself resting on a low wooden stool in the cool stall of a fabric merchant, rubbing silky Egyptian cotton through my fingers, drinking bottled water ordered by the owner and brought to us from the café by the young tea boy. The smell of cloth is intoxicating and I hold a bolt to my nose and inhale. Did you ever stand in the closet as a child and inhale the clothes of your mother; or as an adult, the garments of a lover? I'm wearing that same smile you wore then as I nuzzle the cloth of Mother Egypt.

The old merchant doesn't find sniffing cloth more strange than smelling a baby's neck or a ripe peach, or if so, is not willing to lose a customer over it. He sips his tea through brown teeth, punching out numbers on a calculator still sheathed in its original plastic wrapping to keep the desert sand out of his divisions and subtractions. Two other women, squeezed into the small space, buying lengths for caftans, also hold brightly patterned fabric to their noses after caressing the material that will lie close to their bodies or the body of a loved one. Victoria and her catalogue of secrets has a lot to learn.

The tea boy squats in magnetic silence outside the shop. On and off, between running errands for the alleymen, he's been there the last half hour. He looks up at me like a brown-eyed orphaned pup and his presence annoys me. I don't want a beggar or an incubus attaching himself to me today; I want to be able to walk off my inner exhaustion in my private bubble of silence. I need time and space to digest the words of the Sheikh.

The boy's not outside when I leave, and I'm relieved. But puzzled.

This is a local bazaar, rarely visited by tourists, and since I give the appearance of knowing my way, the locals leave me alone. You look as if you've always lived here, an Egyptian once remarked, and part of me feels I have. And so, when I leave the stall, I turn my head toward the minarets that mark the horizon to decide the direction I'll take. Al-Azhar's scaffolded minaret is but a stone's throw direct, and I wonder what problem the Grand Sheikh is addressing now, whether he is counseling a washerwoman or world leader. This is not my path.

A thought niggles at me. Both the Grand Sheikh and Dr. Mohammed dismissed my intellectual credentials. These learned men threw away the achievements of the mind, more concerned about my heart. I curb a spark of irritation and my mind vows to restore itself to alpha-dominance. Meanwhile, my emotions are humming that my mind has met with the highest-ranked Muslim cleric, give it a rest, but mind and heart continue to struggle with me.

Each end of the curving alley flows into the courtyard of a mosque, and I turn my entire body from right to left like a hand puppet, considering how I will wander. Or, how I am *supposed* to wander. The minaret to the right captures me and tugs me forward, but I resist, testing this Free Will business, reasoning the alley at that end is in full sun, and turn toward the other. I photograph the intersection, the gorgeous hubbub of humanity, the women on errands, etcetera, but all the time I'm looking over my shoulder toward the other sun-scorched mosque. I turn and walk toward it, casually, so God won't notice my change of heart.

A major intersection separates me from the small mosque and its age-stained walls of striped stone, and I join the crowd as it surges through the eddying traffic, carried around, then forward, by its eternal persistence. The wooden gates to the mosque are closed. I weave along the sidewalk, swimming now against the crowd in the unprotected late morning sun, occasionally moving more backward than forward, searching for an entrance. The building is locked up.

A series of amateurish posters handwritten in Arabic, photocopied notices pasted on the stone wall, grabs my eye. On them a wild-looking bird rises into the air, all feathers and flaming wings. It is a notice for a Sufi gathering, a special performance. Someone has penned a notice in English beside it and sheltering under a handkerchief of shade, I fumble in my camera bag for my glasses.

"You are invited . . . ," the pen has written across the wall.

"She is the Fire Bird, Madame," a small voice beside me says in English.

I jump. The tea boy stares up at me, and I want to curse him.

I slam my eyes shut, cutting him out of the picture.

"Piss off. Go on, you little pest. Go away." This I don't say; it comes from an angry voice inside that survived an earlier summer of Egyptian street children begging for money, touching my hair. . . . I like to think I've matured since then. Instead I say, "The Fire Bird? Really?"

The story of the Phoenix is as much a part of Egypt as the enigmatic Sphinx. The ancients associated this fabulous bird, with its brilliant fire-red and gold plumage and haunting song, with the sun, and thus immortality. Heliopolis, the City of the Sun, where the mythological bird immolated itself every five hundred years on a flaming nest of aromatic branches and spices, is just across the Nile, a sprawling suburb of twenty-first-century Cairo.

The Romans, enamored as much by the Phoenix as they were of Cleopatra, carted both birds back to Europe in their bag of spoils. They made the Fire Bird the symbol of empire, but she would have flown there anyway. Ancient Chinese, Persian, Russian, even American Indian cultures have their Fire Bird. She's lodged in our minds—our birdcage of the imagination—and we carry her with us on our wanderings.

This kid's brown eyes are birdlike, too, unshakable. He's an old man in fresh clothing. And I'm the mark.

"Yes," the tea boy says. Serious, old man's face. Jerking English. "Tonight she is dancing."

I don't reply. He is no coincidence. In the Middle East, paranoia descends quicker than nightfall upon those who reject coincidence. This bird-child has followed me here, no mistaking. Did someone send him as a messenger from the Sheikh's office, knowing that I'm looking for mystics? Is this part of a game? A test?

Paranoia is to coincidence as jealousy is to love: stepsisters. Ugly stepsisters. After the recent serial coincidences, I'm wary of buying in too deep. A love that's too perfect, too quick. I'm pulling back. For a second I even consider Leyla's pointed comments about security police, about staying away from trouble.

"Yes, Madame," he says, continuing in English, "I must for to invite you to come tonight."

"Who invites me?" I look over his head, back toward the bazaar. The kid must be some front for a tour group that pulls tourists in to watch the Sufis do their trance thing. Whoopee. No way. I've seen these public artistic renditions of Sufi rituals in other countries performed as interpretative dance routines for tourists, and they leave me cold.

"My friend," he replies in Arabic. "This is a special night. We invite you."

"But, who?" I repeat. The child doesn't reply, just stands there, his hands crossed politely in front of him. He doesn't smile or shift his weight. He doesn't plead or wheedle. His small face is serious and stays on mine. We stand in silence, the din of traffic beating in on us.

I'm feeling suddenly chilled in the hundred-degree heat. I'm swimming close to the edge.

"Not possible," I reply in colloquial Egyptian. "I'm busy. I must work." This is true, but I'm also curious. Who would have sent the young boy with the message? Or is it even a message?

"Inshallah, God willing, I will try," I say to the calm face.

"Inshallah," he says. "God willing," his mouth says, but his eyes blink with disappointment. Damn.

We wander back to the main drag, toward the bazaar where I can catch a taxi going in the right direction, back over the Nile to Leyla's, to Dr. Mohammed's. The tea boy escorts me, watching for traffic, stepping in front of me when another child rides his bicycle too close, winning my affection. I have an urge to kiss his sun-warmed head as I would a younger brother, my own child. Perhaps. Perhaps, tonight . . .

At the corner, I reach into my satchel and fish around for some change.

"Here," I say. "Thank you for helping me."

The child steps back, pulling his hand into his robe as if burned. His eyes bulge.

"No, no," he says. "I am not taking this money, Madame."

I'm confused; street kids never refuse money. And annoyed; I am paying for this conversation to end.

"No, Madame," he says.

No what? No, I'm not in control and this conversation is going to continue? Or No, I'm wrong, and he isn't a street child?

Too tired to think, I thrust the money toward him again.

"I am not taking the money for helping," he replies.

He touches his fingers to his chest and lowers his eyes.

"This helping is from my heart."

At that moment, as shame creeps up my neck, I determine I will not go tonight. I turn and walk away.

CHAPTER 8

Back to the womb

When you have a problem, walk it off, I was told growing up. Geographical therapy. Actually, it was more like, get out of my bloody hair and go for a walk, will you? But it came down to the same thing: When I asked too many questions, I ended up walking. Fairly walked to the other side of the planet, I did—with the help of a few planes, boats and trains—in search of a few good answers.

Walking in Cairo is difficult except in the earliest hours after dawn, not because I'm foreign or a woman, or a blond woman, but because of the math. Seventeen million slow-walking, genetically patient people stuffed into a few miles bordering the Nile. A long-legged female with a thirty-nine-inch athletic stride. Disaster. Swimming is my other therapy, but the Nile is out of the question. Swimming allows me to scream underwater. And blow bubbles. I do it after I teach. Throw myself into the club pool and scream. Not because of the students, but the futility of making the past relevant on a fast-fact planet. But I'm away from that for the summer, so let's keep moving, and asking questions, maybe getting answers.

I change my mind about going back to the apartment. The

meeting with the Grand Sheikh has opened its own intellectual can of spiders. I am a Christian, but I know more about the intricacies of Islam than my own religion. I've studied and taught about Islam, the religion and culture, for half of my life now, a couple of decades. You could say I'm at home in the great house of Islam, comfortable—treated with warmth and respect because Muslims are hospitable—but the house isn't mine. I've always been a guest. A perpetual outsider. And for the first time this disturbs me.

Maybe if I soak up some Christian vibes, I'll get some perspective. Check out the Copts. The Egyptian Christians. The Sons of the Pharaohs.

You can't get much closer to the Christian Church than Old Cairo, the Coptic quarter built into the remains of a Roman fortress. Two thousand years ago, the infant Jesus went underground in Egypt with Mary and Joseph, fleeing the bloody hands of Herod. From the Sinai, down the Nile to the deserts around Asyout in Upper Egypt, the Holy Family dotted the country with future pilgrimage sites. For many Christians, their arrival fulfilled a prophecy of Isaiah that laid the foundation of a living Church in Egypt. Within a decade of Christ's death, Apostle Mark, martyr and recognized founder, officially established the Church in Egypt, which has managed to survive the bloodiest eras of political persecution and internal hemorrhaging of early Christian dogma.

For an historian the Copts hold another fascination. Their liturgies have remained true to the apostolic tradition and include the unique allegory and symbolism they hand-carried into Christianity from the ancient Egyptians and the priests of the Pharaohs. The Copts also started the tradition of camping out in the desert, seeking God in the stars, founding monasteries and communes that are undergoing revival today.

When the country was conquered by Islam in the seventh century, Copt, once a Greek term for all Egyptians, came to mean Christian Egyptians or native nonconverts. Today, the term refers to Christians, predominantly the Coptic Orthodox Church of

Alexandria and Ethiopia, but includes Catholics, Greek and Syrian Orthodox and variant Protestants. In the present face of religious tension, there's also a popular movement among Egyptians to use Copt to describe all Egyptians in the spirit of their shared and unifying heritage: sons and daughters of the Pharaohs.

I can't walk to Old Cairo or ride a donkey as the infant Jesus did, so I leave it up to a supercaffeinated cabbie who hasn't slept since Cleo took the asp.

Cairo is on overdrive. Traffic, noise, horns blare at a drummingly numbing pitch. The taxi, on its last legs, coughs through traffic, choking at a standstill on an overpass where new surface is being laid by hand—no machinery. We are stalled high above the Nile as a band of matchstick men in gallabiyas spread the tar, hot and smoking, with great, rough trowels onto this modern highway that winds down the Nile into the desert. Another man follows behind them sprinkling finely ground asphalt from a basket as if sowing seeds in a field.

Below us the lush fecundity of the Nile holds tight to yet another time. Groves of date palms survive among the concrete encroachment of apartment buildings. A *faluka* in full sail glides across an Orientalist painting. Out there, beyond the haze and out of reach, are the Pyramids, the burial place of the Pharaohs.

The cabdriver takes a scenic detour near the Old City, the meter ticking away, driving around in circles through the noxious dump and running lakes of sewage. The smell is raw on the back of my throat. Mud brick huts dot the landscape like dried scabs. Beside the pockmarked road, under a makeshift shelter of dried fronds, an old man sleeps next to clay water vessels, jars and lanterns with incised patterns, stacked neatly for impulse buying. Tethered to his ankle, a brown she-goat snuffles among the weeds.

This is a different world from the new city center with its skyscrapers and neon. This is urgently biological, the Cairo I remember from my previous visit, where each day I weighed my own weight loss due to dysentery against my desire to stay.

Heat, clear and piercing, almost stinging in its precision, beats through the open windows of the taxi and there is no hiding, left or right, from it. Mind-numbing. I need my mind to be numbed right now. To stop thinking.

Late yesterday when I got through to the cathedral at Asyout where the Nile Bishop once presided, the phone line burred into eternity. I tried the Cairo cathedrals again. One picked up.

The name of the present bishop is not Nuweiba, a voice informed me. I inhaled and forgot to ask if he was dead, thanked the assistant and hung up.

I called her back. Does she know where I can find him, I ask.

"I do not remember him," she replied. She asked someone else in the room, but they didn't remember him either.

It's only been fourteen years and he's evaporated.

I phoned Asyout again. Nothing.

While I'm circumambulating Cairo with an assortment of taxi drivers, one of Leyla's assistants, a young Coptic woman whose uncle is a priest, is working on getting me an appointment with the Coptic Orthodox pope. And Dr. Mohammed has led me to a man who knows someone who knows a monk at the desert monastery where Matta the Poor resides. Later today I'll submit my request to Security for permission to travel to the desert monastery just in case God is willing.

In the backseat of the cab, lulled by the *rik-a-tik-a-tik* of the meter, I finally empty myself and allow myself to be carried forward. There is nothing more I can do. I have no agenda, no purpose to distract me, only to wait for the knots to be tied—or untied.

The Christian quarter is swept clean, doused in sunlight and brave geraniums. Small clots of pilgrims, dazed by heat and holiness, trot along the well-worn paths between churches and gift shop, a few paces behind guides waving flags, and ahead of hawkers waving postcards. I descend into the close darkness of the Church of Abu Serga and rest inside the doorway, adjusting to the change in light, absorbing the fifteen centuries of lingering incense into my lungs. Among stilted icons of stern-faced saints, a riotous celebration of organic vegetal forms wrap their tendrils around column and wall and confirm my personal hypothesis that God is indeed a vegetarian.

To the right of the altars, the entrance to the subterranean cave where the Holy Family stayed is locked but an old guard, a Coptic cross in the shape of the Pharaonic ankh tattooed onto the back of his hand, obliges and makes a show of finding the key. The cave, once on street level, appears sunken as generations of human activity and debris rose above it. A few Greek pilgrims are wandering around with another guard on "overtime." For the intimation of an additional fee, the guard unlocks another door and gives me five minutes alone in the underbelly of the church, closed for general tourism. This is the holy cave where Mary and Jesus lived briefly on the run from Herod.

I step back, overcome with awe and disgust. The cave is now a fetid pool. In a fit of primeval reclamation, putrid seepage and slime from the Nile now inundate the holy site. The Garden of Eden is crawling back into the womb.

Surely this is not the future the old bishop was talking about? Return to Egypt and you will see the future? I think of the words of the Grand Sheikh, that without mercy and kindness, without sincere love and kindness for each other, the garden planet becomes a jungle. No, this cesspool belongs to the past.

The guard, mistaking my speechlessness for religious fervor, offers me another wonder for which he holds the keys: the Chapel of Saint George, where the martyr's relics are displayed. In the outer chamber an elderly woman in black, a Greek pilgrim, is wrapping a length of heavy rusted chains around her thin shoulders and chest. These are the chains in which Saint George was wrapped when he was martyred. To wear them is to bring a blessing. Right.

The old woman is sobbing, buckling under the weight and the experience, and another pilgrim, a young bearded man, helps her stand as she finishes her prayer.

The guard glances to see if I want to wrap myself in chains.

I shoot him a look that says, Are you friggin' nuts?!

Superstition. I want no part of this dark superstition—let alone superstition cloaked with bondage—and walk quickly out into the sunshine.

I'm riffling through books in the gift shop, looking for something useful I can wrap my mind around. I'm at a loss. This fecund world of Copts with its cult of martyrs, its living saints, miracles, angels, mystical texts, reverberating chants and ancient rituals is as removed from country-club Protestantism as you can get. The incense-waving Smoky Marys of Catholicism look clinical by comparison.

An introduction to the Coptic Orthodox Church glosses over the mysteries of science and religion that filtered from the ancient Egyptians into the hands of renowned early Coptic mystics of Alexandria. Religion and Science. Good, we're getting somewhere. I read further: the Pharaonic Egyptians may have been working under the guidance of superhumans from outer space, it suggests. Hang on now. I don't have to come all the way to Egypt to learn about aliens in the Pyramids, I could have stopped at the checkout at my local Safeway.

I snap the introduction shut and pick up a harmless book on Coptic art.

The book falls open to an early Coptic icon of a saint, God knows who. Around his head is a huge golden ball, a sun that's supposed to look like a halo, but it's the sun. Out of the sun flies a sinuous, wild-winged bird. The Phoenix of the ancients. The Fire Bird.

I'm sure the color has drained from my face. My stomach's queasy. I look around for the tea boy.

"Where's this?" I ask the assistant. No manners. She directs me to the adjacent church, Saint Barbara, to an altar screen. But the bird's not there, so I sit out my frustration on a bench.

"God, God, what is going on?" I whisper. "What the bloody hell is happening to me?"

I refuse to plead, but I look up to, you know, where Heaven is. From where the Eternal Eye looks down.

Fourteen years ago, after I met the Nile Bishop, I went swimming in the desert. In a spring, in an oasis, in the desert, but we'll get to that another time. This was an ancient spring, gushing up out of nowhere, with nothing around for miles and there, in the middle of the desert, I was looking down on myself, from God's Eye, the Eternal Eye. Yes, I could see myself through God's Eye looking down. In that instant of clarity, I knew exactly where I was on earth.

The point is that moment of clear knowledge, of insight, when the heart leaps and overrules the mind.

Fourteen years ago, for an instant, with pure clarity of the heart, I knew who I was. What has happened? I address the ceiling.

On the ceiling is a painting of a wild-winged bird.

I start to notice them everywhere. In the church. In the square. In the graveyard stele of the museum. Carved into stone walls. Painted into icons. Not the gentle cooing dove of peace. Not even the startled dove of Pentecost. But the muscular, angel-feathered, Fire Bird whose golden egg took life from heat.

An allegory for the Resurrection. For life after death—and persecution. Rebirth. The sons of the Pharaohs just couldn't leave this beautiful image behind and brought it with them into their new religion.

The Fire Bird. I hoot nervously at the coincidence. Then I begin to cry, a deep sobbing river. I am so utterly adrift in life.

I wipe my face on the sleeve of my shirt, blow my nose on the hem, and look one last time for the little tea boy. The square is empty.

Coincidence.

CHAPTER 9

another plane

Saint Kyrillos died one score and ten years ago. Within my lifetime and, yet, only now am I meeting him. Twenty-five, thirty years ago. Approximately. In a country as old as Egypt, time is relative. To a saint time was—is—irrelevant. So I'm learning.

During his long life, the former Pope Kyrillos (Cyril) VI was a worker of miracles. Dead, he has a website, several actually, that keep his name spinning through the ether, but matter, like time, is also irrelevant. To Copts his spirit is as alive now as it was then because, according to the Coptic Orthodox Church, you don't have to wait until you die to become a saint. You become a living saint existing between two worlds like the Pharaohs of old and Matta al-Maskin today in the desert. We all benefit from this intermediary state. This is wisdom.

Okay. I'm trying to learn something new, to suspend disbelief, so work with me.

Less than an hour ago (this time thing is still a tic), a professor at the American University in Cairo suggested that if I'm serious about an inside perspective of the Copts, I should go downstairs and talk to one of his colleagues, the former assistant to a saint.

I can't resist. Apart from my former mother-in-law who was working on her own beatification, I've never met anyone who was close to a saint. Besides, the present Coptic pope, Shenouda, is too busy to see me so this may be as near as I get to learning what it takes to be a spiritual person.

My friend phones downstairs. Talks a minute. Hangs up. The professor has been expecting me.

Time may be irrelevant, but Dr. Adel Beshai, former assistant to Saint Kyrillos, doesn't waste it. Beshai is an international econometrist, a numbers person, a stats cruncher, an unlikely person to be talking about something as intangible as miracles.

"Aaah, Pope Kyrillos, I used to know him when he was a monk," Adel Beshai begins as I snuggle into the semidarkness of his office; Beshai keeps the lights off to damper the sweltering heat. "In those days I was of a very young age. Then he was chosen to be the Patriarch, the pope, you know. Pope Kyrillos VI."

His palms are extended, churning air like a turbine engine. A pair of metal-rimmed glasses flips dangerously from the end of one hand. He's steamed up his small, dark office and pauses to wipe the fogged lenses.

He says Kyrillos in the Italian fashion, savoring the Rs and Ls as if they are love itself.

Among Copts, more than reverence, there is a wonderful affection bordering on love for this Church leader, complete with the goofy grin and dreamy eyes that love inspires. Copts talk of the dead leader as if he is alive, as being both stern and gentle, of his open door and his love of children. Love for him extends past the Christian Church. At the mention of his name, Muslims also become quiet. Miracles, Egyptians say, he performed miracles.

After my experience with the tea boy, I'm curious about what kind of man performed miracles and how this gentle passion continues to stir nearly thirty years after his death. I'm willing to listen—and Adel Beshai is prepared to talk.

"Ever since he was a monk, Pope Kyrillos was a very special person," Beshai says. "He was the only one I know of until today who did miracles. I mean, I have seen it. And the very special thing is this: How was it that everyone that entered to him came out with his face shining?"

He shrugs. I shrug in return. Miracles are not my forte.

In the late sixties, an apparition of the Virgin Mary hovered over the Church of Zeytoun in a Cairo suburb, flooding the night sky with an ethereal light. Thousands flocked to see it. Many were healed. The apparition made international news and you can still view the records in film archives. The tenure of Pope Kyrillos coincided with this apparition and I'm hoping that Adel Beshai will talk about it. To get there, we have to walk his personal path together. I slow my internal pace to match his.

"This is the main thing I want to say," Beshai says. He has the charm and timing of an orator and his English reveals traces of California with overtones of Shakespeare that could sound pompous but for the wonderful Italian-Arabic trill. "The Coptic Church is traditional, very strict, but as a spiritual person Pope Kyrillos was very understanding, very understanding. He was a very, very unusual person. He was very unassuming, a very simple man.

"He was the type of person who could read your mind and you could feel him reading your mind," he says. "And he was the sort of person if you tell him I commit sins, I am nasty and so on, he doesn't tell you, Well, the devil can make you commit sin one time but not the second time. He was like Christ—flexible and forgiving, but in such a fatherly way that made you not commit sins."

My own stepfather used the strap to make us not commit sins, so I wrestle to get a handle on this benevolent, fatherly image.

Black-and-white photographs of a hooded, unsmiling, long-bearded man glare down at me from the walls of Beshai's office: Pope Kyrillos. If you're accustomed to clean-shaven Western Christianity, they're rather spooky. Not fatherly at all. But there is another photograph beside Beshai's desk that catches my eye, and once so, I can't stop looking. Pope Kyrillos is in full papal regalia:

golden crown, encrusted cape, snood, and stands in front of an icon of Saint Mark. He stands three-fourths facing the camera: His full beard is now streaked with white. His eyes . . . his eyes are looking straight into the camera, at you, at me . . . and they're laughing.

Beshai also turns to the photograph. We're both smiling goofy smiles.

"He radiated love and power at once," Beshai says. "You know. Very awe-inspiring, he was. You could be scared of him, but then you were comfortable with him. You see, to be able to radiate this comfort instantaneously is the sign of spirituality. Your body almost shivers and you feel you are getting all the love in the world. He is most unusual."

He uses present tense, and I let it slide for now.

"How's that?" I ask.

"I remember when I was going for my degree at Stanford, to do my graduate degree," he says. "At Stanford in the States. In those days it was difficult to travel and my papers were kept for approval and so on. And one day I went to visit him at an odd time because I was going mad waiting for these papers."

Beshai pulls at his thinning hair in the excitement of reenactment. In front of me, he becomes a bewildered youth with a head of curls.

"So I went at three, three-thirty P.M. , a time when he is resting and as I am entering the Patriarchship—let me put it this way, his door was always open," he sidebars himself. "And his assistant was sitting outside—he's now a monk in St. Mena's monastery—he said, the pope is sleeping. You will wait until he wakes up. He just didn't finish the sentence and the bell rang, which means he woke up, so I entered in a fury. A fury."

Beshai's eyes are popping with rekindled youthful indignation. I'm right there with him, waiting for the Egyptian bureaucracy to grant me my own travel permit to the desert monastery.

"As I was walking to him," Beshai continues, "I wanted to tell him all these things; that I have this departmental fellowship from

Stanford and all that. I wanted to say that and that I want your prayers. But I didn't. You know what he told me?"

I shake my head.

" 'May you travel in peace and come back in peace,' Pope Kyrillos said. Without me uttering a word," Beshai says. "I go back home and relax. Next morning at quarter to nine the telephone rings, the mission's office rings. They say to my father, 'Is this the house of Adel Beshai?' My father says, 'Yes, I'm his father, what's wrong?' They say, 'No, because his papers came approved.' "

"Things like that," he says. "This was Pope Kyrillos."

We drink in the moment of silence. I, because among my women friends we'd say this was intuition, not a miracle; my male friends that it is statistically irrelevant.

"I am talking about my own experiences," Beshai continues. "Pope Kyrillos, I still think of him, talk to him, he is my guide in life. I have through this marvelous experience something that has colored my life and will color it until the last day. I feel there is nothing to worry about because of him."

His face is glowing. Indeed, the entire room is bathed in soft, diffuse light. This strange illumination registers at the back of my thoughts, but Beshai doesn't give me time to understand it.

"Yes, I feel there is nothing to worry about, but I just wonder," he says. "I'm a widely traveled man. I went to China in the days of Mao Tse-tung. I went to America. I studied in England in Oxford, and Italy, in Egypt here, and what sometimes bothers me is that the vast majority of people are good people, good. But this spiritual aspect is lacking in them. Okay, in my case I was lucky to have met him, but I already had preparedness inside me."

The professor sighs, long and deep.

"Our Coptic Church is still a lovely church . . . but I miss the times of Pope Kyrillos. You know what I mean?"

I do. I'm thinking of Sheikh Tantawi, the Grand Sheikh of Al-Azhar, and his unassuming ways, his common touch. The affection he stirs.

"He seems very human. Humane," I say.

"Humane, yes," he replies. "Godly at the same time. All right, professor, I'm a professor. I've lived all my life a professor. I have enough of professors! I need that other thing, you know what I mean. I need that other thing and it doesn't exist now. Now you find priests rushing from one wedding to another with their briefcase and the atmosphere is not as before. They mostly talk. Pope Kyrillos did not talk a lot. These spiritual people, they don't talk a lot, don't lecture. Sometimes he would sit and he wouldn't say a word, but he would radiate so much you would be filled twenty-five years later. Whether he said two words or four words."

"Could you give me an example?" I urge him.

"When I went to the States," he says, "after I came back from getting my master's from Stanford, I don't know, I was not feeling well. I don't know why, it was suddenly the change of culture and then on the way, you know, there was an accident in the plane. It was on the plane that came from Cairo, there was a comet, and the cover of the engine flew off. It was very serious, and anyway, we landed. And I did my degree and came back, and as soon as I arrive, he says, 'Oh, come in.' "

Adel Beshai suddenly laughs. He places his fingertips to his forehead and opens them toward me as if emitting sun rays.

"He always used to pull thoughts from my head," he says explaining his odd gesture. " 'Were you ever—was there an incident that shocked you,' Pope Kyrillos asked me. Although I was going to him, *Nooo,* he was right, there was. It was that thing, the plane, you know. And then he said to take some oil and he anointed me."

I'm having a hard time getting my hand around miracles so I grasp at a more tangible subject: the career track of a saint.

"Did Pope Kyrillos ever tell you how he was called to the order?" I ask. "How he became a pope? A saint?"

"He never tells no one of this," Beshai replies. "No, but his path is very clear, and this is a major point you need to know. These very, very spiritual people, each of them has a guiding saint. For Pope Kyrillos, it was Saint Mena."

Beshai then begins to tell me how the career trajectory of a saint began in generations past.

"The interesting thing I emphasize to you," he says, "is those very special fathers, each one has his guru, as it were. Pope Shenouda doesn't have Pope So-and-so as his mentor, but a saint. And in a way it is nice to have your saint whose name you always mention because this kills your ego. Pope Kyrillos used to chat with Saint Mena when people were with him, used to chat with him!"

Sixteen centuries ago, Mena the Miracle-maker, a high-ranked soldier and son of Christian ascetics, left the military to become a hermit. His conversion coincided with the bloody Diocletian persecutions in which more than 800,000 Christians were killed in an attempt to annihilate Christianity from the Roman Empire. These persecutions are memorialized by modern Copts as the Years of Martyrs.

Mena's body, buried at Mariout in the desert near Alexandria, remains the source of healing miracles. Following the Crusades and the explosion in Western pilgrims, the monastery at Mariout became a spa city known for healing the mind as well as the body. Small clay images of Mena have turned up from Heidelberg to Dongola and confirm his universal fame.

"He was called Father Mena before he was Pope Kyrillos," Beshai says, referring to the pope. "He vowed to retrace the tradition of St. Mena's monastery and rebuild it. When he became pope, the first thing he did was to rebuild the monastery. In a sense, in a spiritual level, Pope Kyrillos is Saint Mena, if you understand what I mean. Saint Mena was known for miracles."

"And miracles of healing, especially?" I interject.

"Yes, of healing," he says. "Even animals that passed by his place got healed. And people used to come from Greece and Italy and were healed and went back."

He becomes quiet.

"Pope Kyrillos, when he was a monk, he was Father Mena the Solitary, Abuna Mena al-Mutawwahid, because he was in a cave, living in a cave."

The hermits of the desert began this tradition within years of the death of Christ.

"He was first in the monastery near Wadi Natrun," he says. "Then he was in a cave near the monastery. Then he lived twelve years in a cave, a mill, in Old Cairo in the hills in Al-Muqattem. And in front of his cave was a hyena always, guarding him. Pope Kyrillos is this sort of person; he doesn't worry about things."

"Miracles," I say. "Miracles are commonplace here."

"It has always been commonplace in this part of the world. Pope Kyrillos always used to say that Egypt is a very special place. I think he said, don't forget that once Christ lived here."

"Did you see any of the miracles of healing?" I ask.

"What is a miracle?' he responds. "People say, 'What it means is this one performs miracles.' But the fact we can walk is a miracle! Miracles are happening every second."

Beshai makes miracles seem so ordinary. Listening to him, I begin to understand how they become part of the everyday. How even the extraordinary appearance of Mary at the Church of Zeytoun was treated without hype. Miracles are treated not so much as the creation of something new or extraordinary, but the returning of something to its normal state. Stasis.

"There was a student of mine here years ago," Beshai begins. "She was born to a rich Coptic family here, and she had parents, father and mother, who were not church people. Her brother was born with a disease and until he came to the age of five, he was in a very bad shape. They were very rich people from Asyout, so they took him to England and to America to cure him. They had enough, they had lots of money. But no way, no way, and then they came back."

Asyout? The bishop on the Nile train was from Asyout. My focus sharpens. Beshai continues.

"A relative of the family said, Why don't you take him to Pope Kyrillos, but they didn't believe in this. As a mother she said, 'Okay, lets go. What else will I do with him?' The day that they were going, that man who was a relative of theirs who knew Pope

Kyrillos, he came to the house to take the mother, the father, and the sick boy. His sister, who was my student here, who's still around living in Zamalek, the day they were coming, the sister screamed in a frenzy, 'Take me with you, take me with you.' She was almost out of breath. Anyway, they said, 'No you're not coming with us.'

"They all went without her. They came to Pope Kyrillos; the man who knew Pope Kyrillos entered, the father and the mother for the first time they entered to him, and bringing the boy. Pope Kyrillos ignored the man, ignored the father, ignored the mother, and called to the boy: 'Come, my son. And when your sister wanted to come, why didn't they bring her? Your sister wanted to come with you, why didn't your parents bring her with you?'

"The mother told me when he said that she was nonexistent."

"Nonexistent?" I asked.

Adel Beshai purses his lips and looks for another word. There is none.

"Nonexistent," he says. "Stopped existing. She was surprised how he knew, you know."

Beshai continues.

"And he prayed for the boy," he says. "The boy was perfect and graduated from engineering and got married five years ago, and things like that."

"And the sister?" I ask.

"The sister was not sick," he replies. "She just wanted to come. But the fact that he said, why didn't they bring her, it was a sign to the parents."

Adel Beshai falls silent, lost in the moment. I wait. He looks up.

"No, Pope Kyrillos was very special," he says. "So really at the heart of it, when it comes to this spirituality it is this: that if you liken God to the sea, the sea is the Infinite in a sense. And suppose you can drink salt water, you can drink it, but you can never drink the entire sea. Also, you can never be the sea, but if you drink it you can be filled with it, you can have the same nature."

Sufi mystics are fond of this allusion of God and the sea. The Sea of Consciousness in which we are one with the One. Jung borrowed heavily from this concept of collective consciousness.

"So Pope Kyrillos just performed miracles like Christ," Beshai continues. "Once he went to the church in Alexandria and there was a mother and a daughter, ten years old. The daughter was born blind. And you know, before our mass, they go around, making the incense, and as he was going around, and he just walked to that daughter, and just put the cross on her head. By the time he was making the turn and entering the altar, the girl started to see."

The professor grabs the edge of the desk and leans forward.

"That *was* Pope Kyrillos! That *is* Pope Kyrillos!"

"So you believe that his spirit still lives on?" I ask, unnecessarily.

"Absolutely," he says. "So, now you know, this is my lineage, I mean. This is the line of the ancient fathers."

"What makes these people spiritual?" I ask.

"Spirituality is not going into details," Beshai says. "Nowadays, they go a lot into details. Spirituality, now they say, if you haven't gone to, what's the word, confession, you shouldn't—now they issue the instructions—you shouldn't attend confession if you didn't attend the reading of the Gospel before the mass, you shouldn't go. They keep issuing orders. But, you know, people like that, God lives in them, also.

"So, Pope Kyrillos, this is what we need in life. This spiritualness, this, not emphasis on details, not emphasis on words. Even here in the Sunday school, they teach them a lot from the Old Testament. What is the longest name in the Old Testament? Silly questions, missing the point. I'd like people all around the world, people to concentrate on the essence, to take one verse from the Bible, one verse and just meditate on it. This is the approach I like."

"Was this also the approach of Pope Kyrillos?" I ask. "To meditate on one verse?"

"Pope Kyrillos's approach was above it all," Beshai replies. "Pope Kyrillos's approach, if you came to see him, you would hear from him two words or four words you would never forget the rest of your life."

"Do you remember a particular message he gave you?" I ask. I expect an upbeat answer from this energetic man, but the question stirs a confession.

"One day I went to get an autograph from him. That was the only time he was tough with me, but I understand. I said to him, 'Could you write to me something? An autograph?' He told me, 'I will *not* write or anything, I will just—I have the book here—I will just make the sign of the cross here on top of it.' He was angry."

Shame and sadness seep into the voice of this middle-aged man.

"Seven years later I met a monk who was a good monk," he says. "Then I understood what he had done. He told me, he was giving you a message that really says concentrate on very important things. It is not words written by him that will guard you. The unseen, the unwritten, the fact that he did as he did is enough."

The monks in the desert monasteries spend their lives in the service of the unseen. Many are mystics who pursue the hidden meanings of the invisible in order to attain union with God. I ask Beshai about Kyrillos and the monasteries.

"Once he became pope he sent all the monks to the monasteries," Beshai says. He waves his hands as if scooting away children. "He said that all the monks should be in the monasteries."

In the Coptic Orthodox Church priests marry and serve the community, whereas monks remain celibate and serve God. Bishops come from the line of monks, and the Orthodox pope is elected from the bishops. Before Kyrillos sent the monks back to the desert, they were spread around saying their prayers in the churches of Shobra, Cairo. He sent the monks back to focus on meditation, but not necessarily to endure physical hardship.

"At that same time, Matta al-Maskin and Father Amiyya and

another monk were here in Fayoum, in the area where you have the waterfalls—in Wadi Rayan. After they were there for two years, Pope Kyrillos said they'd better come back or else their health will suffer. Two came back, the other one didn't come. That was Matta al-Maskin. Later on Matta al-Maskin came. So the pope has told him, 'Ah, you have grown old, Matta.' "

My ears have pricked up at the mention of Matta al-Maskin, the desert bishop who is using the technology of the Pharaohs to make the monastery self-sustaining. The young priest friend of Dr. Mohammed's left a phone number for me to contact him, and we spent late yesterday playing telephone tag. I ask Beshai if there is a difference in the spirituality of these two spiritual men.

"They are the different types but there is something common," he explains. "Matta al-Maskin is the sort of spiritual philosopher who you would ask to give talks in your seminary in Washington for graduate students in theology. Very philosophical, but very spiritual also. His talk, not every one will understand it.

"Pope Kyrillos is à la Christ. Pope Kyrillos would never give you a lecture in your theological seminary. You've seen people who would come and say a word, and just don't, you know, don't analyze, but impart to you a certain power that cleanses you, that opens your eyes and your perceptions. Unseen things that make you happy in the kingdom of heaven on earth. Pope Kyrillos was like that. Pope Kyrillos's path is not the path of the mind, it is the path of the heart.

"Pope Kyrillos differs in that he can take a topic—on the ego, for example—and lecture to you on the ego and everyone would understand. In very simple terms. Someone from primary education would understand and someone like you would understand. Matta al-Maskin? You have to be a philosopher."

"Two different paths," I say. "The heart and the mind." The Grand Sheikh also emphasized the path of the heart over the intellect. I'm becoming concerned that nobody gives a hoot about my intellect; rather, the opposite.

"What about different religions," I continue. "Can there be different paths to God?"

"I would say, given all my experiences . . . religion, see, it is a circle. . . ." Beshai searches for blank paper and not finding any draws a circle on the top of his desk. He points to different spots on its imaginary perimeter.

"You can be here," he says and dabs his finger on the desk. "I am here. Someone is here, farther, and so on. All of them, however, are equidistant from the center. So if we all aim at reaching the center, inside the center is all the same."

"But some leaders say there is only one way to the center," I say. "Through recognition of Christ. Unless other religions come to that knowledge, they are not equidistant from the center."

"Look," Beshai says. "I am a Christian, born a Christian. But, none of us has the right to sort of ask God, Why did you allow in the world so many religions? My own belief is this. We have to accept it as a fact, as a given, that there are so many religions. The idea of changing all these religions into one, proselytizing and all that—it's none of our business.

"I have seen Buddhists, for example," he continues. "They are super people. In Islam there are certain things—I know a little about the matter—where if you look at the Qur'an, the world will be heaven. Heaven."

He decides to give me a personal example.

"I remember there was a Muslim friend of mine and I told Pope Kyrillos he wants to come with me to receive a blessing. He said, 'Yes, yes, bring him.' He said, 'They are all our sons.' He said that. He didn't say convert him to Christianity. This is the very lone effort of a nemesis. Like all those Catholics that go to southern Sudan to convert the animists. Okay, he will be called Philip and Edward, but what have you changed? I mean the idea is . . ."

An absurd smile spreads across his face. He calms himself and continues, softly.

"I have met enough spiritual people in the world who, anyone sitting with them would melt and come to the inner Christ in him, okay? As a manner of speaking."

"There are many ways to the Creator, to the One, then?" I ask.

"There are many ways," he says. "Pope Kyrillos can fast a lot. One of his disciples was imitating him and without saying anything, Pope Kyrillos understood and told him, 'Go and eat, go now and eat.' Which means for everyone there are some things some can do and some cannot do. And the spiritual paths are many. It can be through suddenly meeting one person; for another person, it has to be through the intellect. For a third person it can be through music, or art, or looking at birds. Or being in the desert. So to me it is crystal clear that the paths are many."

Beshai gets a glint in his eye.

"You see, real spirituality can also be achieved by what is in Shakespeare." Here the hidden showman breaks loose with a heavy British accent. "To thine own self be true, and it falls like night and day, thou canst not be false to any man. Truth."

"Tell me," I say after he accepts my applause with a modest grin and a soft bow. "Is life the pursuit of truth? Or happiness?"

"Happiness?" he counters. "Or pleasure?"

"Pleasure, perhaps," I reply.

"Happiness," he says, "according to the ancient Greeks, is a mental activity. Pleasure is transient. Generally speaking, I am not happy with the way people are living in the United States. But of course the United States is a huge place. You have super spiritual people. You have bad.

"Spirituality demands that you must have the contemplative virtues, that you must have time to sit back and to meditate in your own way. But if you are in New York, and rushing and walking fast, and so on, you can't be spiritual. You can't. You can't because you are not giving it time. It is not that it does not want to come to you, or you don't want it, but spirituality calls for coming close to oneself, taking time to sit back and ponder. Taking time to sit back and think. Spirituality demands that one should be almost ashamed at the fact that one has so many blessings. And I should ask myself if I deserve them. Spirituality demands the killing of the ego, trying to kill the ego. Self-importance."

"It would take more than Saint George to slay—" I begin, but he stops me.

"Self-importance," he says. "The ego is the devil. The ego, the devil—'I'—doesn't exist at the level of spirituality. Pope Kyrillos, when people would say, 'Thank you, thank you,' he would say, 'Not me, not me,' and shout at them like mad. Not me. Almost to make them hate him. They were not his miracles, you see."

I nod. I like the idea of shouting and spirituality existing within one person. A saint.

"The mind can be the devil," he says. "People think the body can be the devil; the mind can equally be the devil."

I want to ask him—Saint Kyrillos—Beshai, something personal. The heart. Trust the heart, not the head, the mystics say. But trusting my own heart has led to nothing but pain.

"And what about the heart?" I ask. "Can the heart be the devil also?"

"The heart has the soul," he replies, gently. "No. Never. Untouchable. There is a phrase in Saint Paul where God is speaking to his people, saying Give me your hearts. God asked for your heart, and he never asked for your mind or your body. The heart in the metaphorical sense. The easiest path to God is by the heart, not by higher means. Not everyone can do that—reach God through the intellect—and it takes a long, long, time. But with the heart, it clicks suddenly. For those again who have the preparedness. But there are people who put blocks, you see what I mean, in the way. They block it."

I shift in my seat. Getting no response from me, Beshai continues:

"Spirituality," he says. "People should have less words. They follow too many things. To think and contemplate and meditate. And know that the scientific method is limited, that there is a cause and effect relationship at another level."

"Yes?" I ask. "Like coincidence?"

"There is no such thing as coincidence," he says. "Coincidence is a cause and effect relationship at another level. When something happens you say, What a coincidence. This is not a coincidence, it is meant."

My mind still refuses to listen. I have been in Egypt only three days, and each has been stuffed with coincidence.

"Spirituality is sort of letting oneself be guided," he says. "By coincidence."

Impossible. I put invisible hands over my ears.

"I hate it when I talk to some Americans," he continues. "And I tell them my master's is from Stanford. And they tell me when I got my Ph.D. from Oxford: W-o-n-derful planning, they say. What a marvelous choice you made."

Beshai is rolling his eyes with exaggeration and I can't help but laugh out loud.

"Actually my going to Stanford was unplanned, and Oxford was unplanned," he says. "And the choice? The choice was unplanned. It is these types of things. The trouble is, the more you educate people in America, the more they want to say, I planned it. What a pity about the weather this weekend, because we planned . . . such and such. We planned, I planned, I, I . . . Hells bells!! There is no 'I' that plans life. Just live it."

We both pull up in sharp silence, our motors idling. My rational face is scrunched up. My doubting lips pursed. I'm still not buying this go-with-the-flow-and-live-by-coincidence stuff. Not entirely.

"But at the same time, we do plan," I say. "We don't just sit by and let life wash over us."

"Yes," he says. He's off and running again. "I plan what I can plan. I plan to teach this course in the summer. But I also let things come and wash over me. That's why I'm a happy man. And I am a man who is also in applied econometrics. I am a technician, a statistician, a mathematician, an econometrician. And still I'm able to put this on one side. And I behave like a totally illiterate, simple person on the other. But not many people are like that in this respect, because they will feel it is undignified. This is so absurd as far as I am concerned."

"Someone told me that Americans turn to spirituality because they have eaten so much and found there is no taste," I say. "Whereas people here turn to spirituality because they have suffered so much."

"No," he replies. "Because there are people who didn't suffer and they turned. So this cannot be true. I am an only son and I grew up with no suffering, but why do I turn?"

"Why do you think then that some people turn to the spiritual life?" I ask.

"It is a basic thing in us to try to distinguish between the real and the nonreal," he says. "The phenomenal world and the reality. And as we grow—some people get it even when they're very young, you know—in some instances, some people become very disillusioned. You know, I wanted a bicycle, why didn't I get a bicycle? That's one aspect of it. On the other hand, there is a search inside a human being for the truth. For the reality, for the core, there is this search."

"Is this one of the things that defines the human character or the human spirit?" I ask. "This search for the truth?"

"The fact that my mind has gotten me a Ph.D. from Oxford means my mind is all right as far as my mind is concerned," he replies. "My body, I can play my tennis and I am fine. But then I still feel something is missing. This is the whole idea of the trinity. There has to be three: mind, body and soul. And soul should never, ever, be confused with the mind. That is the worst thing on earth that anyone can do is to confuse them. Many people think that the mind is the soul."

"If one of the defining characteristics of the human nature is to search for order in chaos," I say, "I wonder if that is what we're doing, turning to the tools of the mind, the products of the mind, and away from the soul?"

"I agree with you," he says. "I think this is what has been happening."

"Do you think this will increase as technology becomes the center of our lives?"

"Unless it increases until there will come a point where enough is enough. And then they will go back."

"The best of technology is for the benefit of man," I say. "But then we have such things as pollution—"

"Weapons," he adds.

"How do we balance this?" I ask.

"It is dualistic," he replies. "Things are dualistic. There is always the other side. Like in mathematics. Here."

He looks around again for a blank sheet of paper and I pass him my notebook. He begins to draw a straight line at an angle across the page.

"There is differentiation," he says. "But there is also deviation."

He draws another line that intersects the first. Two arms of a triangle.

"Regrettably," he says, "in the phenomenal world, the two have to exist together, because the word Evil would not exist unless the word Good exists. The word Good would not exist unless Evil exists. Day and night. In the universe, there is day and night. There could never have been darkness unless there was light. That is the nature of the phenomenal."

"And they are each contained within each other?" I suggest.

"They are each contained," he says. "The two are together. The battle is there continuously."

"That's what keeps us moving," I say. "This dynamic?"

"That's right," he replies. "The battle is there continuously. The battle is there."

He returns to the two intersecting lines on my notebook.

"For example, mathematically, by definition there is no convergence unless there is divergence," he says and taps the point where the two lines meet. He runs his pen along the widening angle of the arms. "These two lines would never have converged unless they had first diverged. Otherwise they would never converge. This is mathematics."

"And so that point of contact," I say, "eventually is the result of divergence? And unless we recognize divergence, we do not see the convergence?"

"Exactly," he says. "So there can be no divergence but if you come to a convergence. In other words, I am saying, convergence is not at variance with divergence. Divergence can lead to convergence. Technology can make you invent a small, mini atomic bomb, can make you invent—I don't know what—and goes on until the essence is the essence. It is number one, it has to come about."

We've arrived at our own moment of divergence and as we both prepare to leave he repeats his advice from the saint.

"Be very simple," he says. "If you are sitting in your church and someone you don't know comes to you, tell him to open the Bible at any page and read a verse that speaks for you. Pope Kyrillos, when he used to be Father Mena, when he was free he used to busy himself by taking small pieces of paper and writing verses from the Bible. And to all visitors he used to take one blindly and give it, and in all cases it tended to be the answer to the reason why the person came. It was not he who was doing it, this is the secret. It was not him.

"Don't read too many words," he says. "Be very simple. Take half a line and let them chat about it, and chat about it in a simple way. Don't lecture people. He never lectured. Pope Kyrillos wanted things to unfold within the person, when you realize it later. But not—do this, and don't do that—he didn't follow that approach. Let what is inside you unfold, slowly. Gradualness has to be emphasized. American speed has to be discounted when it comes to spirituality."

"This speed," I begin to say.

He throws up his hands as if he has just heard a scandal.

"This is unreal," he says. "Because time is not real. Because reality is timeless. Time is a succession of thoughts. If you are in one thought in one level in the Kingdom of Heaven then you become timeless. You have timelessness, a feeling of timelessness."

"So time is just an abstract, artificial conception?" I ask.

"Yes," he says. "You see Pope Kyrillos would be feeling different from us because he is in a state of timelessness, because he is all the time in one plane. After all these years he reached the stage where he is in one plane.

"When he was in Old Cairo, and he moved to the Church, people would come from Upper Egypt and spend the night there. One day they woke up and told him, 'You look wonderful and happy. But just look at the tragedy that befell us while we were sleeping.' He said to them, 'What tragedy has befallen us?' They replied, 'Thieves came last night and stole the benches and the jackets,' and so on. 'So what,' he says. 'So what? They steal the nasty things. They can't steal the good things here.' "

Adel Beshai, econometrist and personal assistant to a saint, points to his heart.

"They were dumbfounded," he says. "They couldn't answer."

I stand at the door, my eyes fixed on the slim finger that rests on his jacket. His heart.

"They can never steal what is inside you," Adel Beshai says.

"This you will never forget, this sentence. This sentence."

CHAPTER 10

sex and the cyber-copt

If you really want to know about the future, watch a child grow. Nothing will focus you more quickly. Pope Shenouda, the successor of Pope Kyrillos as head of the Coptic Orthodox Church, knows this. Rather than my talking with another old man, he has made arrangements for me to meet with the person charged with guiding Egypt's young Orthodox Christians, the sons and daughters of the Pharaohs, into the computer age. In his wisdom, the pope has done me a huge favor.

Bishop Musa, Bishop of Youth of the Coptic Orthodox Church, comes from the same ancient line as the famed Fathers of the Desert, so I'm expecting some wild-eyed, God-Driven mystic like the photographs on Beshai's wall, given to high thoughts and holy visions. Like many things in Egypt, however, the reality is more interesting.

In contrast to Old Cairo with its museums and dark churches that service the tourist trade, the cathedral of the Coptic Patriarchate and its administrative outbuildings in densely populated downtown Cairo are the pulse of Orthodoxy. They deal with the vital day-to-day activities of a living community.

Bishop Musa has just finished a television interview and is

waiting for me in his office, a guard tells me. An Egyptian camera crew in black Euro-chic almost mows me down in the corridor outside his office. They're good-natured, rehashing a joke or two, but impatient to get outside and light up their ciggies.

Musa's laughter greets me before he does and I follow its trail down the corridor, craning my neck around an office door in expectation of finding him.

Inside, a flock of young nuns is clearing away Coca-Cola cans and the remnants of a tray of cookies in the wake of the film crew. Like most young women, they're a little giddy from being around television cameras.

"Come in, please, come in," a young nun says in Arabic and waves me in.

I hesitate. Nuns? Seriously religious, celibate young women in long black robes and headgear? I'll wait outside, thank you.

"Doktora," a young woman says as I waver. "You are Doktora Yvonne."

She has the face of gentle authority and is slightly older than the others.

"Come in, please, please, Doktora Yvonne," she says in English "I am Sister Yvonne."

The others are nodding like a Greek chorus.

Yes. Yes. Two Yvonnes. In one room. This is almost a miracle.

Yvonne the Nun puts her hand out. Yvonne the Professor steps in. The fledglings giggle.

"I have never met another Yvonne," she says. "Before this, really. Before I am a sister, I am Yvonne."

I am confused. But not surprised. After the past few days, I am no longer surprised by this rabid coincidence that follows—or precedes—me.

"My birth name is Yvonne," she says. "This is fate."

As if that's enough, or because it is, she puts her arms around me and kisses my cheeks. I'm confounded by this warmth and affection.

One of the fledglings says something in Arabic that I don't

catch and they start chirping again. They're looking back and forth at our clothes and agreeing on something. Sister Yvonne helps out.

"She says, you are also a nun," the sister says.

"You wish!" I reply in Egyptian dialect. And they laugh at my mock indignation.

"No. No. Your clothes," she says. "Look. We are sisters."

We're standing side-by-side. I'm wearing a fashion statement that can only be described as "Early-Convent"—a floating circle skirt of black linen, a black camise and a white long-sleeved blouse, unbuttoned. Black flat shoes. My namesake sister points to our habits, and I join in their laughter.

Bishop Musa, the author of the deep chuckle, walks into his office from a side door. The young nuns swallow, brush themselves off, and return to business. Any semblance of dignity on my part is gone. It doesn't matter.

Musa, or Moses as his Arabic name means, is a tumbled, garrulous bear of a man. His beard, not quite flecked with middle age, stands out from his face like excited coils around an energy field. The long black robes serve as a photographer's foil. His eyes are busy telling you that life has an inner source. He fingers his cell phone like a rosary, and checks his email before—and after— prayers. Bishop Musa is the Coptic Bishop of Youth. He is the Cyber-Copt.

We drink Arabic coffee and cola in his cluttered office, a caffeine kick at the end of another endless heat-wave day. I'm drained, ready to curl up on the cool floor like an old cat; Musa's conversation revives me. He sits adjacent in another of the deep chairs, not behind his mammoth wooden desk piled high with paperwork as other church officials might. He leans forward when he speaks, backward when he laughs, which is often.

I need more room to describe this man, because his presence fills every corner. He spills out of himself. First, his hands. His hands seem too large to hold the fragile coffee cup, which is on the edge of being airborne as he waves it about to emphasize a point. I curb my reflex to duck. His thick glasses, like his shoes, are coated with a thin layer of dust, but then so is everything and everyone in Cairo.

Occasionally the sound of the soccer ball being kicked around the courtyard below catches his attention and he seems ready to toss off the black gown and checkered skullcap to join in. Ten to one he's wearing jogging shorts under those long robes.

My namesake nun sits beside me and holds my hand as we all discuss the future of Egyptian youth. Her hands are pale and cool like marble. Between the bishop and the nun, I've found my bridge across the Nile, from the desert Pyramids to the downtown skyscrapers, from the past to the present. And hopefully into the future.

Let's be straight. We talk about sex and the Internet, a subject or subjects about which Bishop Musa knows a lot. This is not going to be an ordinary discussion, and after a few minutes of warming up, he's ready to play ball.

"What is your vision of the future?" I begin.

On cue, he immediately starts talking about technology.

"They say the coming century will be the teenagers' century," he says, "because they are going to use the Internet on a very wide scale. And because their lives are going to be computerized, this may lead to some kind of computer addiction. As you know, it has already happened."

I nod, pleased with this smooth beginning. He continues on cue.

"The most dangerous thing," he says, "is that the people are going to be perplexed from many types of antagonistic data. Confused. Everybody can say what he wants. It will be a difficult life for our coming generations, because they are going to be confused, they are going to suffer very much in order to choose their way; to make their decisions and decide their priorities."

Then he takes me off guard.

"Add to this also this type of pornography that will be on the Internet."

Pornography? I sit up. Did the Bishop say "Pornography"? I look at my nunnish counterpart, and she's unfazed. He keeps going.

"For sure," he says. "It will cause the following generations to suffer from a life related to instinct and physical senses and not the spirit. Not even intellectuality. They are going to have some intellectual knowledge, yes. They'll have a job, yes. They may have a doctoral degree, yes. But he will suffer a spiritual vacuum because he'll all the time be attached to the body and the senses."

"Excuse me, Your Holiness," I say. "But, ah, about pornography . . . sex on the Internet . . ."

Musa throws back his head and laughs. He slaps his knee.

You could say that Musa is an unlikely character to give me insight into sex. In the Orthodox Church, bishops specialize in the weaknesses of the soul. As a former physician, however, Musa is well acquainted with the frailties of the human body.

Also, the monkish line is celibate. My alter-ego nun beside me is celibate, too, Musa reveals with great pride. She nods enthusiastically. Her face bears the clarity of having made a wise decision. There but for the grace of God, go I.

For a moment I envy her: Hey, hon, I'm tempted to say, good choice. As often as not, sex can wreck a good relationship, I've been told. And what freedom, not having to worry about that ticking biological clock.

For Musa the subject of sex and technology is a natural extension of youthful interests. Sex and exploration. Exploration of the self and of the world. It's also an intrinsic part of teenagers breaking away from the culture of their parents and the past. Sex, technology and youth are therefore a natural match and there's no getting around it.

Musa thoroughly approves of sex and immediately lets me know it.

"We as Christians sanctify sex," he says, "and we believe it is the holy of the holies in this life."

If this were a bar somewhere, I would demolish this as a pickup line. But I'm in a cathedral, talking with a guy in a black dress. Not for the first time in Egypt, I am surprised into silence.

Musa launches into an enthusiastic mini lecture on love and I listen, despite myself.

"It is agape," he explains. "You know, in Greek agape means love. Love can be a sensual love, it can be emotional love, and it can be spiritual love: eros, phila and agape."

Sure, I've heard something like this lecture before. Mrs. Blackwell, my high school religion teacher, used a highly censored version to try and offset the sordid information we were picking up in biology class. She was sure the road to Hell was strewn with fetal pigs.

The Bishop of Youth knows he has captured my divided attention. I am trying to track the projectile of his thought. Our minds are both ahead of the conversation and we are enjoying kicking the imaginary soccer ball around the outer field.

"I am afraid," he says, "that the following generations will suffer a lot from senses and instinct and this is not very constructive for the coming generations."

"And this is related to computers?" I ask.

"I think so, yes," he says. "I've started to have on my Internet young people sending some kinds of confessions about this. That they are spending the whole night in front of the computer for these sex programs."

I am more fascinated that he has a cyber-confessional than about voyeurism. On the same computer you can have both the Ten Commandments and Tammy Does Texas.

"Now voyeurism is something very attractive, and it is a temptation," he says. "Because it is not very difficult to pull such a young person, a teenager, toward these things. He'll find these all the time in front of him on the computer. Once he wants them, he can just get the file and go ahead.

"Therefore, I think there will be difficulties: in intellect, in intellect and in psyche. And even in the body. Because if he starts indulging in fornication and bad sexual practices, he may get

AIDS or something like that, or chlamydia, or something like that."

I've forgotten that the bishop is also a physician and that his take on computer "viruses" is grounded in the physical world.

"With protection," I say, "one doesn't always lead to the other."

"Not always, but because of this type of globalization of everything," he says, "I think the next generations are going to suffer more than ourselves."

"The way you describe it, this pornography on the Internet," I say, "young people will not be actually experiencing physical sex, but watching from a distance. Sex will become exclusively an experience of the mind. Not the body. Or even the senses. The globalization of disease shouldn't be an issue, then."

"Yeah," the bishop says, "but not only the mind. Because sex starts as an idea in the mind, and then an emotion, and then an action. Therefore this will lead to that. You cannot fragment the human personality. Therefore he will think about seeing something, and then he will be excited by what he is seeing, then he will go and do something."

Musa is also thinking ahead.

"What to do?" he asks. He extends his surgeon's hands toward me. "We are moving even without our will. Now things are moving like a car without a direction, without any control. This is concerning the information and the communication."

The connection between sex and technology is not new. Before coming to America from Australia, my own image of the Lady Liberty was informed by the postcard versions she sold of herself to the rest of the world through movies and advertising. The car, the darling of American popular culture and physical mobility, played a major role in this self-promotion.

For Americans the car has always been more than a vehicle. Getting into one presented the possibility of being carried away to somewhere dangerous, even forbidden. If you believe present television ads for cars, the line between sex and religion is becoming more confused. The modern American auto can give you a mountaintop experience. Its supercharged xyz engine and fuel-injected such-and-such with video screens, surround sound, satellite tracking and no-spill coffee holders will take you to Nirvana.

In America, land of the automobile, parents recognize the new world their teenage children can enter once they are old enough to drive. Egyptian parents face the computer and the Internet with the same trepidation for, through them, their children can travel outside of their control and reach. The new vehicle of choice, the computer, is alien to many parents but they still hand over the keys with mixed pride, knowing that it is inevitable. They hope and pray that all they have taught by this point—discernment, values, respect—will be enough, and that they will not be abandoned in the dust.

Egyptians have also discovered that, like the mythic red Mustang of America's Boomers, the computer has a steamy backseat. Musa plugs into the concerns of parents when he speaks of pornography on the Internet. He's a firm believer in the mind as erogenous zone and that, in the hands of young people, the Internet has the potential of becoming an expensive adult sex toy.

Evidence? Apart from emailing him their confessions, young Egyptians have also entered fantasy games, talked with freaks, and bared their souls to strangers. This doesn't rattle Musa. He's more concerned that some confess that, in their addiction to the Internet, they're neglecting their families and friends.

As youth turns her back on family and community to face the global computer screen, she touches a cultural nerve: There is no equivalent for "alone" in the Arabic language. In many cultures, but particularly Mediterranean ones, isolation of the individual is an unnatural state of being. It is a place to which the group banishes you for punishment.

You don't choose isolation, with one exception. To withdraw from human physical contact is to enter the metaphysical. In Arabic, Alone implies All-One with The One. God.

The place these young people are entering is not the spiritual realm. It's a table for one. It's self-sex.

Since the discovery process is inevitable, the Bishop of Youth prefers to actively participate in it. He claims that knowledge of the world, as well as each other, is the key to openness.

"But openness and experimentation at a cost," I say.

"This is why we feel our concern in the family, in the church and in the country," he says, "to educate our young people on how to build themselves spiritually, intellectually, psychologically and physically and socially."

He counts these off on the fingers of his extended hand.

"In these five areas," he says, "to help build themselves, to become somebody having his own strength. Then he can take a stand and say No to all these things. It is very difficult, but through the power of God and the will of the human being, they can work together in choosing the right direction."

"You talk about choosing," I say. "Some people object to the word 'choice.' They say that young people should not be taught that they have a choice. They are to be taught there is right and there is wrong—and they are to stay away from wrong. Period."

"I mean by choice," he says, "to discern what is right. This is right, this is wrong. Although I feel some attraction toward the wrong thing, I should withdraw, I should say No. I should have some sort of struggle against the wrong things or else I will be going everywhere. There is nothing called freedom, actually."

His face lights up with an idea to offset my reaction. No freedom? He's never listened to Janis Joplin, then.

"Yeah," he says. "Because if you are driving the car, you are actually not free. You are free to go anywhere, but you should be aware of the traffic arrangements or otherwise you are going to destroy yourself. This is what we teach our young people—that, yes, you are free, but you should have some sort of limitations coming out of your own free will. That this is something constructive, otherwise life will be destructive."

Okay, point made. He's listened to Janis.

"In the West, the family's breaking down," I say. "There are rapid changes in society. Where will responsibility lie for teaching young people discernment?"

In order not to relinquish its position as mentor, the former physician prescribes that the older generation do more than conquer the new technology.

"I think everybody has a role," he says. "The family has a role, the church, and the government, and the media. There should be some sort of brain trust for this world."

"A brain trust?" I ask.

"Yes, a brain store to have some sort of strategy for the future generations."

"Do you mean guardians for the next generations?"

"Not guardians—because we are not going to be able to impose ourselves on the next generations," he says. "No, but to give them the opportunity to come with us into dialogue and discussion. To select the right things and to neglect the wrong things. To be convinced that this is constructive, this is destructive. Out of their own free will, as their personal decision."

"What can we possibly teach them?" I ask.

"For sure, sin is destructive," he says. "We are not only speaking on a religious basis, we are speaking on a scientific and practical basis. Whenever you see a drug-addicted person, he is destroying himself. Smoking, he is destroying himself. Even if it is very slowly, it is destroying his will. At least his money. These types of different sexual disorders, they may be destroying. Therefore, yes, we should come into dialogue with the next generation and give them the opportunity to decide for themselves."

Musa is an idealist, but conscious of the risks. Egyptians across socioeconomic level, class and religion are taking to the Internet with unexpected energy. Also, young Egyptians are proving to the Egyptian government that in this age of technology and global communications, the once-tight boundaries are now porous.

"I want to tell you something," he says. "Among our young people, we have a special group called the intellectual group, and through it we are studying everything in the world. Communication, globalization, different cultures. This is with an open heart and open mind to everybody, selecting from the

Western civilization and from what is coming over the Internet and the satellites."

The bishop doesn't subscribe to segregation of knowledge. He is concerned that Egyptian youth in general, Muslim majority and Christian minority, should be reading off the same screen. Although not unified, religious leaders and groups, Muslim and Copt, are trying to build a sense of citizenship and nationhood that promotes unity and de-emphasizes differences between them. Musa, for example, regularly brings together young Muslims and Christians so that they can explore common ideas and concerns of the future.

"We cannot live in a prison," the bishop says. "And we should communicate with everybody. In our education we always speak about this globalization, even in the economy, not only politics or culture, but the economy. We are always giving them this motto: Select the best. Even from your own culture select the best, because we have many things negative in our culture. So select the best in your own culture and in every culture."

"These are difficult choices," I say. "For young people. For anyone."

"Yeah," he says. "But we should move positively and tell them what to do."

"There are subjects that are controversial even in the West," I say. "As a physician, you must be interested in this whole question of cloning."

"We say that if you are spiritually, intellectually, psychologically, and sociologically in the best way," he says, "we can study everything. Study everything and select the best. Therefore we had many conversations concerning cloning, concerning transplantation, concerning the external fertilization, and so on. For all these things—euthanasia, everything—we are now always, always, discussing everything, because we are not isolated from the world.

"This is good sense, this is wisdom," he explains with determined enthusiasm.

I wonder how much he is saying to convince himself, as well as me. I watch his eyes. They are impassioned.

"Through love we are going to build a unified country," he says. "It will be a progressive one. And if it succeeds we will be the first ones to benefit."

"And if it fails?"

"If it fails, we are the first ones to lose," he says.

He lowers his eyes, and removes his glasses as if they are suddenly too heavy. It gives him a chance to look inward. The boys have stopped playing in the courtyard. The sound of traffic drones by like some strange insect mating call. His assistant, my namesake, leaves us for a few minutes and returns with water and pastries. She pulls back the drapes. The sun is finally setting and effects an illusion of coolness.

Egypt wishes to be an example to others in the region. Knowledge of the world, as well as each other, is the key to the openness that Musa foresees for Egypt. The question is how to integrate this knowledge. For him, youth is the obvious vehicle.

Musa's head-on directness toward technology reminds me of the similar views of the Sheikh of Al-Azhar. They would both agree that it is up to the individual to select with both "an open heart and an open mind" from what comes over the Internet and satellites.

Indeed, on some topics these leaders appear more receptive than their Western counterparts. They are able to encourage this attitude because they believe that the traditional values of the family and the community, the bishop's "traffic patterns," continue to provide a moral base for young Egyptians. They advocate and encourage discernment, not censorship. Subjects that we steer away from, they approach directly. There are differences, however.

"Many young people, as well as older people," I say, "are concerned with the state of the planet. Water, industry, pollution. McDonald's and globalization of culture—"

"I think we should notice some kind of difference," he says, "between the rich world and the poor. For the rich world—the States and Europe—it's much different than in the Third World. We consider this type of concern for the ecology a luxury."

I look at him quizzically.

"Luxury?"

"Yes," he says. "Because we don't find things to eat and water to drink in many parts of our countries. Therefore when you speak about the fluorocarbons and so on, we say, 'Oh, you are speaking from another world.' Because we are suffering a lot. We are suffering oppression, we are suffering a lifting up from our roots. And we are suffering terrorism, fundamentalism, poverty, illiteracy, overpopulation. Imagine."

I don't need to imagine. Yesterday's contrast between the bustling new economic center of New Cairo and the muddy streets of Old Cairo a few miles away is stuck in my mind.

"But," he says, "we are very glad that this ecology or ecological interest is growing in Egypt now. All the time it is in the newspapers and we have our special department for ecology now with some rules, some trials to get rid of the waste from the buses and the cars, and some concerning the Nile, and so on. We are glad about that. But, you know, the people here are very poor, and that is a type of luxury in their life. They need the basic needs first."

"Is overpopulation a luxury?" I ask.

"No," he replies. "It is a disaster. We are increasing by 1.3 million per year. Imagine how can we get for these people an education, health, social welfare. It is very difficult. We are trying a lot to restrict this overpopulation and we are now on the road. We have started, and they say we have started a bit to control the birth rate."

The Coptic Church is committed to birth control and contraception and has centers for contraception all over Egypt.

"At the same time," I say, "population control would seem to work against Copts as a minority."

"Yes," he replies with a grin. I've forgotten I'm talking to a celibate. "We become less in number, but we say that quality is more important than quantity."

He and Sister Yvonne exchange a knowing grin.

Information, sex, knowledge; conflict, disease, isolation; the list continues to grow. Globalization means access to all of these. These are concerns parents throughout the world share.

Musa has definite ideas about what can be done for the daughters and sons of the Pharaohs, but what can we in the rest of the world do? What advice can the Bishop of Youth from one of the world's oldest Christian sects, a minority that connects us with an even more ancient world, what can he give us?

"How does a young person lead a good, moral life?" I ask softly.

Musa pauses to consider. As quick as he may be to laugh, the future is nothing to joke about. Any message to young people is a serious matter. His black-and-white cotton bonnet has slid toward his eyes and he pushes it back.

"Because I am a youth worker," he says, "always I put in front of them four mottoes: One. Nourish yourself spiritually, and intellectually, and socially. Pray, read the Bible, play sports, have a hobby, serve in the church, serve in the community. All the time have a full life, spiritually, intellectually, socially, and so on.

"The second is take care of your senses and relations: What are you watching on the TV, on the videotapes, what are you reading, what are you speaking? And your relations, who are your friends, are they going to teach you something wrong, and so on. Take care of your senses and relations.

"The third motto is to resist sin as much as you can because it will destroy you. It is not something beneficial at all. Any sin mentioned in the Bible is not beneficial. To lead an immoral life is something destructive, it is not constructive. It is something apparent.

"The fourth motto is, never give up or feel despair. Have hope in God, the Lord will support you. And if you fail today, there may be a good triumph tomorrow—if you have this package of nourishment, discernment, resistance and hope."

These mottoes are not new. I sense Musa can recite them in his sleep. For some, they may even pass for ageless wisdom. Perhaps that is their simple beauty, I try to convince myself.

But I'm not satisfied. In fact, I'm disappointed. We've both wound down. There doesn't appear to be a second wind.

I'm looking for more from this man who represents the future of a small part of our past. For more than I can get by walking into a suburban church or turning on the television. I want to hear from the high bishop, not the local priest. The servant of the universal soul, not of man and his petty little problems.

For me, Musa holds a unique position in the world from which to contemplate its future. He is from a lineage of saints. Their role as guardians of the spirit is virtually ageless. Surely there is more than this.

The Bishop of Youth insists we embrace the future. But what about the past? We've always played around with history, but now we can do it so much more quickly and decisively. We can reinvent or delete the past with a click of the mouse. Musa and his ancients can become irrelevant overnight.

I press him.

"What will happen to young people when they have unlimited access to the ideas of the world?" I ask. "Aren't you concerned that in becoming globalized these bright young people will lose not only their Coptic, but their Egyptian, identity?"

He forms his large hands into a tent in front of his mouth. He could be praying, except that his eyes are open, although glazed. His mind is off traveling somewhere and I wait. I imagine he's sifting through the dusty files of the ancients for some splendid wisdom to impart. Again he surprises me.

When he speaks, it is to reveal that his thoughts have not taken him back into the past, but halfway around the world to the young Egyptians who are now first- or second-generation Americans. He visits them and their communities once or twice a year. He speaks of them to bring home an issue the world is struggling with. It is as old as civilization. Pluralism. But pluralism with a modern twist. Once we have become part of a progressively globalized culture, there remains the question of how we will live together yet retain what we believe to be unique about ourselves.

"We say to our young people in the States or in Canada," he says, "What is your *identity?*"

He begins to count off on those big fingers again.

"You are Christian," he says. "You are Orthodox. You are Coptic in origin. You are American. These don't cancel each other out."

He has struck a universal chord. In our world of alienation, of serial monogamy and split families, of social mobility and multiple career moves, we all want to belong. Yet we all wish to remain unique and identifiable.

Like Adel Beshai, who talks with his circles and angles, Bishop Musa uses geometry to illustrate his idea.

"These are Circles of Belonging," he emphasizes. "You belong to Christianity. To Orthodoxy. To Egypt as your roots. And to America as your land."

Circles of Belonging. His words are simple, yet profound. These circles, he explains, are neither static nor exclusive. On occasion they may be concentric or overlapping. They are multidimensional and inclusive.

Implicit in Musa's words is the key to clarifying our conflict of identities in this next global age. He tells us we can reconcile our new identities, our changing loyalties to country, family, faith.

While Copts, like other minorities, struggle to maintain their integrity within a larger society, their concern is universal. They don't wish to be absorbed. They are trying to define their Circles of Belonging.

The history of the Copts is also the history of Egypt. Through her ability to adapt, to include new peoples, and to adopt ideas, she is an inspiration for America. Over the millennia she has been invaded by Persians, Greeks, Arabs, and Europeans. She has integrated them all while incorporating both Nubia and the Mediterranean into her psyche.

America claims Egypt as one of our own original Circles of

Belonging. But now Coptic faith and Islamic Egypt both face the possibility of being absorbed by that larger American culture. As the Mother of Civilization, Egypt finds strength in history, however. The youthful upstart, America, she believes, will grow wise with age and experience. This is a truism of history.

"Does history contain a lesson for the future?" I ask as I reluctantly prepare to leave the quiet halls of the Patriarchate for the turbulent world outside.

"We have a long history," Musa replies softly. He speaks of both Egypt and the Coptic Church, a circle within a circle. He is quiet now, a contrast to the jocularity that has preceded. "Our history is on our minds. Always. We must never forget the past."

Copts may be deeply rooted in history, but their minds are sharply focused on the future. Perhaps if we embrace the future, you almost hear this Egyptian minority reasoning, we will survive to become part of it. They are betting on becoming part of the global village. They access this world not only through books and satellite television, but through the Internet.

At the same time that new technologies threaten to test their ancient beliefs, they may be the answer to their survival. Copts hope that the rest of the world will become interested in their history and therefore their future. Rather than erase the past, the new forms of communication can help to keep it alive.

Musa's confidence in the combination of new technologies and youth is also his hope for the future. He's grabbed the wheel of the red Mustang convertible, top down, ready to feel the hot wind riffle through his beard.

PART TWO

syria

CHAPTER 11

Damascus Gate

High above the Syrian desert, I drift between two vast black layers—the sky of stars and its mirror, the desert, studded with an occasional electrical light or village constellation. I am awed by our ability to fly, by our striving through machines to do what a bird does effortlessly.

On the plane from Cairo to Damascus, I've been reading Assad Ali's *Happiness without Death*.

> *I, the Desert,*
> *woke in the arms of night*
> *and wondered, O night,*
> *how do you embrace people and things?*

Only a metaphysical flight could have inspired the Sufi poet to write such words about land and air unbounded. Hopefully, I'll ask him in person soon enough.

I lay my glasses aside and rub the sand from my eyes. The past week of chasing wise men around Egypt is wearing me down, not the action—for I thrive on action—but the stillness. Each interview—the Grand Sheikh of Islam, the Coptic bishop, the Sufi masters, the secretary to the saint——has asked far deeper questions of me than I of them. Each has looked inside me, into the core of my soul.

And just as I'm getting used to the spiritual strip search, the topic of miracles and the metaphysical keeps cropping up to challenge my academic training. Can't have that.

Yesterday, getting out of Egypt seemed like a good idea, but as the plane bumps along the runway, I'm already reassessing my decision.

Something about arriving in Syria jump-starts the reptilian part of your brain. Entering Syrian air space you expect the steward to hand you an invisible card that says, Welcome to Paranoia. There's good reason. Syria is a dictatorship, after all, and on the international terrorist list. Also, Syrians are as old as sin and hold the original patent on the game of dice.

You also expect trouble because you're not quite sure of the rules, who is making them at any particular moment, or if there are several sets of rules going on at once. You know there definitely are rules: Look around. Everyone's just waiting for you to make your move. It's Monopoly without the instruction booklet.

And everyone has power: to keep you waiting for hours, or to throw you into jail, you're never certain which. Hanging off the worn belt of every bureaucrat are the Keys to Purgatory.

I wait in line at customs, resigned that even though I've filled out every form in triplicate, had each page stamped and signed, and done everything instructed, when I get to the guy in uniform, he'll shout, "Ha! Those rules apply only to days without the letter Y in them."

Late night feeds the paranoia. The airport is tired-looking. Cigarette smoke softens the socialist architecture with sepia wash but adds no charm. The cleaning lady pushing the gray mop across the cracked bathroom tiles is beyond tired. The khaki shirts of the customs officials on last duty are rumpled, sweat-stained, and fagged out, as are the long faces of the men who wear them. Even the ubiquitous posters of President Hafez al-Assad look worn-out and tired. He's waving, but his smile is drained. Perhaps it is the death of his eldest son the previous year that has made him so tired.

Everything in Syria appears tired, but I can tell you it's just a cover. Even in sleep, Syrians are poised. But poised to do what? Until they know, their minds work overtime. They live in a suspended state of hypercaffeination, ready to pounce on or leap aside as opportunity demands. The eyes that watch you from that tired exterior are a giveaway: They are sharp and inquisitive and quick.

This is the first time I've been in Damascus by myself. The several times I led delegations of professors and journalists I was surrounded by a cloud of semiofficial security. Within whispering distance a few drifts of secret police followed us like a thought bubble in a cartoon. On those visits I was treated like a princess with all muddy hurdles cleared before my silken feet. Tonight there are no assistants to lead me through VIP passport control, no guided tours and no damn responsibilities. I'm on my own. Yes!

I know from experience, then, that I am being watched in the airport. I can feel the eyes. I turn around and smile, trying to affect innocence. No one meets my gaze—I told you they were quick. The fluorescent light above has a severe tic and I blink in empathy. I stop when I realize it makes me look nervous. From experience I also know that security police sit behind the thick, mirrored wall near the customs officers. Watching. Not blinking. I look into the glass and tuck a few strands of sun-bleached hair behind my ear. I, too, look tired.

But why am I so nervous? Egypt has exhausted me with her hospitality, but Damascus is like a second home. I know her back streets like the twisted destiny line of my palm. Blindfold me and my nose will lead me to that plate of fragrant green olives, walnuts and pomegranates waiting at my favorite Syrian restaurant. Above the din, my ears will sense that perfect oasis of silence from which to savor a monument, a Roman column, a pyramid of fruit on a roadside stall.

A quick gut check confirms that my physical self is comfortably at ease, thank you. At peace, even. The problem is God.

Hon, she says (God often does a Bette Midler to get my attention). Hon, she says, trust me. Re-e-la-a-x. That immediately makes me suspicious. God should know better. I am incapable of relaxing.

True, in Egypt I finally agreed with God to go with Flo, her New Age cousin. There seemed no point in struggling. Still, a thought continues to heckle me. God may walk with me through the Valley of the Shadow of Death, but will she be on her cell phone when the wolves attack?

Intellectually I understand where I am supposed to go, and I even want to go there. I'm trying to meet this great Sufi poet, Assad Ali, whom a friend in Washington has connected me with. I've never met the mystic or been to his mountain enclave. He could be a madman. Some warped superdervish with snakes and whips, who sleeps on nails and eats blond Australian academics for breakfast.

No, I'm not afraid of anything physical—of being hurt, kidnapped, murdered, raped, beaten up and or even being forced to dance naked at some cultish ceremony. This is internal. My fear is that when I finally get to wherever Flo is taking me I will somehow fail. Fail to pass the test. Make a fool of myself.

The customs official has finished reading my passport as if it were a sordid best-seller and nods me through. I exhale with relief and silently thank him for not resorting to one of the many alternatives at his discretion. That's when I reach into the camera bag for my glasses to check the address of the hotel where I'm staying.

My glasses are not there. The case is empty.

I search the camera bag again. Then my shoulder bag. I pat my pockets. Left pocket, right pocket, of my cotton jacket. Deep pockets in my trousers.

My glasses are not there. I was using them on the plane, my new beautiful glasses without which I cannot see clearly or read, and reading is my life, or at least my escape from life. Besides, they cost a small fortune. They were my new statement. My paper thin, purple rimmed, "Ain't these cool" glasses. Damn.

A few hundred feet separate me from the plane. Plus a customs official reading a newspaper and a few unshaven guards, a corridor and plate glass window. My glasses are there—on the floor, down between the seats, perhaps in the hands of a steward or a cleaner who's this instant pocketing them to sell on the black market. Between us stretches a wilderness of bureaucracy, of paperwork in triplicate, carbon copies, application forms and precious time.

I am about to try the impossible—to talk the customs official into letting me go back to the plane. I have a problem. I don't know the Arabic for eyeglasses. Do you? They didn't have them in the tenth century manuscripts I was trained to read. And Egyptian colloquial is a foreign language here in Syria where a pure and florid dialect reigns supreme. When I worked on a dig in Jordan, the local Bedouin thought my Egyptian accent was the biggest joke on earth. Anyway, I don't know the Egyptian for glasses; the Pharaohs didn't wear them, but I do my best.

"Please," I say to the guard. "Please, I left my 'eyes' on the plane."

I'm making round shapes in front of my eyes to signify glasses.

"My eyes. Somebody might take them," I add, hoping he'll let me back into that no-man's-land to retrieve them, or else he'll send someone to fetch them for the Princess, realizing that without official status I will no longer be treated as a Princess. I am trying to exude residual princessness.

"Lady," he replies, "in Syria, nobody will steal your eyes."

Certainly, there are no thieves in Syria, I reassure him, and explain that my glasses are not in Syria, really, but on the plane, just down the corridor.

The world conveniently stands still for a moment. My glasses are more than the lens through which I experience knowledge; they are a shield behind which I can hide. I am literally naked without them. Moreover, I can't crib up on the poet's biography before I meet him, nor an anthology of Damascus Sufis so as not to appear a complete idiot.

I begin to understand what is happening.

The Grand Sheikh in Cairo had warned me about too much book learning. The old mystics kept harping on about experiential knowledge. Sure, I said. All the talk of miracles, of believing. Of seeing from the heart. Sight has always been my primary, dependent, sense, and now I will have to rely on the others. Or learn a new one.

Because I had asked their help and allowed them to look into my heart, each had led me forward on the path, to this particular place and moment at which I have now arrived: I still have to walk through the Valley of the Shadow of Death, but without my glasses. Oh great.

"Which plane?" the customs official finally asks.

"EgyptAir," I reply.

"EgyptAir?"

He shrugs. His body language is quite vocal: What? You left your eyes with the bloody Egyptians and expect them to give them back? Fer-get it, sister. We are Syrians, not . . . not Egyptians.

At any moment he'll strike up the Syrian national anthem, but he only shrugs again, and sucks down on his unfiltered cig.

"Inshallah—hopefully," he finally says, "God willing, the Egyptians will send your eyes to your hotel." But he holds out little hope for either the Egyptians or my glasses.

I wait at the taxi desk, laughing to myself, ever so softly.

It's dark. I'm alone in Damascus. I'm exhausted. I can't see or read. The only thing that's clear is I will not need my glasses for whatever is about to happen.

Okay, God, I'm not sure what you've got in mind with this sight thing, but let's get on with it.

The taxi rushes toward the city and I begin to relax. The windows are open. The air is cool and moist with the smell of warmed, fertile soil. I am sensing the landscape as would a blind poet.

We drive through the Ghouta, an area once renowned for its

gardens and orchards, and under the veil of dark night I experience the landscape through odors, sounds and fleeting lines of poetry that have clung to my memory.

Oh Damascus, Yours is the caravan of the Sun
wherein God is the Preserver and Protector of the One.

Protect and preserve me, oh God, I add.

The taxi whisks me past midsummer orchards of peaches and cherries, and fields of the fragrant roses of Damascus that the Crusaders introduced to Europe on their halfhearted return. After the desert of Egypt, I crave the smell of damp earth. I close my sightless eyes to let it all seep in. Roses and the summer fields are intoxicating, but the smell of history transports me.

As a child in Queensland I would suck the smell of rain-soaked air into my lungs until they were on the point of bursting. And then push that breath down, down into my body until every corner of me was filled with that glorious air. You see, a teacher had told me that traces of the air you breathe today stay in your blood for seven years. At that time, seven years was more than I had experienced. It was an eternity.

Now I suck the air of Damascus down into my lungs, and hold that breath, pushing the oxygen into my blood to feed my being.

The small, welcoming hotel is a pleasant change from the crowded fleabags I've stayed in before or the glitzy chicken crates that cater to the Western tour buses and Saudis looking for a little game. My travel agent in Washington, a wonderful Egyptian, has found it for me. The decor, Syrian-Modern, is that eclectic mix of old tiles, polished marble—and two-way mirrors.

A mosaic fountain laps under silk palm trees in the foyer. A couple of middle-aged Arab businessmen are sprawled out on a sofa and look up from their intense conversation as I walk to the reception. They keep a side eye on me as they return to their discussion, their cigarettes and bowl of pistachios.

The desk staff—two handsome, smiling young men in dark

suits and spotless English, fresh graduates from tourist school—is waiting for me. It's after midnight and they're relieved that I have finally arrived.

They offer me a "special room" with a Jacuzzi.

No bloody way. Paranoia has followed me from the airport. A colleague in Abu Dhabi once advised me never to accept the offer of an upgrade of the honeymoon suite in a Gulf Arab country. He claimed leering firsthand knowledge that several international hotels in the region videoed the antics of the occupants with secret cameras.

On second thought, I could do with the full-Cleopatra and a long soak after surviving the sands of Egypt. I go with the Jacuzzi. This is Syria, not Abu Dhabi.

The young agents take my credit card and American passport and check me in. I keep my Australian passport with me.

My travel agent in Washington wants to be notified of my safe arrival, they tell me.

"Did he say why?" I ask. "Has anything unusual happened in Syria?"

I may have missed an attempted coup or assassination mid-flight. In the main square on the way to the hotel, I had recognized a man getting into his Jeep with an entourage of gun-toting heavies as an infamous Kurdish terrorist. The Syrians were giving him safe harbor against the Turks. But this was not unusual.

The young men look at each other and shrug.

"Nothing unusual," one replies.

I mention the situation with my glasses and they nod toward the young woman at the side desk. Lost glasses are obviously a girl thing.

Her head is down. She taps out accounts on a hand calculator with a pencil so as not to chip her long, pink fingernails. A mass of dark hair is fashionably streaked with blond and held up by large plastic clips. She's wearing an inexpensive copy of the chic lime green suit that's sweeping Paris this year. On the collar is a badge identifying her as Hanna.

Hanna looks up with her magazine-painted face, her cool black-frame glasses, and fixes on me for a second. She's checking me out with the thoroughness of a holy man, except, I assume, she is interested in the external. I am Western Career Woman in real life, not one from Star television, the local equivalent of MTV. And what a disappointment with my sun-blemished skin and unkempt hair, my rumpled T-shirt, cotton trouser suit and sneakers covered in Egyptian dust. Right now, those purple glasses would rally a good impression for the women of my culture.

Her makeup melts into a warm smile. She will call EgyptAir for me.

The hotel manager has sent a basket of fruit and a bottle of 'arak to my room—I have an idea my travel agent has told them I'm a travel reviewer. I pour a generous portion of the anise-flavored alcohol, add bottled water and watch it turn milky white. Lion's milk, they call it; gives you the courage of lions, they say.

I take a good slug for courage and head for the Jacuzzi. As I sink down among bubbles in the marble tub, I give the boys behind the hidden camera a little wave. After you've exposed your soul to a roomful of Islamic clerics and a Coptic bishop or two, then a couple of wankers with a jerk-off camera are small fry.

CHAPTER 12

syrian fire bird

hree rounds of soft pecking at the door muddle my sleep. I wake confused. Birds are chattering in trees outside my window. The streets are silent. This can't be Cairo.

A shy attendant stands in the hall with a thermos of Arabic coffee and another of scalded milk. The newspapers she brings are all a useless blur without my glasses. Morning in Damascus, and I have no idea what the hell is going on in the world.

After several grunts and a futile stab at a meditation—what's the point when God is right here in the room with me?—I start my cycle of calls. No one is home. I leave Assad Ali, the Sufi poet, until last.

The phone burrs on the other end for an eternity.

In the Middle East people answer their phones either within a heartbeat, as if the phone is surgically attached—they expect disaster—or else they let it ring forever as they slowly finish their conversations, feed the canaries, water the geraniums, then finally pick up the receiver. For them, time is relative. Assad Ali's phone belongs to the latter.

A young man, Assad Ali's assistant, yells over the crackling line that the mystic poet is not there.

"When will he return?" I yell back, expecting to be told, Later today.

"Inshallah, tomorrow," he replies, and giggles. "Inshallah, God willing, next week, next month. I do not know. Only God knows."

Damn. Damn. I have only five days in Damascus. He has to be here.

I yell the hotel phone number in careful Arabic to the young man; he yells the numbers back incorrectly and we continue yelling at each other until we finally get them straight. He promises to pass my number on to the poet at first chance. I can only hope.

Today's Friday, God's day off in Syria, so I get a chance to sneak away. No exhausting interviews. No lessons. Just playing tourist.

The stores in the Ottoman Bazaar and the Old Quarter are shuttered, leaving me a ghost town to explore. My feet lead me over familiar territory. I thread the darkened, winding alleys of the market, happy as a tapeworm in some grand intestine, emerging into the blinding sunshine of an ancient and holy square.

This one square is both humanity's unfinished canvas and well-worn paint box. In front is the Umayyad Mosque, an imposing exclamation in stone and mosaic built by Muslim conquerors nearly fourteen hundred years ago. A model of Islamic eclecticism, the mosque tacks itself onto a Christian cathedral, itself built on a pagan temple, and is rimmed by ugly Socialist-style office blocks of the twentieth century. Today being the day of Islamic congregational prayer, only Muslims are permitted beyond the mosque's ornate gates, so I lean back against a column of Jupiter's Temple, content to capture the faces of history on their way to worship The One. The Mesopotamian eye of a woman as she tucks her hair under a scarf, the Phoenician glance of an old man as he greets a friend, the Semitic gesture of a father as he carries his son, the Turkic cheekbone of a young girl in a confectionery dress, the African nose of a grandmother in sensible shoes. Add Greek, Circassian, Crusader, Persian and Arab in unexpected, daring permutations and keep painting, until you've designed the butterfly's wing.

This square is stitched onto my soul, the destination of day-dreams. Late one memorable night several years ago, two muezzins interwove the haunting call to prayer from ornate minarets outlined against a full-mooned sky. I am, as then, mes-merized in the square below.

Memory shunts me forward along my favorite route from the square. A grape arbor shades the tomb of the chivalrous Kurdish ruler, Saladin, who rid the area of the tiresome Crusaders. I drift through the old caravansaries and artisans' workshops into a narrow cobbled street that crosses from one side of the Roman Old City to the other, a street so straight, it bares that strange name. The blinded Saul of Tarsus, the later missionary Saint Paul, walked this Street Called Straight. With my squinting eyes, I am in good company.

The stalls of the coffee roasters and spice dealers are shuttered for the holy day, but the air hangs fragrant with residue. Vines, their thick-knotted trunks like peasant thighs, wind affectionately across old brick and stained clapboard buildings. Huge carved, wooden doors, two horses wide, once an entrance to a grand storehouse, are freshly painted green and blue.

The once thriving Jewish quarter is now almost empty. Residents who lived here for God knows how long recently migrated when given the choice, leaving behind only a few elderly who refuse to leave the streets in which they and generations before them were born.

Almost two thousand years ago, early Jewish converts to a small heretical sect later known as Christianity, also lived along this road. Today's Christian quarter, now a multitude of sects—Catholics, Assyrian, Greek Orthodox, Protestant—stands near the Eastern Gate of the Romans, which sharply divides old Damascus from new and serves as terminus for the Street Called Straight.

I traverse this cultural stew toward what I figure is my destina-tion: the home of Barnabas, now a church, where Ananias led Paul. My mind has made a desperate link between losing my glasses and the church where Paul regained his sight. Ha ha! I've got God worked out on this one. That's the solution to this mystery. Something's bound to happen there. It's a logical plan, under the circumstances. I just haven't checked it out with God.

Outside the market, the cobbled street widens enough for one car and one overloaded donkey cart to carefully squeeze by each other with the instruction of onlookers. To the right, a young boy is wiping the dust off carved bedsteads lined up on the sidewalk at a carpentry shop and looks up.

"Hello, lady," he says in English.

"Greetings, little master," I reply in Arabic, and we both smile briefly into each other's eyes.

A few yards along, across the street, a decrepit wooden building that was once an old inn or caravansary begs my attention. I stop.

The carved edifice has shed its paint and darkened with neglect. A lopsided balcony alcove juts out over the street. Windows, tall and handsome, are patched in places with newspaper and crusted with dust. The studded door to the courtyard rests slightly open.

My curiosity behaves like the stray cat she is and drags me across the street.

Who lives here, I wonder, Who used to live here?

Midstream I change my mind again and walk on several yards before turning, drawn back to the old house. I step back and forth, confused, not able to make up my mind.

God and I are having some control issues. This is my day off, dammit. I'm exhausted and need time alone to think. No tests today.

I'm pacing back and forth like a lunatic, twisting myself into a storm.

I will not go inside that gate. I have a meeting with destiny at the church to regain my sight.

Finally, I step beyond the gate.

Inside the courtyard, I measure the shadows of the old house and imprint it on my memory. The voices of women startle me and I turn quickly and leave, determined to maintain some control over my life. The shadow follows me and darkens my mood. I do not like being unable to see clearly.

The Christian quarter is eerily quiet and offers little distraction from my thoughts. The shops of craftsmen and artisans are boarded up for the afternoon. Workmen have dug a deep sewage trench down the center of the alley and left for the weekend. Hillocks of sand, rock and clay impede the sidewalk but I plough on determined.

Ever since the old house I'm dangerously irritable. The rest of Syria may be enjoying the weekend, but God is not giving me the day off.

When my younger brother was in his brat stage and wanted to get a rise out of me, he would gently prod my arm. He'd usually wait until I was reading or lost in thought. Over and over. Tap, tap, tap, with his finger until I could no longer stand it and turned to slap him one. I can feel God's finger prodding me now, but slapping God's hand is not a good idea.

My determined footsteps echo in the alley leading to the Church of Saint Barnabas. The place is deserted. Even the wretched old nun who usually collects the entrance fee is not there, and I slip through the unguarded door, down the stairs into the grotto.

This small subterranean room is where Saul was led by Ananias and hidden when he regained his sight. He wasn't missing much. The space is damp and dark and claustrophobic. Moss grows on the stone walls encouraged by a bare, low-watt bulb. An old priest once told me that the early converts used to meet in such miserable basements to avoid persecution. Their depression is catching. I spend an hour chasing away visions of crucifixions and being buried alive.

I light a taper to chase the gloom and place it with the flickering row of prayer candles by the stone altar, its edges worn smooth and polished by the touch of supplicants. Once, the same old priest told me, this altar was used in a pagan temple for human sacrifice. He had shown me the channel for the blood. I run my finger along the edge and the hairs on my arm ripple.

I'm alone as I wish, waiting for destiny, but I'm as satisfied as a one-night stand. Instead of inner peace, I'm fixating on externals.

A wooden bench this old should be worn to perfection, but it isn't. Some of the hand-printed signs are misspelled. A rhythmic shadow crosses the stairwell and pauses on the cobbles above.

The soft, uneven tap of footsteps continues. Tap, tap, tap. Two thousand years ago, martyrs hid in this same room, holding their breath, waiting for similar shadows to continue on their way. Since I'm not a bloody martyr, I surface.

At the top of the stairs, the old familiar nun has returned from lunch and paces, waiting to collect my exit fee and to sell me post-cards. She doesn't have a revelation for me and I give up on being receptive to the inner voice. I second-guessed God, and I was wrong. I decide to backtrack to the old house with the open gate.

Outside in the street, a few Christian schoolchildren in uniform are inspecting the sewer trench. They're sharing packets of candy, talking quietly and holding hands, hugging the shade of the alley to avoid roasting in the afternoon sun. Innocence and laughter is an antidote to the dank basement and I willingly fall into step behind them.

When their pace quickens, mine follows. By the intersection of the Street Called Straight, they start running toward an old church as if they're late for class, but it is not the bells of heaven that call them. Under the Greek columns that mark the ancient city walls, an ice-cream vendor has pulled his pushcart into a sliver of shade and rings his bicycle bell. Children crowd around him, making decisions, ringing the bell, tearing off wrappers, gently teasing each other and horsing around.

I am lost in the universality of it all, when a hand touches mine.

A young girl, perhaps ten, smiles up at me. Her eyes are clear and bright, like a young sparrow's in midsong. I can almost hear the tune going on inside her head, a sweet hum without specific words. I've hummed this song many times myself. A pink plastic headband holds her brown hair off her face. She's wearing a light cotton caftan covered with small bright flowers. On her feet are blue plastic scuffs emblazoned with the word *Adidas*.

"Hel-lo," she says in halting English. "What is your nim?"

She is fresh and clean and open-faced, not a street-ripened waif with wares to sell or places to guide me. Her hand rests in mine as if I am her older sister. Unlike in the West where children are told not to talk to strangers, children here adopt you as part of their extended family. You are given an appropriate name or status: Aunt or Big Sister, for example.

"What is yours?" I ask.

She tells me her name is Lena. Lena is also the name of one of my favorite friends in Washington.

"I must speak English, to learn," she says, matter-of-factly.

"Yes, you must," I reply. I have entered her game.

"Then you are pleased to come with me," she says and gently tugs my hand.

"Where?" I ask.

Am I supposed to go with her? I ask myself. Is she a messenger sent by the Sufi poet whose answer I'm waiting for? After the tea boy in Cairo I am less ready to dismiss her, but the paranoia of Syria continues to rattle my cup.

My self-noise lasts only a second. I stand still. And listen.

I sense I'm standing within the circle of a perfect moment.

"You are a teacher," she says.

"And how did you know?" I reply.

Without speaking, she taps her heart and shrugs her shoulders at the same time.

My Middle Eastern paranoia bubbles up again and I push it back into the box. What if it's just some tourist trap and there'll be an ugly or at least, uncomfortable scene? What if I'm led into some other kind of trap? What if the security police want to see me?

Lena's waiting. Take your time, she seems to be saying.

I look down at her again and surrender. So be it. I'm in her hands. Down the Street Called Straight the old house waits with its open gate. There's no doubling back on God's timing. I shrug and follow the little girl.

She begins to lead me to her home, or toward where she says is her home, through back alleys that I'm sure I'll never retrace.

Small houses plastered over and painted bright yellow and blue. Geraniums and Damascus roses in recycled vegetable oil cans. Women in floral caftans hanging out laundry of blue jeans and striped shirts of their menfolk. They pause to look at us.

Lena leads me forward, smiling proudly as if she has won first prize at the fair. She chirps along about school and her family and I chirp back, asking questions while trying to observe landmarks, to check the position of the minarets on the horizon, just in case I need them to get out.

We step down off the sidewalk into a small room, neat and clean and freshly painted sky blue, with flowery curtains to keep the blazing sun in check. Against the wall a daybed serves as a sofa, and is covered in another flowered fabric and white embroidered cotton pillows. Everything looks starched and smells of fresh air. I feel sweaty and dirty among all this cool hard work and innocence.

In the far corner is a single red upholstered chair with wooden arms, obviously for visitors and guests of honor. Lena ushers me toward it. Remembering Dr. Mohammed in Cairo, I also decline the seat of honor in favor of the family daybed.

Lena pads barefoot across the old stone floor, furrowed near another door, and disappears behind another floral curtain that separates the kitchen and living quarters from the front room. A bird trills and the child whistles in return, setting off a cooing interchange that snags on a memory of flocks of budgerigars and other parrots that would greet us in the Australian morning. And of my younger brother who would patch up and tend the broken winged and ill, talking to them softly as he opened their temporary cages. There was something so poignant about the way he would hold a broken bird in the cup of his large hand.

A beak scratches against metal, followed by the sounds of a grate lifting and water splashing as Lena tends to her friend.

A heavy refrigerator door creaks open, then shuts with a solid double click that brings to mind the old ice chests we had growing up in the tropics. The ice man—Jimmy the Greek, who also owned the fish and chip shop—drove up once a week in his deliv-ery truck loaded with huge blocks of frozen gold. He'd whack them with a huge scimitar to wedge a block loose, then haul it with tongs, large enough to hang a sheep on, into the ice box on our verandah. We kids would clutter around the back of his truck, excited yet trying to be well behaved, hoping yet not begging, for some chips of ice to suck on. These mouthfuls of frozen water were the sweetest thing we'd ever tasted.

Filled with sadness, overwhelmed with the burden of child-hood, I swallow hard. The last thing I need is to start crying in front of this little girl.

On a shelf on the opposite wall in an obvious place of honor is a gilt frame with a black-and-white photograph of a young man in military uniform. He could be Lena's father. Or her brother. Even without my glasses there is definitely a resemblance. Next to it is a plastic radio and a postcard of the Virgin Mary. There is no television.

Tacked to the wall is a series of childlike drawings. Angels or some kind of winged creatures, fairies perhaps; I'm not sure from where I sit.

We've left our dusty shoes outside the door and Lena brings me some plastic scuffs and a glass of cold water on a saucer cov-ered with a crocheted napkin. The scuffs are her brother's, she says and then nods at the photograph of the young man in his military uniform.

We sit together in silence for a minute, her English temporar-ily exhausted, my mind just taking in the room, the peacefulness, the pencil drawings on the wall. I bathe in this calm moment, a respite from the frenetic swirl of the past weeks.

"Yes," Lena says as she follows my thoughts more closely than I, "the birds, she is mine."

Our conversation is drowsy and unfocused so I nod absently at the non sequitur. Yes, yes, the bird in the kitchen, I nod. She insists on showing me.

Lena returns not with the canary in the kitchen, but with a

ledger, the everyday kind with the marbled edges they use in the market. She curls up on the daybed beside me, puts the book on my lap and begins to flip through the pages.

Once, my baby brother and I curled up against my mother as she read to us. It was mid-September, heavy tropical rains drummed on the metal roof, and the three of us were on her large bed, drawn together under the protective veil of mosquito netting. I remember this because it was unusual that my mother showed affection and because I sensed she was afraid. She was about to go into labor with my sister; my stepfather was away and a neighbor would drive her to the country hospital. As the pain sharpened, she pulled us close under the tent of netting and read us fairy tales. My sister was born in the middle of a fairy tale.

I pull Lena into my side.

All the pages of Lena's book are slightly discolored by musty water damage. The beginning, the back, of the book is covered with the flowing Arabic of an adult hand in ink. Midway, childish letters in pencil take over. And then she turns to the drawings. I squint to see them.

With my imperfect vision, the drawings on the wall appear to be angels. But within comfort range, I see they are a giant seated bird, its huge wings unfolding above it in an arc, two hands in prayer. There are pages of such birds, progressive in accomplishment, embellished by imagination. In the later versions it is surrounded by an illuminating halo like a Christian saint or New Age aura. In one she has drawn stars and a moon.

Lena has given the feathers a life of their own; one bird has wings like palm branches, another reveals the pet canary as model. She has drawn the head both in profile and straight on. Its eyes are outlined and upturned like an Egyptian god or a fifties movie star. In each, however, the incredible bird is either seated on a nest with an egg, or simply on a decorative circle.

"She is the Fire Bird," Lena says.

The Fire Bird? I drop the book, as if it is fire itself.

"Yes, yes, I know," I reply, slowly. "The Phoenix."

I know all about this fiery bird, I want to tell her rather smugly. The tea boy invited me to see the Fire Bird dance in the Sufi lodge. The Egyptian Phoenix rising to life off the walls of the Coptic churches. My own self-immolation and ability to rise out of the ashes. I survived the fire in the Turkish village when someone tried to kill me. Tell me, hon, I know all about the Fire Bird.

Lena looks at me, cocks her head, then dares to correct me.

"No, teacher," she says. "She is not *your* phoenix. In our country, the Fire Bird, she is different."

In broken English mixed with Arabic, she explains how this fantastic giant bird, as fiery as the sun, hovers above us, invisible. Being invisible, it can talk to people but they can't see it. Whenever a circle of good-hearted people comes together, however, the magic bird materializes from their collective desire for goodness, and brings prosperity and peace to them. But the bird has to wait, and wait, for good people to find each other. Then it comes to life and the wishes of the good people are realized.

The Fire Bird in her last drawing sits on a golden egg. Lena has colored it fiery orange and attached pieces of tinsel to it.

I ask her about the egg.

"This is the circle of good people," she replies simply.

"Waiting to hatch?" I ask. "To become a Fire Bird?"

"Inshallah," she replies. "God willing."

For her they don't need a reason to exist.

"How do you know about this bird?" I finally ask. "From the old paintings and buildings?"

The rich architecture of the city is enough inspiration to fill the head of any child with such fantastic creatures. And there are books. There are always books.

"No," she says.

"From books?" I ask.

She shakes her head and looks up at the photo on the wall.

"From my heart," she says. "When my brother died, she came to my heart."

CHAPTER 13

Dr. Khayyam

A message is waiting at the hotel desk when I return from Lena's. A sullen, weedy night clerk has replaced my favorite boys. He wears the look of a mother's least favored son and does his best to share his calumny. He keeps his eyes down as he hands me the note.

Hanna, the young accountant is there in glam-orange, gold bracelets jangling up her wrist as she jabs at her calculator. She catches on my swollen eyes, curls a black brow into a question mark and frowns. Nothing escapes this woman, and her attention has begun to bother me. I'm not in the mood for a new best friend.

Dr. Khayyam,* personal advisor to the Sufi poet, Assad Ali, will meet me in the hotel lobby at 6:30, the note says. That gives me ten minutes to wash off the dust and clean up my tear-stung face. A douse of cold water and my professional mask says cool, calm, and back in control.

Downstairs in the lobby, three middle-aged men in gray business suits are sitting under the silk palm trees by the fountain. Two I recognize from the previous evening, and in one uninterrupted, balletlike movement, they look up, give me the full body search, and go back to their cigarettes, pistachios and huddled conversation. The third has already leapt up, hands held extended in welcome, and strides toward me.

Dr. Khayyam's talking away before he reaches me.

"Welcome, welcome, Doktora," he says.

Not sure whether to treat me as a colleague or a long lost family member, he does both, vigorously shaking my hand and patting my back at the same time in the familial hug of an Italian uncle.

"Our friend said to be expecting you, sister," he says. Our friend being Abdul Aziz in Washington, who has faxed the poet of my arrival.

We sit, we talk, we drink water and half-gossip like old cronies, talking in that Middle Eastern code that assumes you know the subject (as well as object) of the sentence without going into too much detail. We're checking the landscape with a probing nonchalance I've become accustomed to, both aware that the two other men are sucking on every word.

The men finally leave.

Dr. Khayyam raises his bushy eyebrows toward me, slides his gray eyes sideways, and cocks his head in that unspoken question, Do you know who they are?

I reply with a twitch of my own brows. No.

He taps his ear and nods knowingly.

"Oh," I mouth.

He motions slowly. Secret police.

I glance up at the desk and Hanna is smiling at both of us. Oh. I suppose she also knows. Or is one herself?

We continue our conversation but less self-consciously, filling the blank spaces in the sentences with words and names.

"Mawlana," Dr. Khayyam uses the honorific title to refer to a spiritual leader. "Mawlana, Our Master, is not here, as you know."

His huge, sad eyes register a definite loss. He is sincerely sorry.

"It is according to the Beloved," he says and points upward. "The One."

I am expecting the worst, an accident, illness. Don't tell me the poet's dead.

Dr. Khayyam explains that the Sufi master is in seclusion, that he is fasting and meditating and may be gone for quite some time. However, because I am "a special friend of a special friend," he may leave his retreat to see me. He is praying about it.

"God willing, tonight. God willing, next week," he says. Time is so old in Syria that nobody quibbles about a few days.

Meanwhile, Dr. Khayyam has come to check me out in case the mystic poet needs backup.

Dr. Khayyam is a retired lawyer, a lover of words and literature. A trusted friend of Assad Ali, also a lawyer, he is the Sufi poet's translator. His English is as beautifully florid as the Arabic I fell in love with in grad school. My first Arabic professor had been a squat Egyptian playwright who would close the classroom door, turn off the lights and do dramatic readings of ancient poems filled with long, delicious, melodious words. Even before I learned the meaning of the words, I loved their sound. The transformation of that little professor's sweaty, unshaven face when he recited poetry was almost beatific and if I close my eyes today, I still see him with a halo. Unfortunately, our high saint of drama neglected to teach us any grammar.

Dr. Khayyam has that same love of language. When he wants to capture the quality of a word in English, he pauses in his enthusiastic sentences, closes his eyes as if sniffing a full summer rose, smiles, exhales, and then presents the word as a gift of rare wonder. And from his mouth, the words are beautiful, because they have been chosen among all words for their meaning and beauty. Or full-of-beauty-ness, as he says. It is disarming.

He glances at his watch, then stands abruptly.

Apparently he has received some kind of message.

"Come," he says and he starts out the door. I grab my notebook and camera bag and scurry after. Alice with another of her White Rabbits.

We drive with subdued urgency toward an area of Damascus

off the tourist track. The car windows are down, rushing us with humid air, and we raise our voices above the bleating traffic to keep up with our 100-mile-per-hour conversation. We talk about Mawlana and his poetry, the beauty of the Syrian countryside, the revolving residences of the Syrian president, the barren mountain that looms above the city, and for each subject Dr. Khayyam snatches poetry out of the air.

European villas and wide boulevards from the French regime give way to narrow thoroughfares and storefronts with signs entirely in Arabic. The pace changes. Donkey carts and beaten-down cars leisurely weave between small knots of working-class families crossing the dimly lit streets. Unlike the center of Damascus, there is no need to hurry; everyone is already home.

Smoke suddenly blurs my vision. Clouds barreling off the sidewalk engulf the car and absorb the headlights. I sniff the air. Burning wood and flesh. For a second I'm transported back to last year's fire in Turkey, and I grip the dashboard.

Dr. Khayyam crunches the car against the curb, and I jump to my senses.

Rows of small restaurants with open spit-grills and wood ovens tumble over into the street. Whole lambs and chicken are hand-turned over the chars by young boys with wanna-be mustaches.

"Here," he says.

"Here?" I ask. I look around for someone who resembles a Sufi poet. "Is Mawlana here?"

"No," he replies. "But the fresh lamb comes off the grill at nine o'clock."

He taps his watch proudly. Nine, spot on.

"You must feed the body as well as the soul," he says and guides me into the haze.

I am still shaking as I enter the restaurant.

The acrid smoke of the kebab house stings my eyes, but I gradually reach equilibrium. The noise of families and workers overrides any meaningful conversation we might have, but we didn't come here for conversation. Dr. Khayyam sits opposite at the rickety table savoring his forbidden favorite—charcoal-brazed lamb slices, smothered with yogurt sauce and onions, wrapped in flat bread hot from the oven. I've opted for the vegetable version and lick the thin trail of warm butter that escapes into my palm.

"My wife," he says and wags his finger. "She does not approve. Kol-les-ter-rrol."

I return his grin and become a conspirator in the war against hardened arteries.

"When do you think it is possible to meet the Master?" I ask after we hose down at the washbasin.

"We don't know when," he says and points to the Big Man Upstairs. "But you will know."

I'm catching on. I've read about what is happening, some California friends have told me about it, but I've never experienced or been part of it.

It's a strange phenomenon.

There appears no reason for much of what my new friends do with their time, no organization, no sense of urgency, no pinning them down. They don't even have lists.

You go and have a kebab because you are not receiving an internal message to do otherwise. You don't sit by the phone, unless instructed, because you have a more perfect, equally invisible, form of communication. You go about the day, brush your teeth, attend to the mundanities and responsibilities, but you're not double-guessing yourself.

You will "know" when it is time for something to happen, if it is to happen at all. "You will hear," is the other expression they use. If you are still, you will hear the voice within. But just because you are listening doesn't mean something is supposed to happen. Sometimes nothing is a happening. And that's enough.

"I will know," I reply, but shake my head nonetheless.

I spend the next day in pursuit of sight—and distraction—while I not-wait for some message. The accountant Hanna has introduced me to her optometrist across the square, an elderly

Armenian who cobbles Dior look-alikes from nothing but cunning and cannibalized parts. Lest I maintain any hope of seeing clearly before I leave, my glasses will not be ready until the day I depart.

Distraction comes from a woman friend, Rheema,* the niece of my Washington colleague. She's a hot-wire lawyer, and we're out having such a rowdy time that I almost miss the Sufi's small, quiet message.

CHAPTER 14

Enclave

The house of Assad Ali, the mystic poet, sometime lawyer and professor of literature, rests high in the mountain above Damascus. The room where we will meet is bare-lit by flickering neon and, at ten at night, still sweltering. Sparse, hand-calligraphed verses of the Qur'an dot the desert colored walls. The furniture—armchairs, side chairs, coffee tables—is all as worn and mismatched as the half-dozen guests who wait for the Master. There's not one Flower Child among us.

A faint stirring fans through the room. The middle-aged Muslim businessman looks up, then the Armenian physician beside him. The attractive woman next to me, a pharmacist and the physician's wife, sniffs the air, then smiles, as if a pleasant odor floats in on a breeze and stirs a memory. The young man on the other side of me, a trim high school teacher, smells it too. A memory of a breeze that comes off the ocean in midsummer, perhaps, and tells you that a storm is approaching. I too, smile, as the electricity builds.

As a child, I played with siblings and friends on the sandbanks of Queensland, lost in imaginings, herding anemones, crabs and fish around coral ponds, living in the moment. At that age, the future meant tonight, or tomorrow, or perhaps if pressed, next week, but that was difficult to imagine. Midsummer afternoons, a silence, almost imperceptible, would descend. Palm trees hushed. Parrots swallowed their song midsquawk. And for a moment, even the waves held their breath.

That silence before the storm was both frightening and exhilarating. We had but seconds to run to shore from the reefs and sandbanks before the blinding downpour and rising waves threatened to pull us into the ocean and drown us. We were not afraid of the storm, for after the initial burst and the fury softened, we would run half-naked, glistening with cooling rain, dancing like the little savages we were, in celebration of ... what? Wonder, perhaps. The lack of fear?

The tension in the room is much like that. Children waiting for the arrival of a storm, awed yet excited, to dance naked in its majesty.

"He's coming," they say, and with their looks they fold me into their excitement.

I nod in return.

Yes, I, too, can sense the massive energy of the storm as it approaches.

Assad Ali glides into the room. He glows, almost transparent, a human salamander still carrying the reflection of where he has been. He is surrounded by light and grinning ear to ear. There is no other way to describe him. He is tall and lean and wears a long creamy robe. His hair is short and silver, his skin is almost pearlescent, devoid of lines against which to measure depth or life.

And his eyes? What color are they? Sea color, like warm, deep, encompassing water.

Is this what a drowning person sees when pulled into the ocean by the storm? An alabaster statue of Pan come to life? If so, he and I are delirious.

The Sufi poet is greeted like an unexpected visitor to his own house. The others clearly love him and want to fuss about him, but stay at a distance.

He raises the index finger on his right hand, and points upward. One. The One. God. The Beloved. There is no god but God.

He turns fully toward me with this wide, devilish grin. His face is sexless, ageless yet childish. Impish in its open joy.

As I step toward him, I am pulled back by a strong hand on my shoulder. There's no one next to me, or touching me. Still I can't move forward past an invisible barrier. It's not a struggle. I simply stop because I'm peaceful and stand in a place of calm. I have this overwhelming urge to close my eyes and to smile. I feel warm and safe, and at home.

My mind kicks in. What the hell are you talking about?

But I keep looking at him and thinking, this is the face of a man who has been with the angels. This is a man who dances naked in the storm.

Oh hell. Don't tell me I'm going to be dancing naked by the end of the evening. It's been years since I did anything like that, and I only did so because someone paid immense amounts of money—on a dare—in art school. Which makes it okay.

These are not rational observations. I try to focus, to compose myself. I've come here to ask a great intellectual, a renowned poet, who just happens to be a Sufi mystic and master, about technology and faith. I'm here not as a person, but as a professional. I am not here to feel anything or to participate. Let alone to feel safe and warm and at home.

Still, I cannot move forward and I'm happy to stand where I am, a child in warm, wet underpants.

Please, please sit, the poet motions and we pull up our chairs and bend toward him like sun-starved plants.

He is still glowing. And everyone in the room appears to be, also. I'm trying to frown.

"Our Master welcomes you," Dr. Khayyam begins, once again using the honorary title, Mawlana, given to religious men. "Our Master welcomes you and also apologizes for not coming forward to take your hand."

The others in the room buzz with agreement. Taking my hand would definitely be a bad thing, bad thing, the woman beside me says.

I'm not surprised by his action, however. Religious men in the Middle East have pulled this dead-hand trick on me before; some who believed that the root of evil lies in a woman's palm and therefore refused to shake my long, callused hand. I was expecting the same explanation.

"You see," Dr. Khayyam continues, "our Beloved Master has been . . . away from us."

He indicates the sky, and the others laugh gently at this inside joke.

"He has been away from us on a retreat, fasting," he says, "and has only returned from his meditation to meet with you. This is a great honor."

I swallow hard and thank him.

"And when our Beloved returns from swimming in this Sea of Consciousness, this meditation . . ." The Sufi poet speaks slowly, smiling, as Dr. Khayyam's voice echoes after his, two voices interwoven, calling the faithful to prayer from a minaret. ". . . the power is too strong. It has been known to knock a man across the room, yes. That is why he does not shake your hand or even kiss us, who he knows like children. We must wait for the power to go down, to subside. We—who are his children—must wait and be patient."

There are distractions as Assad Ali settles and tea is brought in, along with sodas and glasses of spring water. The room is charged and, despite the antiquated fans pointed in all directions, we sweat profusely. A young assistant in a striped cotton caftan places a large rattling fan behind me and adjusts it several times. A couple of latecomers arrive and more chairs are squeezed in.

I set up my tape recorder, and another assistant, a graduate student, places another recorder beside mine. Assad Ali's guys will also be taping our conversation. Over my shoulder, the pharmacist is setting up a video camera. Without glasses I cannot see enough to keep notes, but I contribute to the activity and open a notebook on my knees. This has become theater, and we are all equally onstage. Assad Ali is clearly the director in this rumpus.

The poet sends the student assistant to retrieve a sheaf of papers, which he places on his lap. Even without my glasses I recognize them as the faxed copy of my résumé.

Assad Ali puts on wire-rimmed glasses, turns the pages forward, nods, turns back a page quickly. He takes off his glasses and closes his eyes.

After eternity he turns to Dr. Khayyam.

"Are we ready to begin?" he asks.

I nod, others agree. The room falls silent for the first time since Assad Ali's arrival.

Assad Ali begins speaking, and the translator bends closer to catch every word. He jots down a few words on a notepad to cue his memory.

Turning toward me, Dr. Khayyam is briefly ruffled by the video camera, gathers himself, then continues.

"Again, our Beloved Master welcomes you," he says.

I begin a florid reply, but Assad Ali motions that he does not want to be interrupted.

"Our Master welcomes you," Dr. Khayyam continues, "and says that he is impressed with your résumé."

I thank him, but the Master is not smiling.

"However, he would like to know where in your life is there room for your heart? He does not see it here on this piece of paper. And your family? Do you have a family?"

I pause, stunned. My mind races. That is what it's trained to do. To race. To compete and win. I'm trying to understand the question. From every angle. At once. And formulate a reasonable response.

My heart on my résumé? You are not supposed to include your heart on your résumé. And my family? Academics are not supposed to have one.

This is not how I expected the interview to go. Just who is interviewing whom? I'm supposed to be asking the questions.

That little defense mechanism in my brain takes over. Of course my heart is there on those bloody sheets of paper. That is my work. That *is* my love. I have poured my heart and soul into it. How can he not see my heart in such titles as "The Immense and Universal Importance of Whatever, in The Long Ago Whenever, to Long Dead Whomever, in The Faraway Lost Kingdom of Something-or-Other?"

Look at what I've accomplished, what I've achieved, how far I've come. Especially for a woman in the field. And a natural blonde at that. Look at all my awards and honors.

I've trained with the best in the world. . . .

I've given up. . . .

I've gone without. . . .

I've fought. . . .

I've poured my heart into . . . fighting to become the person summarized on that shitty piece of facsimile paper sent by invisible airwaves from the other side of the world.

How does he know my heart is not there in his hands?

His eyes dance with watchful humor.

There is nothing for me to say, so I remain silent. He has read between the lines of my soul.

For the first time in my journey, I am uncomfortable in my nakedness and vow, as I did with the tea boy in Cairo, that I will not dance tonight.

The poet takes the sheaf of papers while keeping my eyes tacked to his, folds it vertically, and with operatic flair opens a small book that has lain hidden on his lap under the papers. A mischievous pucker now on his face, he places my folded résumé between two pages of the book, sealing it with a magician's flourish.

The others around us murmur approval. I'm looking for the trick mirrors.

It is his book of poetry, *Happiness without Death*, which I had been reading on the plane when I lost my glasses.

I, the Desert,
woke in the arms of night
and wondered, O night,
how do you embrace people and things?

"May you find your heart," Mawlana says and passes the book and papers to Dr. Khayyam to pass to me with a word of instruction.

"Mawlana says, 'What is the use of gaining knowledge of the whole universe if you lose your self?' " Dr. Khayyam adds. "These are the words of Christ, no?"

I take the Fifth. My defense team has stepped out of the room.

Dr. Khayyam leans toward me and speaks off script ever so quietly.

"Mawlana does this so that the papers, and the life it represents, will be imbued with the spirit of the book," he says.

The Desert embraced by the Night?

"This is a great blessing," he assures me, and turns back to his duties.

"Now," Assad Ali says, and claps his hands, ready for the entertainment to begin. "Now we begin our discussion."

The group agrees it's time for some gentle sport and adjusts their seats for the best view.

"Those who seek knowledge beneath the words," Assad Ali says, "are very endeared to God."

My hopes disappear of ever getting in a question.

"So let me ask the Doktora," the Sufi continues. "What is the English word for *qalb?*"

"The heart," I reply quickly. The two men confer, looking back and forth at me as they do.

Finally Dr. Khayyam says: "Because you answered so well, Mawlana thought that I might have inadvertently mentioned something about this to you, but I rely on your intellectual power. So maybe because of this intellectual power you have sensed something."

"No," I reply. "The heart is a well-loved subject in Arabic."

They laugh, and I relax.

"Mawlana also says something concerning the word *heart*," says Dr. Khayyam. "In English, this is to be read from left to right, from the West to the East. Let us now try to read these foreign letters, or Roman letters, from the East to the West."

The concept of reversing the letters of words, or assigning numerical value to each, is widely used among mystics who savor words as the direct communication of God. Or among the more pedestrian who just love word games. I'd entertained myself for hours this way as a child. My puzzlement is that *"traeh"—heart* spelled backward—doesn't make any sense. Also, my mind is racing ahead in a futile attempt to outsmart the mystic.

"First we pronounce it *'haart,'*" the Sufi instructs. "Keep this *sound*, not the letters, but the sound, in mind. Now try to say it from East to West."

They are not only switching letters, direction and language, but now, the senses.

"*Tr-aah*," I say.

"*Ter-aah*," Assad Ali rolls the word on his tongue. "Yes, *Ter-aah*. This translates in Arabic as 'You see it,' 'You meet it eye-to-eye.' So the heart is the vehicle, the medium for seeing."

The Sufi claps his hands like a grand maestro. Everyone in the room is laughing with delight. I'm smiling at this nimble game.

"This means the heart's function is to see," he now says softly, moving forward with the game.

"But you first have to translate the words with the mind," I add. My expensively trained mind is determined to maintain primacy over my ragtag heart.

He pauses for a moment over my comment and puckers his brows before continuing.

"In the heart of the heart, through the reversing of the reading," he says, "we can come to other things. Now, we have a game, a puzzle, as you say. I want each one of us just to try and shut our eyes and try to see a certain word, a particular word. What word would we see if we shut our eyes now, right after this experience?"

The timekeeper is Assad Ali. He wears no watch.

He instructs us that there is one particular word he has in mind and he has just dispatched the word through his heart to all of us. He wants to see if we can pick up the word.

We contemplate in silence. The faces around me glow softly with a love-drunkenness.

"Now, our eyes are open. What is the word?" the Sufi master addresses me. "You need not be the first to answer if you wish."

One by one, the others in the room give their answers in Arabic. Many are the sacred names of God. Dr. Khayyam translates them.

"What he saw was the word 'Light.' "

"He saw 'The One,' 'The One Being.' "

"And he saw 'The He, *Hua.*' "

"She saw 'The Light.' "

"He saw 'The Hearer.' "

"I saw 'The Most Kind.' "

So far, none has correctly answered Mawlana's puzzle.

"Now, what did you see?" Assad Ali asks me. "What is 'The Word'?"

Dr. Khayyam suddenly gasps. He has solved the puzzle, and gives me an excited look, then closes his eyes again in an attempt to transmit the answer.

He wants me to look good. He wants me to get it.

"Peace," I finally say, drawing the letters out into an elongated sigh.

"Ah," Assad Ali says in English and Arabic, "P-e-e-a-c-c-e. Salaaaaam. Listen, it is a longing breath from her heart. P-e-e-a-c-c-e. Listen how it comes out from her heart."

The others nod. P-e-e-a-c-c-e, they say quietly, and the room fills with sibilant echoes of my own longing.

The room closes in, and I lower my head, slowly breathing in and out through my nose. The sound, P-e-e-a-c-c-e, wafts around me and I begin to float. When I look up I see myself in the eyes of the others as if they're a mirror and I flow in and out of their faces and bodies.

Assad Ali's voice pulls me back, but I continue to float.

"These are each our concerns. We each saw our own concerns," Dr. Khayyam says. "And you are all wonderful, the most wonderful. But you did not explicitly say that particular word Mawlana dispatched to you during the experience.

"Mawlana says, 'I dispatched The Word, and The Word in the Qur'an is Christ. Because Christ is The Word.' "

Ahhh.

"This is the way he tries to open us up," Dr. Khayyam says to me directly. "I tried to help you when I discovered the answer."

We're all caught up in the good humor that I'm not expecting the next question.

"What is your experience with Christ?" Assad Ali suddenly asks.

"Experience?" I ask. What a curious word, experience. "My religious practice?"

"Your experience," he replies.

I stiffen. A bubble of resistance perks through my glorious haze. My experience with Christ is private, mine alone. Then I glance at the mirror of faces around me, and understand that I am no longer separate.

I begin to tell Assad Ali of an experience I had as a child. How, alone on my bed one afternoon, I prayed to Jesus for help. My stepfather was a violent and angry man, and I, like my brothers and sisters, was the focus of his rage. I couldn't protect them, or myself. My mother had her own troubles. I prayed.

In the middle of praying I saw myself as if from above. I saw myself, a child, on the bed. A strange warmth ran from my head to my feet. I saw myself lifted from the bed and could feel a presence. A light. And in that light was a glowing presence.

If I think the mystic will be impressed by my revelation, he is not.

"Did you *feel* the presence of Christ?" he asks. "Or did you *see* him."

"Felt," I reply, puzzled. "But I also looked inside the Light and he was there. I saw him with my heart. No, with my senses. As a presence, not a person, that drew me forward and reached for me at the same time."

"And you knew it was Christ?" he asks rather abruptly.

"Yes," I reply. "By the peace that filled me. I can't explain."

The room is quiet. Assad Ali murmurs.

"The atmosphere is now filled with this peace which you have just expressed," Assad Ali says.

Dr. Kerim, a young physician, leans forward, his hands folded on his knees and begins to speak. The others agree, and then look toward me.

I'm sitting in a limbo.

"Dr. Kerim's impression," Dr. Khayyam translates, "about what you have just said. He can feel the truth flowing from your heart, through God, Allah, Christ. The Light. . . ."

I'm sure he thinks I'm mad. I sigh deeply but with calm. There's nothing I can do. The experience happened. The words are now out in the atmosphere and have become part of the out-spoken and in-breathed universe. If I'm mad, so be it.

Assad Ali speaks softly. He's reading my mind. Or rather, he has pierced a permeable barrier that contains words and images and thoughts.

"Blood in Arabic is '*Dam*,'" Dr. Khayyam says. "Mawlana reverses it to 'Mad.' In Arabic, 'Mad' is the word for 'Matter.' Spiritually, this is the sustenance, the maintenance, of the spirit. And materially, it also means the 'Ink.' In Arabic, we call Ink *Mad*, also."

Mawlana speaks directly to me, ignoring the soft applause of the others in the room, but I'm dazed, trying to understand what he is saying.

Writers are madmen?

He smiles. As a writer himself, he's tasted this insanity of ink.

"A well-known Tradition of the Prophet is: Of all the favored of the tasks is to be a worker of words, to be a teacher, to write." He adds, "You have been blessed."

Assad Ali now claps his hands loudly. Right, the time has arrived to talk about technology, since that is the reason I have come to visit him.

"Yes, Mawlana says that, the universe, all the population of the world, is looking up to the skies," Dr. Khayyam says. "They are looking up to the spacious universe, this celestial universe, because they originally came from that celestial spacious universe. This universe is also living within them, inside them. But they have this feeling, this yearning, rather, to go back to their original territory."

"Is this the enveloping Night of which you write?" I begin to ask, but he continues.

"I try to enlighten the hearts of the universe through such treatises like *Happiness without Death*," he says, "and another book called *The Policies of the Heart*, and a third one, a volume about the policies of the souls. Rather, not policies, but the government, or instruction, or management of, the souls. Here our intent is to traverse these differences between government, the state, and religion."

"Reconciling these differences can lead to mad-ness," I say.

He registers my attempted pun with a smile, and continues.

"If every individual in the world was governed by that great love for himself," he says, "for his relations with others, and for this contact and relation with the Source, the Beloved, everybody would be living in peace."

"Our love of technology," I say, nodding toward the camera and sound equipment that surrounds us, "does this distract from our search for peace?"

He raised his eyebrows. Definitely not.

"We also believe," he says, "that the trend toward the Internet and in scientific channels is to help us reach that spacious universe, and will really help us immensely to reach our goals for human happiness."

"But, should happiness be one of our goals?" I ask. "I mean, isn't that reserved for the afterlife?"

"The Qur'an is composed of about 76,000 words," he says and stirs the air with his hands, scattering them around us like stars, "and the word 'difficult' never occurs there. The three letters of the word *s'ab* do not occur in the Qur'an. This indicates that our existence, our life, our problems are governed by the term 'easy,' 'simple,' 'simplicity,' but not 'difficult.' "

There are rules, he says, and uses the same image of cars and traffic rules as Bishop Musa in Egypt.

At 3:00 A.M. , Dr. Khayyam and I head back out into the traffic ourselves. We're light-headed. From lack of sleep. From the intense concentration. From the energy-charged embrace of Assad Ali as we leave.

The early morning streets of Damascus have a life of their own, but definitely a man's life. Young and middle-aged men gravitate around the doors of past-prime nightclubs, which wearily hump away like lovers in the last minutes of a pay-by-the-hour motel. Men sit on curbs, sharing cigarettes and silence. Some have come in from the outlying towns to break the hopeless same-ness of life; others, from their severe haircuts, are on leave from the military. A few donkey carts clop by. A neighborhood patrol-man leans against a wall pasted with a poster of the president and drinks a glass of tea sold by a street vendor.

At the hotel, the sullen clerk is on duty. He takes his time searching for my key that should be hanging on its hook in front of him.

My entire body is grinning like a drunken oaf. I am supremely at peace and nothing can bother me now. He can take all the time he wants because time is meaningless.

I float to my room on the second floor. My door is already unlocked for me. Perhaps the oversight of the night maid, but not important because in Syria, with its strict police system, nothing ever gets stolen. Unless . . . it's the police who want that some-thing.

The bed is turned down but no chocolate on the plumped up pillow. Bugger.

A night breeze stirs the drapes and I sniff the air as I did earlier tonight, sensing a presence.

Some heavies have been polluting my space.

A cigarette butt is ground out in the ashtray on the desk where I'd normally sit for writing. The foil chocolate wrapper is balled up beside it. I pick up the butt and squint at the label from arm's length. Syrian, not imported.

Oh hell, guys, not tonight.

Only security police and farmers smoke the government brand. This ain't no welcome committee from the Melon Growers' Cooperative of Syria.

I pull my travel bag from the closet and crouch on the floor to inspect the few contents left packed. My notes from Egypt are still there. Thank God. The tapes are in my camera bag I took with me tonight. And without my glasses, I haven't been able to write since arriving in Syria.

Why, why, why?

They know everywhere I've been. For God's sake, they lounge in my lobby. Follow me in the streets.

I search again. God's already taken my sight, so there's nothing much left.

My Australian passport is gone.

The little shits have stolen my birth identity.

Awww. They're feeling left out.

CHAPTER 15

The carpenter

Nabeel and I hurry along the Street Called Straight. His body demands that some part of it be moving at all times. If his feet stop, his hands take over. His mind zaps the horizon like a tetherball and his mouth never reaches stasis.

"Yeah, yeah, Doktora," he says. He combines American movie colloquialisms with unconventional English. "I know the exact peoples for you."

Hands, feet and mouth are moving together, underscoring his excitement.

So far, I've met only highly educated individuals who are believers in the mystical. No complaints, especially since I'd expected the opposite, that mysticism was the realm of the superstitious ignorant or of isolated hermits. But when I told Assad Ali I wanted to talk to some ordinary people who've had mystical experiences, some men and women in the street, he volunteered Nabeel as guide. Nabeel, a tall, pale Christian with a wispy mustache, has experimented with Buddhism and teaches English Lit at Damascus University.

"Yeah, yeah," Nabeel says as we scurry down the cobbled street, "you will meet Abu George, and then Sister Salma. They will show you about miracles."

He pulls to an abrupt halt and gestures toward an old wooden building, its crooked balcony overlooking the street, dusty windows papered, gate slightly ajar.

Like Saint Paul, I stand transfixed. It is the same old house and courtyard that drew me the day I met Lena. The house I refused to enter.

Nabeel motions for me to enter the courtyard.

This time, there is no pacing back and forth. After the meeting with Assad Ali last night, I'm holding my impulse to arm wrestle God and, instead, push on the heavy wooden door and enter the shadows.

Inside the spare courtyard, Nabeel hails a young boy crouched under a mammoth fig tree in the midst of a game with friends and sends him to tell his grandfather we are here.

The young boy smiles as he rises.

"Hello, lady," he says in English.

"Greetings, young master," I reply.

God is having a great time. It is the young carpenter's apprentice who was dusting off the bedsteads in the street. Three days in Damascus is a thousand years of renewed friendships.

On the second floor of the building, approximately where the crooked balcony had earlier captivated my attention, we leave our shoes outside a door and enter without knocking.

"Uncle," Nabeel calls into the dark room. The old man is not his uncle, but he uses the term with affection. "Uncle, uncle. We are here."

Tall windows over the courtyard shutter the room from the afternoon sun and even before my eyes adjust I sense it is tranquil and well tended.

Abu George, about seventy, walks shyly out of a door to the side of the room in which we stand. His face is freshly washed and the track of a comb still runs wet where he's tidied his thin, short white hair. His pale blue eyes are a little unfocused behind his thick glasses. We've disturbed his afternoon nap.

He kisses Nabeel on both his cheeks in welcome and the two men embrace both before and after I am introduced.

"A sister from America," is how Nabeel refers to me.

For the first time, the guest-of-honor chair is not offered and the two men lock eyes in perceptible relief when I settle into a small, upholstered armchair in front of them. Their eyes return to the worn brocade chair to the side of a daybed and they smile in unison. The guest chair carries an invisible reservation sign.

Old man and young man sit comfortably side by side on the daybed, backs resting against white embroidered cushions. Nabeel holds one of the carpenter's knotted hands. The carpenter holds prayer beads in the other.

The broad, slightly stooped shoulders hint that the old man was once strong and tall, but his hands, the outsize hands, are the only remnant of a life spent bending wood into submission. From this distance I notice the water splashes drying on his freshly pressed striped cotton, short-sleeve shirt. A woman's care—but not a wife's—shows in the neat trousers and in the methodical arrangement and contents of the room.

The apartment consists of a single room with a kitchen alcove I glanced on the way in. There's a small washroom behind me. The carpenter came out of it when we arrived. The daybed serves as both sofa and bed. Family photographs are arranged behind the daybed on clean, whitewashed walls. I squint at a faded turn of the century portrait of a proud and prosperous couple with children; a black-and-white studio portrait of a young couple, newly married; another of a young man in military uniform; then another of him as part of a smiling couple (this time in color) in a wedding portrait; and children, framed snapshots of shy, smiling children, one of which is the young apprentice from the carpenter's shop.

As I take in my surroundings, sweat drips off my face and down my legs under my long linen skirt. Keeping up with Nabeel in the streets of Syria has been a marathon. My soaked T-shirt could enter a Florida nightclub contest without me.

The young carpenter's apprentice, Abu George's grandson, brings us each a glass of refrigerated water and, with a kiss on his forehead from his grandfather, returns to his game downstairs.

"Our friend would like to hear your story, Abu George," Nabeel says to the old man.

Abu George lowers his head. His fate is to tell this intimate story to strangers, and he has accepted his fate. When he looks up again, he speaks softly.

He first relates portions of his story to Nabeel, who nods—uh-huh, uh, yeeah—and then pours out his translation, growing more excited with each word. Their interaction is affectionate and colloquial and the telling of the story weaves together into a joint effort.

"One night . . . ," Nabeel says.

But as soon as he is a few words into his translation, the old carpenter interrupts to untangle a thought.

Nabeel inserts the new information.

"Every day," he says, "Abu George wakes up at three o'clock in the morning to pray. This is his habit, okay?"

I nod. Okay.

He takes up the thread again.

"One night, it is five minutes before three," Nabeel says. "Our friend is lying here in his bed and he sees an old man calling him."

"Get up, my son," the old man says to Abu George. "Get up."

"Abu George is terrified and he draws a cross on himself. He looks up again and he sees the old man is still there and there is an aura around his head. And his beard is long, to his belly, and he is carrying a cane. In this room, here. Yes."

Nabeel pats the daybed where he and the carpenter sit. This is also where the carpenter sleeps.

"And the old man says to the carpenter, who is on his knees praying, 'Get up my son. I am Saint Elias.'"

The carpenter is respectfully stunned by this news: Saint Elias, Elijah, was one of the most remarkable prophets of the Old Testament. He is considered by Eastern Orthodox as the second

"Forerunner" to the coming of Christ (some believe Jesus was the returned Elijah) and was present with Moses at Christ's transfiguration.

"And Abu George replies, Welcome, my grandfather. Please sit down."

The two men point to the mysterious guest chair in which I didn't sit.

The saint sits down in the guest chair, places his cane against the daybed where Abu George sits, and starts telling the carpenter about all the problems of the people. They don't have faith. They don't have patience. They don't pray. And so on and so on, they commiserate.

Alone in the morning quiet, the saint and the carpenter are just two old men talking about the problems of the world. The saint is as real as flesh and blood can be.

After some time, the saint asks the carpenter for a glass of water. He's thirsty.

"Our friend brings this very glass," Nabeel says, and holds up a worn, plain glass. "It looks a little used now."

I'm trying to show interest, not sure where this is going. Unlike conversations with the religious leaders, my intellect is disengaged. This is not a philosophical debate, but a song of spirit. I can't squeeze a note out of a flute, but am no less respectful of those who can. Last night with Assad Ali, I had a part on the stage. Today I sit this one out and listen to the riffs. And suspend disbelief.

Nabeel turns back to the carpenter and confers. They nod in agreement.

"Just a simple glass from his kitchen over there," he says and continues the carpenter's story.

"Abu George pours some water from his jug, a lot of water, and brings it to him. The old man, the saint, takes one sip—one little, tiny sip—and then tells Abu George to put it near the holy place."

Nabeel points with his forehead to the kitchen alcove behind me.

"Where all the pictures are now draining holy oil," he says.

The small open kitchen, its counters, walls, shelves, sink, and refrigerator, have been taken over by the Holy Family. Framed pictures of Mary and Jesus, in various life stages, separate and together, with and without halos, layer every available space. Statues, small vessels, glass jars and icons add further layers, with printed verses, beads and olive wood souvenirs filling in the crevices. Under a small, framed portrait of the Virgin sits a saucer, with what appears to be olive oil. Small clumps, like clear discarded chewing gum, stick to the wall and some of the pictures.

The carpenter continues with his story, and Nabeel becomes more excited as he translates.

"And then the apparition says to Abu George, 'Do you want anything my son?' "

The carpenter shakes his head.

" 'I will go now,' " Saint Elias says. And then, he leaves.

"The next day . . . ,"

Abu George touches Nabeel on the arm to add a detail that flits across his mind's eye.

"When the old man left," the carpenter says, "he walked a couple of steps with his cane and then just disappeared."

Abu George looks at me directly for the first time during his story and shakes his head. He still doesn't know how it happened.

"In a very magical way," the carpenter says, and shrugs, "he just disappeared."

He tells me that the next day—that night he couldn't sleep—in the morning, he went to church to pray. He returned to his room, but he felt something mysterious was happening to him. He felt unsettled, unstable. He had a feeling that the old man, the saint, would come again at night. He kept praying and praying and praying.

That night he tried to sleep again but couldn't. He noticed that by two o'clock all the neighbors had turned off their lights and the quarter was dark. Except for a small lamp, he'd turned off the lights of his room. At three, he got up and turned on the main lamp in the center of the room so he could pray.

"While our friend is praying," Nabeel says, "Saint Elias returns and begins to talk to him. Very natural, like we are now in this room. Many things, he tells him. He will show him a miracle, he says. Through Jesus Christ he, Saint Elias, has also been given the same blessing to change water into wine. Just like Jesus at the wedding in Cana al-Jadid."

The saint then picked up the water glass he had left on the altar the previous night and took a sip. When he put it down, the water had turned to wine.

The old carpenter's face is as troubled as it is awed by this event. He is out of his depth. As am I.

"And while Abu George is praying," Nabeel continues, "Jesus also talks to him, as well as Elias, and many others."

The carpenter was uneasy with all this going on around him. Saint Elias was there as in real life. The others he recognized as visions.

"And our friend says to his guests, 'Please, what you are giving me? I don't deserve it. I am a simple man. And also, I think people would not believe me when I tell them what has happened. What should I do?'

"Saint Elias says, 'Don't worry. We are with you. Just tell them what happened. This is your cross to bear and we will be with you. Be patient.' "

Jesus then spoke to him. Nabeel speaks slowly as he repeats the words.

" 'People will curse you, will say bad things about you,' " Jesus says. " 'When I was on earth, I mean, in the body, I was also cursed many times. People would say bad things about me, throw bad things on me. You have to be patient, the way I was.' "

Saint Elias then gave Abu George a sign on his right cheek.

The carpenter is pointing to his cheek as he explains to Nabeel and me. In the shaded light of the room, I can make out a scar in the weathered shape of a cross, but without my glasses it could very well be the indentations of old age.

"It used to bleed a lot," Nabeel explains. "Saint Elias gave him this sign and the blood was coming out of his face as an indication of what happened that night that he turned the glass of water into wine."

"Fifteen hundred people have drunk from this wine," Abu George adds. "Fifteen hundred!"

As the glass emptied, and the wine was drunk, it filled up by itself.

"That is what happened," he says, "and then it dried up."

"Do you know why it stopped, Uncle?" I ask.

"Because the people's faith is very bad," Nabeel replies after conferring with Abu George, "it stopped giving wine for some time. And then it came again for some time, and then it stopped. Three times it came and then it stopped. But his friend, Abu Matu, filled up one liter of this wine and the old carpenter filled up two Coca-Cola bottles."

"*Thalatha*," Abu George says directly to me, in Arabic, and holds up three fingers for emphasis. "Three times."

"*Barakat Allah*," I reply. "The blessings of God upon you."

His lack of guile wins me. I've been around enough religious charlatans to make my blood curdle at 100 paces. It's my own fault—I'm attracted by charisma—okay, power, and many religious leaders (like political and cultural leaders) just ooze it. But oozing is a messy state of being, and mess without substance bothers me. My guard immediately goes up when I meet a self-proclaimed holy person, and I step backward.

Abu George and I are starting to warm to each other and, as if in confirmation of my thoughts, he stands up and motions for me to follow.

"He has some of this wine now," Nabeel says, his eyes stretched to capacity at this unexpected bonus, "and we can drink a little bit. He can give us a little sip. You will drink of this wine. This wine is equivalent to the wine Jesus made 2,000 years ago in Cana al-Jadid at the wedding. You will see, this is the gift of Jesus."

"Here. Just drink," Abu George instructs me. "Take all of it."

The wine is heavy and sweet, a hearty village vintage.

Several years ago a group of Syrian skeptics sought out Abu George's miracle wine.

"They were not very much believers," Abu George relates. "They don't have strong faith. They said, 'Okay, can you let this glass be filled up while we are here? Show us that. We don't believe, but we have to see.' "

Good rational citizens of modernized Syria that they were, they decided on a scientific experiment.

" 'Let's go outside, all of us—you, too, Abu George—outside the door, outside the room,' " they said.

Before they left, they searched the rooms—living room, bath and kitchen alcove—under the bed, in the closet, in the cupboards that would not hold a cat, even under the carpets for a trapdoor. All to make sure a coconspirator wasn't hiding. Finally, they synchronized watches. The experiment began.

After five minutes they sent one person inside, and he found the glass full. The glass was even flooding over, and the saucer in which it stood was full of wine.

"Just to prove their faith is not good," Abu George says. "They were surprised. Then they realized it was a miracle. Fifteen people left the room and this happened in five minutes."

I'm nodding, amused at this simple attempt at a scientific proof of a miracle.

"Yes," Abu George interrupts my quiet musing. "Some peoples want to see before they are believing. But sometimes seeing is confusing."

"Go on," I say.

"The first time he saw Jesus," Nabeel relates, and pats the daybed, "Abu George was sitting here, and Jesus and Jesus were sitting here."

He's indicating the space on the daybed directly right of the old carpenter, and again the velvet chair of honor. I'm a little confused. I've been following the simple Arabic as well as Nabeel's translation, but they're not making sense.

"Wait a minute," I say and hold up two fingers. "Two Jesuses. Two? *Ithnein?*"

Nabeel is pleased that I'm interested in this puzzle. He nods, wide-eyed.

The puzzle is larger than two Jesuses. I think of the old bishop on the train and his puzzle to me: Return to find the future. Is one real, and the other an imitation?

"Yeah. Two Jesuses, sat here," he says. "One here and one here. And they talked to him in person, not in a dream or vision, but visited like us in flesh and blood. They said, 'One of us is the real Jesus. Which of us, which one of us?'

" 'I don't know,' he said. 'Give me a sign or so.' "

"Like the wine?" I ask.

They both gave him the same sign, but he still wasn't able to discern the real Jesus.

"He says to himself, 'I know Jesus is only one.' " Nabeel says. Abu George is nodding. " 'I know Jesus is only one, why are you two?' And then suddenly the Virgin Mary appears here, and Jesus, the real Jesus, he makes a cross on himself in the presence of his mother."

The Virgin Mary then bent toward Abu George.

" 'The one who made the sign, the cross sign,' " she said, " 'is the real Jesus.' "

And the false Jesus disappeared.

"Which chair did the real Jesus sit in?" I ask, still interested in the guest chair.

But Abu George sits on the daybed and shakes his head. He's still trying to work out how it happened. Not that it happened. But how.

"And then they were gone, both Jesus and Mary, and he doesn't know how," Nabeel says. "He thought it could have been a dream, but then he turns on the light and realizes that he has a cross engraved on his forehead and one on his belly. And this, another one on his arm. Look. Look. And they were bleeding."

When Abu George closes his eyes and reposes his face, I see the form of a scar on his forehead, but it is nebulous. Nabeel grabs the old man's right forearm and pulls it toward me. A small, raised cross of about two inches faces down his arm.

"Yeah, but it is Jesus who drew it on him," Nabeel adds, almost wistfully. "Every Friday, it drains, it leaks, fresh blood."

I look at the fresh scab on the wound and Nabeel catches my raised eyebrows.

"When are you leaving?" he asks. I will be gone by Friday.

"Nabeel, I don't need proof to believe that he believes this," I say. "This miracle was for Abu George, not for me. It is enough that he believes it."

"Yeah," Nabeel says with uncharacteristic calm. "But it is Jesus who gave it to him, Doktora. A real cross from flesh."

The two men elaborate on the stigmata, Nabeel more calm but still more animated than the old man. They tell me that sometimes the cross on his head appears after prayer. Other times, he bleeds from the head while he is praying, because Jesus also gave him a thorn from his crown.

"So sometimes when he is praying," Nabeel says, drawing a circle around his own scalp, "blood comes out of his head."

They show me a white handkerchief and urge me to look closely at the dried blood on it.

"See, here is a picture of Virgin Mary," the old man points out. "And Jesus is here."

But my mind—or my heart—is unable to discern what they're showing me. I'm clearly not seeing what they are.

They take a piece of bloodied tissue from inside a box and point out the shape of Mary and Jesus that appeared in the blood mopped from his head while praying in a cave in Lebanon. During the war in Lebanon, he had taken refuge in Mount Mantara in the south. When he started praying, blood flowed from his forehead and he saw the image of Mary and Jesus. When he dried his head, the image was on the tissue.

Nabeel next places a simple yellowed handkerchief with blue borders on my lap.

"And this is a cross," Abu George says quietly as he leans over the young man. "And the crown of Jesus."

I look down at the imprint of the cross in blood, and crown of thorns, with the imprint of three large thorns twisted among a row of smaller barbs.

I touch the dried blood with my ring finger, then rub it gently against my thumb, asking myself, "Is this real?" followed immediately by, "Does it matter?"

The blood may be real, but there are deeper images within the blood that stir the believer.

"Many things happened to him but he does not tell anyone about them," Nabeel continues. "He has something else to show you."

Abu George has gotten up and beckons me once more to the kitchen alcove, where he has begun picking small, translucent globs from the wall. Amber colored lumps, like dried sap, punctuate the ceiling, the walls, and even the framed pictures of the Virgin Mary and Jesus.

"While he is praying, incense falls on his head," Nabeel says. "It comes from nowhere. He will show you some."

Abu George places a piece of golden sap in my palm. While running around the backwoods of Oman, I've come across the spindly trees that seep this liquid gold that empires have fought over and built fortunes on. What more beautiful aroma to lift a prayer to heaven, or cleanse a musty medieval church?

When dried, the sap has the feeling of stone and the look of gnarled quartz. While I study the physical attributes, Nabeel waxes ecstatic about its metaphysical power.

"This incense has blessing, energy, special energy," Nabeel says. "See, feel how big this energy is, mashallah."

He closes his eyes and inhales the universe.

Abu George interrupts his ecstasy to show us an especially large piece of incense. When this piece hit his forehead, he bled.

Nabeel is nonchalant. He's experienced many incense showers and seen Abu George bleed often. He points out the incense on the crucifix on the wall and tells me that when it comes, it is hot and sticky, and after it sticks, it cools.

"Like sometimes, you have some woman who has a problem with her son, or such and such," he informs me. "She talks to the carpenter and he prays. He asks Saint Elias to do something, and Saint Elias brings a piece of incense for her to carry with her."

Abu George presses another piece of incense into my palm and gives Nabeel specific instructions for me.

"Carry it with you wherever you go," he says, "to give you some kind of protection."

The carpenter then brings another piece and gives instructions again.

"This is for you," he says. "This is a piece of incense come from Saint Elias. During prayers, it fell on his head and he is giving it to you. A little gift, a little tiny gift. From Saint Elias. Of course, this has a lot of energy in it."

As I roll the rock of dried sap between my fingers, the warmth of my hand draws out its perfume. Pine. And lemon. And roses. I scratch it with my nail and sniff it, drawing a long breath down into my lungs, willing it to stay part of me for seven years.

"You can swallow it," Nabeel says.

I raise my eyes to his in question, then look at the glob that resembled chewed gum. I'm not convinced.

"Swallow?" I ask. This is turning into a regular Communion.

"It will give you a lot of blessing," he says. "You can swallow it and it will give you a lot of help."

I look into the eyes of the old man and understand this deep shadowy place inside him where light dances on water. Perhaps Assad Ali is correct. Perhaps writers are insane.

I place the golden sap on my tongue, bite into the pungent mass, and swallow.

The incense warms a track into my belly and I exhale perfume as I speak.

"Uncle," I ask, "do you know why these miracles happen?"

He looks sadly at his feet before he answers.

He doesn't know why, they just happen, he replies as we sit.

"It is a secret, maybe," Nabeel translates. Even he is now subdued. "Sometimes . . . He doesn't know. To prove to the people that faith is good for them, perhaps. That they are away from spirituality and religion, so when they realize what happened to him, maybe they have more faith."

The two men look at each other.

"But he was chosen," Nabeel says. "Once in a while, someone is chosen, and he was chosen. Why? This is just the way it happened. It was not his choice."

He wasn't a spiritual man, before this, they tell me, and didn't go seeking a miracle. He didn't wish for water turning into wine, or incense, or visitations. He didn't have an interest in the spiritual, he was just a carpenter with a small business. He never even went to church regularly before. He never prayed before all this started.

"About eight years ago, not long," the carpenter says directly to me in Arabic, "that all these things happen."

Nabeel echoes him. Jesus first appeared to him in person five years ago.

"For five years," Abu George says, "since Jesus appeared to me, I wake up at three o'clock in the morning to pray."

I'm curious about the timing, about Saint Elias appearing to him in prayer when Abu George wasn't yet in the habit of praying. But the men continue and I have no time to question this lapse.

Since then, they tell me, blood has been coming out of his hands. Also, from the marks on his belly, his forehead, his arms. Many have witnessed the stigmata, even the head nun of the revered Convent of the Lady of Saidnayya in the mountains outside Damascus has seen it. And she has proclaimed it a miracle.

While we've been talking in the alcove, a woman in her thirties has arrived with a young girl. She sits cross-legged in her housedress on her father's daybed, after first smoothing out wrinkles in the floral cover, and then begins to shell peas into a bowl that rests between her knees. She passes me a pod to chew on. She brings an air of domesticity with her. This is the daughter behind the scene.

She introduces me to Myriam, a beautiful child who kisses me on the cheek in welcome. She has a perfect V-shaped face, with thick eyebrows, bright almond-shaped eyes, a straight nose and a smile that rivals a Cheshire cat's. Her skin is as pale and luminescent as porcelain. She wears the universal gear of kids her age: jeans, a snowy white T-shirt, with an embroidered vest. She's poised and graceful and when next to her grandfather the tip of her head reaches the slope of his shoulder. Her features echo in his.

She smiles up at him with adoration. He smoothes her dark hair and smiles back.

"My granddaughter," Abu George says, with pride.

"Myriam," I ask the young girl, "do you understand your grandfather's gift?"

Nabeel translates to her.

She nods and tries to reply in English.

"Yes, I know," she says, then turns to Nabeel to translate a difficult word.

Faith.

"It is faith," Myriam repeats the new word.

She takes her grandfather's hand, and shrugs.

"Because he has strong faith, things happen like this."

keeper of the word

W hat does peace look like to you?" I ask the holy man in front of me.

Pope Zakka sits in a gold-encrusted chair in a fading cathedral in the Old Quarter of Damascus. Next to mine his chair could be mistaken for a throne, but I hesitate to use the word as it conjures up visions of grandeur and opulence. And the trappings of power.

The power of this holy man is not contained in a chair. Nor in his extensive title: His Holiness Moran Mor Ignatius Zakka I Iwas. The power of Pope Zakka rests in words.

We're drinking sweet tea from small glasses and eating cookies from the Armenian bakery, and have come to a quiet moment in our discussion of the state of the human soul, a subject slow to elicit quaint anecdotes. Heavy drapes occlude the morning sun from gigantic windows. The air is weighted with centuries of residual incense and prayers. A priestly secretary, an occasional monk, skirt our peripheral vision as they carry ledgers, books, and trays of tea through the grand hall, and quietly open and close the heavy doors, letting in fresh air and light, respecting our hour of private conversation.

I'm feeling a little rocky after a late night of carousing with Rheema and her friends, so the slow pace, the hot tea, and heavy drapes are just what the doc ordered.

With all the talk of The Word, I have sought out the one man who should be able to help. Pope Zakka is the Patriarch of Antioch and All the East and the Supreme Head of the Universal Syriac Orthodox Church, the planet's second oldest church, founded by the Apostles. As intriguing as the longevity of the institution is its charge to keep alive Aramaic, the language in which Christ spoke. That is, the words in which The Word spoke.

Assad Ali has made clear words have consequence, but few take words as seriously as the man before me. Whereas the Sufi bends words into sinuous poetry, the Patriarch guards the dictionary. We all know one phrase in Aramaic: Abracadabra. Childish magical gibberish to the rest of us, loosely translated from Aramaic it has a vastly more serious meaning: Create what I speak or May my words be brought to life. These are not men who dangle their participles.

His Holiness wears the garb of his ancient office, a heavy, long, red brocade robe. He must be suffocating in this airless room. A red padded cap. Three gold chains and precious medallions hang from his neck and rest on his generous torso. A carved and gilded staff. These symbols are all in order. His wild snowy beard and scuffed shoes, however, indicate a life too busy for city niceties, or perhaps the short notice of my visit.

I am overcome by an urge to put aside my formal questions and tell this old man in the red robe and white beard what I'd like for Christmas. Which, in a way, I'm doing. This is how I've come to ask him about peace.

Ceremonially poised until this question, he now slumps. He sighs deeply and grinds his forehead with the foot of his palm.

"Ayyy. Peace, you ask?" he says, slowly. "Peace is a tired, old man."

His Holiness knows all about being tired.

The church has come within a breath of extinction at least

twice in its long history, and its survival is a miracle. In the sixth century, following doctrinal splits in Christology, the church was down to three tattered bishops hiding underground from persecution. Empress Theodora, daughter of a Syriac Christian priest and wife of the Byzantine Justinian, intervened, giving the green light for Jacob (after whom the church is often mistakenly named) to establish missions and bishops throughout the East, into Arabia and Ethiopia.

In the early twenty-first century, the church and the language so intimately linked to it again struggle to survive. This time it has found an oddly modern ally. The Internet.

But back to the tired old man called Peace.

"Let me say," the Patriarch continues after a long sigh, "in my opinion, first there must be peace with God. Through Our Lord Jesus Christ, we made peace between God and human beings."

Peace is a given. It is we humans who don't accept the gift.

Since Assad Ali's word game, the subject of peace has become personal. So my ears prick up when the Patriarch begins to talk about the internal struggle.

"Peace *within* ourselves," he says, "within myself, means that I am fighting myself. But how can I have peace within myself? To be honest. To be sincere to the teachings of Our Lord Jesus Christ. We should also have peace with one another as human beings, because if I don't love my brother who I see, how can I love God who I don't see?"

Well, I've managed to solve that problem fairly well. I just don't see my brothers. Or sisters. The thought is meant to be a flip aside, my self-defense against homilophobia, but it settles on me with deep sadness. The Middle East does that to me. I miss "family." Seems illogical, but I divorced my first husband after being in Egypt around affectionate and loving families, and seeing fathers hold their children with open tenderness and love. I realized that I had never seen my husband or his own family show tenderness to a child—or to each other. Assad Ali's remark about my not having family still tweaks.

"Perhaps we prefer to struggle with others than with our-selves," I suggest.

"Perhaps," he replies. "It is difficult. True."

"What is the state of our planet's struggle at the moment, then," I ask him, "on a human level?"

"The world is changing and changing fast," the Patriarch says. "And I'll say that now there is less faith than there was before, less faithful than there were before. Of course we, as Christians, should be trying with our faith and our deeds to make the world want to follow the road of Our Lord Jesus Christ. That is the happiness of the world, really."

Philosophical friends and every Australian pub rat will tell me that happiness of the world is best discussed over a few brews. The morning after a night on the town is definitely not. Any constructive thoughts I have on world happiness are muffled by lack of sleep and a keen aversion to sound.

"So," I say, falling into the cadence of the Patriarch's patois. Pope Zakka, born in Mosul, Iraq, studied at NYU and was a Fellow at the Lutheran School of Theology in Chicago. "So peace and the survival of The Word? The two go together."

"That's right, that's right," the Patriarch replies. "You under-stand."

I'm not sure I do, but I'm damn glad he thinks so.

We converse without the buffer of an interpreter, which frees us to tumble about in English, French and Arabic, with smatter-ings of Greek, Latin, German, Farsi and whatever else we run into, to describe the importance of a language on the brink of disap-pearing. We are our own Tower of Babel.

Given the abracadabra syndrome, I'm trying to be particularly careful with what I say.

"The most important thing is that Aramaic was spoken by Our Lord Jesus Christ," the Patriarch says. "That's why we love it. It has been the liturgical language of our church from the begin-ning of Christianity and, of course, it was the ancient language of Syria before Islam. That's also why we love it. And we feel it is our duty and responsibility to keep it alive because we can't imagine that, one day, the language spoken by our Lord Jesus Christ will be forgotten. It's something we can't imagine."

President Assad, himself an Alawite, a member of a small, heterodox (some say a heretical) sect of Islam, has been supportive of religious diversity in Syria. It's in his best interest, especially when, in the case of the Syriac Orthodox Church, the minority has profoundly strong Mesopotamian and Syrian roots. The state's dubious imprimatur and the church's cultural links to an ancient pre-Christian heritage has helped its survival, but its presence in the predominantly Sunni streets of Damascus is sotto voce.

"Thank God," Pope Zakka says, "we here in Syria are free to teach our language to our children, and to come to the church, not only to learn religion, but to study the language of their forefathers. We have hundred thousands of us whose mother tongue is Syriac-Aramaic."

The ancient language of Aramaic officially died out around the seventh century but continued in the colloquial form, Syriac. Today's native speakers live in southeast Turkey and in the north of Syria among the Arab tribes of the region as well as in Damascus and Aleppo. Others have migrated to America, Australia, and also to the Netherlands, each of which has a bishopric.

As migrants assimilate and adopt new languages, as the See encourages them, Aramaic risks becoming a liturgical, not a living, language as did Latin in the Catholic Church. The difference is that (although Rome may disagree) Christ did not speak Latin.

The Patriarch recognizes this problem. He encourages the migrants to retain their mother tongue, but the reality is that Syriac-Aramaic is taught as a classical language "which we pray in, and in which our fathers have written their books."

Small enclaves of the living language remain in Syria. In Saidnayya and Tekla, the ancient convents built into the mountains outside Damascus, you can still hear the surly nuns chant the Lord's Prayer in haunting Aramaic. In the streets of those enclaves you catch snatches of Syriac from the children who shoot baskets off the walls or from the geriatric shopkeepers who sell cola and cassettes, but these are small, precious pockets.

Monks and holy scholars have kept the flame alive for almost two thousand years, but can they survive the tornado of Western culture? Syria has been isolated from much of the recent technology and communications boom and it is yet to be seen what will happen to these protected enclaves when exposed to global culture and technology. I ask the Patriarch whether he fears this will be the final demise of the Word of God.

The Patriarch may look like Santa Claus, but he is no Luddite. The Internet, with its disrespect for man-made borders, is his ally.

"Technology has always been with the human being," he states. "Those who believe the world was created by God, they will always be loving God through Our Lord Jesus Christ."

With the help of technology—and the savvy leadership of the Patriarch—Aramaic is undergoing revival among members of the Syriac Orthodox Church connected across the globe, and scholars attracted to its cerebral mission.

"We have many scholars here and there," the Patriarch says with enthusiasm, "and they learn the language and they teach it and, of course, we are proud of those people, too. And grateful, too. Yes."

Although he admits he doesn't fully understand the new technology, Pope Zakka has just visited Los Angeles to bless it. The Syriac Orthodox Church of Antioch, formed in the time of the Apostles, has its own website, with libraries, chat rooms, youth groups, and CDs of liturgical music for sale through Amazon.com. Pope Zakka has his own webpage where you can access copies of his encyclicals and writings. The Syriac-Aramaic language project has a worldwide center that the peripatetic Apostle Peter, first bishop of the church, would definitely approve of.

For the Patriarch also, globalization and technology are positive developments.

When I ask him about the commercialization of the globe and the loss of individual identity, he shrugs it off. I'd forgotten that Syrians are hardwired as world traders—just check out the chambers of commerce from Buenos Aires to Brisbane. The first information highway was the famed Silk Route, which moved goods and ideas from one side of the known world to the other and terminated in Syria.

The Patriarch immediately identifies the positive and sellable side of Damascus.

"We may not have McDonald's here," he says, "but we have much to offer. The spirit. Nature. This city is a blessing of God. We call it the City of Saint Paul, of course, because when he came to Damascus, he had the experience of the faith."

Apostle Paul is instrumental in explaining the openness of the Syriac Orthodox Church (as well as others here) toward technology and new ideas. The church was grafted from Jerusalem onto Antioch, the former capital of Eastern Rome (now Antakya in southeastern Turkey), by Aramean and Gentile converts among the local Greek population. A simple and central act of the Antiochians inspired Paul in his writings on inclusiveness: Converted Gentiles and Jews broke a pre-Christian taboo by eating together at the same table. The locals coined a new term for these peculiar church members—"Christian"—and thereby introduced a new word into the planet's lexicon.

Inclusiveness and multiculturalism are historical characteristics of the Syriac Orthodox Church. An early branch of the church was established in Kerala, India, by Apostle Thomas and the Apostles left their imprint on Edessa, ancient capital of Mesopotamia. Conversely, Indian and ancient Mesopotamian influences abound in the liturgy and symbolism of the modern Church.

More important to the survival of the Church has been its early relationship with Islam, going back to the Prophet Muhammad. The revival of the Syriac Church in the sixth and seventh centuries into Abyssinia (Ethiopia) and Arabia dovetailed with the arrival of Islam. When Muhammad traveled as a young child with his uncle, a merchant, and later as a merchant himself, to Syria's dynamic international markets, it's quite possible that with his early religious bent, Muhammad met and listened to the famed Syriac Orthodox mystics and monks in Syria. In a nice turn of events, the Christian ruler of Abyssinia protected the early followers of Muhammad who had been forced to flee Arabia and, according to the Patriarch himself, the tribes of Medina who invited Muhammad to oversee their disputes were Syriac Orthodox.

This info I can't confirm, but something I can is that favors are not forgotten in the Middle East. And this is a pretty loaded deck of favors. In return the Prophet Muhammad established an early treaty of protection with the Christian and Jewish tribes as People of the Book, and also reciprocated the earlier kindness of the Christian holy men with a special treaty of protection given to all monasteries, hermits and priests. To this day copies of the treaty still hang on the walls of several monasteries in the Middle East that existed at the founding of Islam.

I've read about, studied and translated some of these agreements and texts, but never spoken to anyone to whom they had meaning. To the Patriarch, this history is alive and part of his daily life, not some minutiae stored in some dusty museum or archive. In the streets of Damascus this historical continuation is a reality. Former traveling companions to Damascus have commented on the special feel of the city, on the inexplicable sense of "blessing," its mystical underbelly, even people who would not describe themselves as religious or remotely interested in religion.

Inclusiveness has contributed to the quiet survival of the Church and the preservation of the language. The Patriarch greets the advent of Westernized culture with the same careful openness.

"We have Coca-Cola here, already," he continues on his discussion of globalization. He shrugs. "It is the same all over the world. If they don't have Coca-Cola, for example, they have something similar to that. People always try to get the best."

Then adds, quietly: "I think we don't have our lives in the bread. We have it in the spirit. That's something very important."

The Patriarch's concerns about the future are larger than fast food and Western movies, or even about the continued existence of the Syriac Orthodox Church in Syria. His concern is for the continuation of the Church on this planet.

"We have a very big question mark if we are going to exist within a few years or not, as churches," he says, taking a more serious turn. "Not just my church, but other churches here ask this question. Yes. And the West, it will be more dangerous than here because it does not have religion. At least Islam as a people, for example, believes in God. Or Jews, as a religion, believe in God. But there in the West, we feel that the believers of God are very few. Very few. We believe that Satan is the enemy of God. And that is very dangerous to the churches, to us as individuals, as believers in Our Lord Jesus Christ."

The Patriarch believes that in the West, Satan has convinced people he does not exist and the West's state of denial worries him. He explains that in the West (and South America) Satan worshipers are trying to attract people against Christ and his followers. Here, Muslim and Christian leaders, men and women in the street, will all tell you that Satan worshipers are not necessarily members of a dramatic, blood-drinking cult. Satan worshipers are simply people who have cut their relationship with God. They have no belief.

"If we cut this relationship," he says, "that means we are his enemies, we are far away from him."

I don't need to stick my hands into the campfire to be convinced about humanity's capacity for evil on a global or personal level. This is a bogey-mine area for me, one I'd rather not tread unless prepared to go the distance, which I'm not. I may become emotional. After the roller coaster of the last few days, that's a good bet, so I steer the conversation back to more comfortable ground.

"How do you see the family in all these changes, I wonder?" I ask him. "Families in the West are concerned that children no longer show respect for their fathers, mothers, or for the values of the family. And they blame a lot of it on technology."

"Here, in the Orient," he replies, "we still respect the family. Because the churches try to help the families, and we give them the light of our religious advice and lead them to Christ.

"We are sorry," he says, "that some of the parents in the West feel that they should let their children be free, to have their freedom. They don't even baptize them, they don't bring them to Sunday schools. Yes, they have sports and games, and they are free. But we can't know if we are leading them to be enemies of Our Lord Jesus Christ, not to be friends. And that's why we see every day, a new event outside the law and Our Lord Jesus Christ.

"I don't want to judge . . . I don't want to judge others, really. But we feel sorry if you don't give your children faith and love of God. If you don't give them the real spiritual food, they will get it from others. But it will hurt them, because it will not be the real food. It is something we believe here in the Orient."

"What do you tell young children about the future?" I ask him.

"This message is for all human beings," Pope Zakka replies, "but especially for we the believers in Our Lord Jesus Christ. That we should be close to Our Lord Jesus Christ otherwise we will never be happy. You know, we face many difficulties in our world and if we don't have a helper like Our Lord Jesus Christ, who promised to be with us, who we know is strong and can be with us, we can never be happy. At all."

"And for children of the planet who are not of the Christian tradition?" I ask.

The Patriarch returns to his earlier discussion on peace.

"To be honest, sincere, that is something always I say, to all children," the Patriarch replies. "To feel we are human beings and part of others as others are part of us. To forget and forgive the past. They should believe in their present and be good to others. And I wish for their search for God, and they have the faith, especially in Our Lord Jesus Christ."

The Patriarch describes the communal relationship between family and Church, and the special role of the priest between family and spiritual leaders. According to Syriac Orthodox tradition as Coptic and Greek Orthodox, parish priests should be married. Monks and nuns are not married. Bishops are selected from monks, and the patriarch from the bishops.

"The priests don't take care of the children only, but of all the members of the family," he says. "When he visits the family—and we do visit the families—we call the priest, Father. He is considered to be father of all the families, that's why he should take care of all of them spiritually, the parents, the children, the aged and so on."

"With such a strong and loving emphasis on the family and marriage," I ask, "do you find men and women willing to live in isolation and celibacy as nuns and monks?"

"Yes, but we are not surprised. Why not?" he says. "Thousands and millions of people are not married but that does not make them unusual."

The conversation with Bishop Musa, the Coptic Bishop of Youth in Cairo, comes to mind as we speak. He had pointed out that in Arabic there is no word for "Alone." Aloneness (unless with the One) is not something you wish for, because it means you are outside of society. In the United States, living alone, however, independence and individualism are signs of strength.

"What is different," he continues, "is that those monks and nuns live as families, as communities, and they support one another. The nuns in the nunnery, in the convent, they feel that this is their home, and they help one another, they love one another. And the monks in their monastery, do the same.

"They also serve the community—they not only worship God—they serve the community, but indirectly. First, in the seminary, for example, they teach those people who are going to be clergymen. And the nuns in my church, they have their own courses for the young people—yes, it is all right—for the young people, men and young ladies, of course, to teach them

Christianity. And they are a good example for young people, too. How to sacrifice, how to love God, how to love the people, and to be honest, and of course, sincere to your country, and how to cooperate with other churches."

"Other churches?" I ask. "What about other religions?"

"Other religions, too," he replies. "Not only our religions and other churches, but also with Muslims, for example. We try to be good witnesses of our Lord Jesus Christ among them."

As I listen to this wise man, I begin to wonder if perhaps in considering the effects of globalization we have been one-sided in our thinking. The East, and here I refer to the Middle East wherein lies my checkered experience, abounds with values that we appreciate and perceive as disappearing in our own culture. Family life. Respect. Community. A graceful pace of life. And an appreciation of the inner world. These are values that are embodied in the families that migrate to America. Sure, some in extreme.

I wonder if the Patriarch sees the loss of his local community as a strengthening of the global pool and the eventual revitalization of the Church.

He smiles.

"We encourage the faithful of our Church, wherever they are," he replies, "to be examples of good citizens, to love their new country, their new home. If you are Lebanese, and you go to the United States of America or Australia, or another, you should know that is your country, your own home. But in the meantime we feel that those who are good citizens for their new country are sent by God to those places and they should be honest, and sincere, and good examples. And we encourage them, too, to be involved in politics, to try to work hard for the progress of their new country, not the old one, but the new one, and in the meantime to be sincere and not to cut their relationship with their Church."

"So you think its possible to be a good Christian and a good politician at the same time?" I ask him. I'm thinking of the recent scandals in American government but I'm grinning as I ask.

The Patriarch begins to laugh. I'm sure he's got a few wicked jokes up those ancient sleeves.

"That's right," he replies. "If you are not a good Christian, you will not be a good politician, at all."

"Some people don't think that," I reply. "They think you can only be a good politician if you work in ways that are against religion, or against good ethics, or good morals."

The Patriarch becomes serious.

"They are mistaken because if you are not good as a human being, you will never be good for your fellow citizens at all. That's what I believe."

When I ask if he has advice for other leaders, he pauses to reflect. The pace of the day is quickening as the sun races to its peak. In a couple of days it will be the summer solstice. Telephones ring in the back room.

"I think of our job as Christian servants of people, people of God, people of all the religions," the Patriarch says. "I feel that our task is to help the world to raise the new generations, in faith and in the practice of virtues, because these generations, or some of these generations, will help us to serve the earth and bring it into a better situation.

"If we are successful in our task, the future of the technology, of course, will be for the benefit of the world, not for destroying it.

"Our Lord Jesus Christ, God Incarnate, he knows what we need," he continues. "He will be with us always if we come together in his name. Of course, if we try to complete the mission which was given to us of serving the people of God—*all* people are people of God, when I say this—I think we can help to bring those people in believing of God, to having peace with God, peace within themselves and with their fellow human beings."

"Do you believe there is more than one path to God?" I ask.

"Yes, there are many paths to God," he replies. "Many. But we Christians, we have Our Lord Jesus Christ, the Path, the Way, the Light and the Life."

The Church has a reputation of inclusiveness, so I decide to throw in an open-ended question.

"And outside our planet?" I ask. "What if we succeed in discovering other forms of life in the universe?"

What I'm wondering is whether we will wish our half-brothers and sisters peace, or whether we will wrangle with history and borders. How will we see ourselves when the mirror of life takes on another dimension, the dimension of the truly alien?

"Well, I think Man was created in the image of God," the Patriarch replies thoughtfully. "God has given him this power to explore the heavens and the universe. And we are pleased when we hear about the blessings of technology, with space. This is something not against religion at all."

He leans forward and continues quietly.

"And I will not be surprised, if I am alive, and they discover that there is life on one of these planets. God, he knows what he has created. It is his job, not ours."

I also lean forward. I'm sitting on the front porch of the universe with a man who keeps one of our oldest holy traditions alive.

As a planet, we don't deal well with strangers and other aliens; his own Church almost reached extinction, and his perspective on how we can treat others is therefore unique. I don't want to leave without it.

"But, really, Your Holiness," I ask as I brush the crumbs from my skirt. I'm trying not to sound like Barbara Walters. "Let's say we discover brothers and sisters in space. What would you *really* do?"

The Patriarch rocks back with delight and chuckles.

"Why," he says, and slaps the knee under his long red robe, "why, I'd teach them Aramaic, of course!"

We both start laughing, and he begins to walk me to the door. Our hour has spilled over.

I pause halfway to the door.

"People here have been telling me about miracles," I say. "Water into wine. Stigmata. You know."

I watch closely for a reaction. If I mention these to some of the local clergy back in Washington, they'll at least look at me strangely. Or call for an exorcism, if they believe in them.

"Why not?" he replies. "Not only in Damascus, all over the world, miracles are happening. And we as believers in Our Lord Jesus Christ who made many miracles, of course, or gave power through his apostles to do so, we should believe in miracles. I do believe in them, of course, but I can't say that this is a miracle or that, because I haven't seen it. But I believe, especially those people who have good behavior, and they do that in the name of Our Lord Jesus Christ even though I don't see it. When they tell me it happens, I say Why not? Why not? That's all. But it is not only in Damascus. All over the world."

"Do you think these miracles are related to the sense of insecurity with the future?" I ask. "Expectations of the Messiah? Millennium fever?"

What millennium fever? his look clearly says. We walk with Christ and with history every day.

"Perhaps, the media, nowadays, helps to increase the knowledge of such things," the holy man acknowledges. "But it has been always through the generations like that. Why not?"

Why not? Those words again. My hands are becoming full of the why nots I will carry with me when I leave.

CHAPTER 17

sister salma channels jesus

Sister Salma offers us a cold drink, homemade, the essence of flower petals, slightly perfumed. Nabeel first wipes the dripping condensation from the glass with a handkerchief before taking a sip. I hold the syrupy red liquid to the light and watch the swirls intermingle.

"The color of Jesus' blood," she says.

Sister Salma is a broad, hearty woman. Her thick, gray hair is lopped short and two white wings pull it forward from a prominent widow's peak. Her face beams with contentment.

She sits back on the daybed, hands folded comfortably on her lap, short thick ankles protruding under her tidy, dark floral dress.

She doesn't look like a woman who channels Jesus.

I could just as well have gone to Casadega, Florida, if I'd wanted a palm reading, but Nabeel insists I meet this special lady, and I'm not receiving any pressing inner signal not to.

Nabeel again is translating. Unlike yesterday, where he was familiar with Abu George's story and wove himself into it, he listens carefully to Sister Salma like a young nephew. The story is hers alone, free of his enthusiastic interjections and editing.

"In dreams I saw Jesus," she says. If she's picking up any of my skeptical vibes, she's not holding it against me. "Many years ago now, but only in dreams. I saw the Virgin Mary, too, yes. The first vision was seeing Jesus and his disciples distributing bread in the Mountain. This is the story of when there are 5,000 people and he blessed the bread. This is the first vision."

"A dream or a vision?" I interrupt Nabeel. "I mean, was she sleeping, or meditating . . .?"

He confers.

"She is just praying when she has this vision," he says, and then continues as the voice of Salma.

"Slowly, slowly, Jesus started talking to me in real person," Salma says, "and he talked to me about examples, about life and spiritual things. You see, I cannot read. I cannot read the Bible to know how to be a good Christian. So Jesus comes to me directly and gives me personal instruction."

By her own admission, Salma was not a good woman before this. Jesus gave her lessons about spirituality, about patience, about how to love her enemies. And her husband, too.

"All these lessons in the Bible, he showed me himself," Salma says, "so that I could see him and listen as well."

She couldn't see him at first, she just heard his voice like on the radio. Then came the full visuals. Spiritual television. And finally, the real presence.

She smiles broadly as she relates her visits by Christ. She's not speaking of a high mystical experience, but almost as if say, Elvis got out of his Cadillac and sat on the front porch with her talking about the best way to cook catfish. She's just thrilled that the local boy who's made good has taken some time with her. He's a good boy. His mother should be proud of him.

This everydayness continues and not much later the Virgin Mary begins to visit her as well.

Salma tells me that Mary first entered her domestic life when her younger daughter was sick with a fever, a time when women turn to other women for help.

"I prayed," she says, "Christian prayers of our Heavenly Father and, peace be upon her, the Virgin Mary. I fell asleep and in my dreams I saw the Virgin Mary come with Jesus. And she came and she touched my daughter."

After the dream, Salma woke up and went to check on her daughter, and found she no longer had a fever.

As Salma talks, a young woman enters the room. She's about nineteen, and wearing a blue cotton housedress, a caftan, with simple embroidery around the neck. Her long hair is freshly washed and pinned back, her face scrubbed. She's beautiful in a soft, wholesome way.

She greets Nabeel and me, climbs quietly onto the daybed beside her mother, and kisses her cheek without interrupting the story. She pulls her feet up under her caftan, opens a small box on her knee, takes out a pumice, and begins buffing her nails as if we are family and I'd just popped in for tea and gossip.

I also pull my bare feet up beside me, sip the icy red concoction, and relax into the cushions. I'm sleepy, a little drugged by the serenity, and could easily doze off without Salma being offended.

"I once had this beautiful experience," Sister Salma says in a soft lullaby. "I had to go to a Christian group meeting in Tobali and I asked the Virgin Mary to help me because I had some work in the kitchen that hadn't been done. My daughter here, Hunayna—she was a girl then—was at school."

She pats Hunayna's knee.

The angle of the young woman's head, her hair, prompts a ghost of a memory that passes before I can capture it.

Hunayna looks up from buffing her nails. She catches on me for a second with direct curiosity, then smiles, struck by revelation, and returns to her nails, applying a brilliant pink layer of polish.

Salma begins to relate a confusing story. I'm following along, but the pronouns are tripping me up. Nabeel stops her and has her retell it several times. The pronouns are also tripping him up. Salma repeats it until he gets it right.

"Aaahhh!" he finally says to her. His face lights up.

"Wow!" he says to me. "This is fantastic! Listen."

He tries to help out the translation by putting invisible quotes around some pronouns.

"When my daughter came from school about one o'clock, she saw 'me' in the kitchen doing all this cleaning."

" 'Her,' Salma, you mean?" I ask, trying to clarify the quotes. "She saw Salma, her mother?"

"No, she saw 'her,' the woman she thinks is her mother."

"Go on."

The story becomes more entangled as Salma changes pronouns at will.

"She sees 'her' cleaning and cooking and she says, 'Hey'— because she thinks it is 'me' in there. 'Hey, Mum, what are you cooking?' my daughter says. The woman in the kitchen says, 'Beans.' And my daughter says, 'I don't like that.' And the woman she thinks is me replies, 'Don't say that. It is a blessing from God, Why don't you take the clothes and spread them on the balcony to dry?' "

The young woman nods in agreement. She wears a peculiar grin, as if a trick is being played. And I'm beginning to hope it's not on me. I look at the sweet red drink and wonder what they've put in it. Nothing makes sense. As I understand so far, Hunayna came home from school and began talking to a woman in the kitchen who she thought was her mother.

"About two o'clock," Salma continues, "I am coming in from outside, dressed very well, very sharply."

Salma gestures toward her clothes, and pats her face to show me she was all made up.

"You?" I ask. "Not 'her?' "

"Yes, me."

"Okay."

"And my daughter here says, 'How come you are coming in here through the front door? You were just inside, I was just talking to you in the kitchen.' "

"That's right," agrees Hunayna. "I thought it was my mother in the kitchen."

Salma continues.

"And I say, 'Oh well, this may well be our Mother Mary. I prayed that she would come and help so that when you come home the food is ready. And everything is ready.'"

For Salma, the Virgin Mary's cooking beans is a normal occurrence. I'm saving my judgment.

The young woman blows on her long pink nails as she studies me closely. Her fixed gaze gives me sympathy for a mouse waiting for the cat's paw to descend.

If it weren't for her mother's presence I'd ask her what she really saw. It must have seen someone else in the kitchen—an aunt, perhaps, a neighbor—but she doesn't want to publicly challenge her mother's story.

There is no need to wait. She has caught my intention and we begin our own conversation as Nabeel and Salma relive the story.

"You do not believe in the coincidence?" Hunayna asks me in English. There is a slight challenge and bemusement in her tone.

"I don't think so," I reply.

"Hmmm," she replies. We sit in silence. She looks inside me and my face burns as if caught in a lie.

"I saw her in the kitchen," she says finally and tilts her hands wide as if to say, Believe me.

Sister Salma continues, ignoring our side conversation.

"And then my daughter, she talks to my husband. She tells him, my daughter, to her father, 'Father, that's what happened,' she says. 'The Virgin Mary came today and she was in the kitchen and she worked for Mum.'"

Hunayna adds to our side conversation.

"That happens so many times with me," she says quietly. "So many times I call her and I hear the sound of dishes in the kitchen, cleaning, or doing something like that. And then I see my mother passing by, and when I go after her, I don't see anyone. So then I have this feeling that it is the Virgin Mary doing these things."

"See how simple she is, the Virgin Mary," Salma is saying, her face all lit up with pleasure. "How nice she comes in a very modest way to help, and a very real way."

Nabeel is in awe. He pats his shirt pocket as if searching for a cigarette.

"The Virgin Mary?" he says. "She cleans your dishes?"

"She cleans dishes," Salma says, "and a lot of people don't believe that."

"Mashallah," Nabeel replies. "Mashallah."

In return the Virgin Mary asks only that Sister Salma light incense for her in the morning and at night. One day Salma was washing dishes and she didn't light the incense, so the Virgin Mary came into the kitchen.

"She is annoyed," Salma says. "She shakes her hand at me and says, 'Leave the dishes, I will do the dishes, but go and light the incense for me.'"

And Salma went and lit the incense.

I'm being charmed by this delightful storyteller. The appearance of Mary is so real to her, it's almost real to me. I can almost see the Virgin Mary here in this room, throwing a snit at Salma for not doing the one simple thing she has asked.

"One night," Sister Salma continues, fueled by her captive audience, "I go to sleep without lighting the incense, so the Virgin Mary was unhappy with me. I know because I see her in my dream. She said, 'I am packing up and leaving your house, Salma! Enough! I am not staying in your house anymore because you forgot about me.'"

Salma gives a look of simultaneous horror and contrition as when she realized she had taken this divinity for granted.

"So, I say, 'Okay, don't worry,'" Sister Salma says to the Virgin Mary, "'Please, please don't leave. All the incense I have is for you.'"

Salma then tells me about when Jesus took her to the royal kingdom, where she saw happiness and pleasure indescribable on earth.

"Was it beautiful?" I ask. I'm prompted by my own experience I related to Assad Ali.

"Very beautiful," she says, elated by the memory and begins to frame the experience in her own terms. "You feel happy when your son passes an exam. You feel happy when your son or daughter gets married. You feel happy, but then the happiness is finished. But there, in the sky, there is no ending to happiness."

"Salma," I ask, "how does this happen? I mean, the . . . miracles. These visits."

She looks at me, and then explains simply.

"When we believe, we are like a bird flying in the sky," she says. "When I think of earth, I fall down quickly. So I always need to be like a bird flying, always thinking of the highest and the highest and the highest."

Hunayna watches me closely while her mother talks, and even seems to be trying to get my attention, to tell me something. I try not to look at her, but my mind is unsettled.

She stands and kisses her mother.

"You do not know who I am," she addresses me. "Do you?"

I'm feeling awkward.

"No," I reply. I shake my head.

"You do not recognize me?" she asks, this time raising an eyebrow. She turns in a circle holding the hem of her caftan. "You sure?"

I stand because I am uncomfortable with her towering over me in the close space.

I look at the dark eyes, the lush dark hair with the blonded ends. The beautiful skin. I have met so few young women in Damascus and she resembles none and all at the same time.

"I am sure," I reply.

She makes a *tak-tak-tak* movement with her neon pink fingernails as if operating a small machine.

"I am Hanna," she says.

"Hanna?" I ask.

"From the hotel," she says. "You are surprised, no?"

"Hanna? Hunayna?"

I look at Salma, who had called her Hunayna, and then back to her daughter. Without makeup, the painted eyebrows and carefully styled hair, I barely discern her features.

She pulls her hair up on top of her head as I inspect her, turns her face sideways, and flutters her lashes comically.

"I am different, yes?" she says and laughs. She's pleased with her deception.

Understatement. The smile and the gestures are pure Hanna.

"Hanna is easier for foreigners," Hunayna says.

She begins to hug me, but I can hardly return the affection.

What the hell is she doing here? I ask myself. I've felt her watching me closely, too closely, since I arrived at the hotel. And I am now shamefully suspicious. Another thought racks me. How could I not recognize her? Have I become so used to flash identifying individuals by their external appearances like a series of hieroglyphs that I don't recognize the person beneath?

"Yes," she is saying, replying to a question I didn't voice, "this is my mother. I knew when we meet in the hotel that God will bring you here to my mother."

"How did you know?" I ask.

"It is God," she says and shrugs.

Hunayna leaves to transform herself with the help of Revlon and Spandex into another neon fashion statement before heading to work.

Sister Salma continues with stories from daily life, but I'm hardly aware of what she's saying. There have been so many strange occurrences, coincidences, both in Egypt and Syria, that they couldn't have been orchestrated. Paranoia flashes for a second, then subsides. But what's the point? Why me? Why go to all the trouble to set up such elaborate coincidences?

Also my ego still stings that I hadn't recognized Hunayna. I feel like the old carpenter with his two Jesuses. I'm also so exhausted that I could be forgiven for what I am to do next. If it actually happened. Which it didn't.

Sister Salma and Nabeel have decided it's time to pray, to

channel Jesus. She will ask him for guidance as we enter the new millennium.

Nabeel is as excited as a wet pup. Salma has never channeled Jesus when he visited before. We agree that he should focus on the moment and we'll tape the prayer and translate later. His male technology gene kicks in and he prods me to check that my tape recorder is on, and then decides that I should put in a fresh tape so we can copy and transcribe it more easily. He wants his own copy of this amazing event. I comply.

I check and then he rechecks for me, as I still don't have my glasses. The tape is spinning. We can hear it and we're ready to go.

Nabeel is ready to high-five. The air around him tingles with excitement. I'm not sure how Jesus would take the familiarity, but then he and his Mum know this household pretty well.

Salma starts to pray on bended knees before a statue of Jesus. Nabeel kneels beside her. I sit on the edge of the settee and bow my head. After a few minutes Salma begins to transmit a message.

Her voice becomes stronger, louder, but it is her voice. She pauses, listens to an inner voice, and speaks. Pauses and speaks—words, sentences, paragraphs—then pauses to listen again.

Nabeel is not translating, but he's concentrating nonetheless, trying to get it right. This is Jesus speaking. The Word.

I'm not listening, or rather, I'm letting the sound enter me, but my mind is not following. I'll listen to Nabeel's translation in the calm of my hotel room. I'm just soaking up the pleasant sensating swell in the room and the cadence of Sister Salma's voice.

Words filter through, here and there. Peace . . . Love . . . President Clinton . . .

Salma's voice blends with street noises. A donkey cart clops by. Birds. Children. I can imagine the Virgin Mary here in this calm domesticity, quite happy, preparing beans in the kitchen, washing dishes. And I'm thinking about Hunayna. I've been so focused on the secret police watching me that I hadn't thought that God has his own security watching out as well.

Salma finishes and Nabeel turns to me, glowing. He's back to the excited persona of yesterday.

"Yeah," he says. "Man, can you believe this great blessing?"

I don't answer. I'm still thinking about the Virgin Mary.

"Play it again, Doktora," he says, "and now I will translate."

I push the rewind button and wait.

Salma stands next to us, her hands loosely crossed in front of her stomach. She's pleased to have helped me, and smiles maternally.

The tape clicks off at the end of the rewind.

I push Start.

We wait. There is nothing. And wait.

Nothing.

Panic gallops across Nabeel's face.

I'm disembodied, trying to figure this out, rationally. I fast forward the recorder.

It's not possible. I've lost Jesus' message for the millennium.

Nabeel tries to grab the machine to check, but I hold on to it and press the replay.

"Listen," I say. "Ssshhh. Listen."

On the tape, a donkey cart clops by in the street. A bird sings. A child calls to another.

The sound of life.

Nothing else. Not even Salma.

This is the still, silent voice of Christ.

Nabeel circles me as we walk in the street, trying not to blame me for screwing up the recording.

"I know, I know," I say. "I lost his message."

"You are smiling too much," he says.

I stop. Yes, I'm smiling. It all makes sense. Why not?

"Do you remember anything?" I ask. "Do you remember the message?"

He's walking back and forth, biting on his thin mustache.

"It was about us being children of God," he says. "About his love . . . about . . . I can't remember. Except his best wishes to President Clinton."

These reminders about God's love are constants, and as for the message to the president, well, if he's checking in with God occasionally, he'll get the message himself.

"Then, it happened as it happened," I say.

"Yeah, Doktora." I haven't convinced him.

Nabeel leaves me in a crowded square in the center of Damascus. Polluted, crowded and noisy.

Rheema, my lawyer friend, is waiting in a café across the square. We hug, she grinds out a half-smoked cigarette, snaps the locks shut on her Chanel embossed briefcase and we leave instantly. She wants me to catch the last session in court.

The state courthouse is a gray, old, turn-of-the-century building with pretensions of modernity, surrounded by grand old banks and official institutions. Quite close is the once-mysterious terminal of the Orient Express, where a former Mata Hari, now a sad old dowager, operates a tea and fortune-telling business in the remaining few carriages out back.

The courthouse is easy to miss because from dawn to late evening crowds of dusty men spill out onto the streets, and you walk around them, trying to avoid the oncoming traffic. They are generally unshaven, unslept, and wearing out-of-date suits. They've come to pay fines, renew licenses, stand in line for hours waiting for the Syrian nod of the head that says, You are free to go.

You can smell the same acrid combination of lack of sleep and fear at the University of Chicago's Oriental Institute when graduate students are defending their theses. It's the smell of powerlessness. I had forgotten about it until returning a couple of years ago during exam season. My eyes burned and my stomach knotted before I reached the carved Assyrian lions on the stairs.

Together we push our way up the outer stairs through pods of men and women, past uniformed security guards and into the crowded building. I'm trying not to lose sight of her as I'm bombarded by faces and noise. Everyone seems to be shouting orders or requests over my head to someone else and the stone walls echo them back. Grandmothers in village dress are the most vocal and one almost takes out my eardrums as she yells to her son across the mob. She's lost hold of her grandson and they both start calling for him.

The place is seething with commotion. We press up another wide staircase, like salmon swimming upstream, and then another. I notice other official and groomed women in lawyerly suits who greet Rheema on our forward push. Some come out of open doors to join us in the swim for a few minutes, then step aside at a convenient corridor to let the crowd flow on. Her male counterparts light up when they see her, one or two men flirt carefully, but she deals quickly and businesslike with the issues they discuss as we keep pushing forward.

We reach the main hall and are almost thrust through the large doors, so great is the pressure behind us. The room we enter is only slightly less noisy than the halls we've left and just as dark. Yellowed blinds are pulled against the sun, which still filters through the cigarette-clouded room. Here the dominant noise is whispering, a buzz that stops and starts in waves that follow the progress of Rheema's short yellow skirt and the blond foreigner down the central aisle to the front of the room where the lawyers sit. Five hundred pairs of tired eyes are getting their fill.

With her long blond hair and sophisticated clothes, Rheema looks nothing less than a movie star. To the poor people in the room she's walked straight out of a television commercial. She's from the local line of strong women—Zenobia, Cleopatra and Sheba, to name a few—where beauty is a weapon and intelligence is a peacemaker.

Everything about Rheema says that she will not take "No" as an answer. As we walk down the center aisle of the long hall, her black patent high heels click loudly on the marble floor and, instead of treading lightly as I would to avoid attention, she sets up a nice undulating rhythm. I fall into step and try to become invisible while I absorb the room around me.

The far right of the hall is taken up by a raised promenade of barred cages. In them, thin men with thin cheeks stare out into the dark, seated crowd searching for faces they know: their fathers, mothers, wives and friends, who are there to catch a glimpse of a loved one about to be sentenced.

"Prisoners," Rheema says quietly. "Waiting for the judge."

Her voice is noncommittal.

One prisoner sits alone, rocking back and forth. A few huddle in a group talking quietly through adjoining cages. A guard whacks at a prisoner's hand that reaches out through the bars for a cigarette held out by a man in the crowd.

The judge and assistants sit on a series of raised daises at the front of the room. There's a break in the procedures as they compare paperwork for the next case. They look up at Rheema's approach, and instead of immediately signaling an apology for her disturbance, she gives a 100-watt smile. Then bows slightly. I'm in awe, but not because of her audacity, but because she is herself.

A colleague signals Rheema from the farthest seat at the side and we climb over a row of lawyers and briefcases to squeeze in beside him. They put their heads together and start a quick whispered discussion. Other colleagues turn around or lean forward and add comments to their discussion.

For the next few minutes, Rheema and her colleague search the faces on the other side of the room while I take in the subdued mob around me. These are the secular courts of Syria, that is, the law of the land. The Islamic sharia courts of old no longer hold official power but still operate.

Before I get a chance to ask Rheema what is going on, she suddenly rises with her colleague. They've found the person across the room they've been looking for and we're all leaving.

Oh, God no, I whimper. Walk down the aisle through that seated crowd again, when they've just settled down. This time we'll be facing them. I haven't felt this wretched since I was an understudy doll in the *Nutcracker Suite*. I suck in my breath and pretend I'm a bloody colonial princess, and feel very, very horrid for all the sins of my forefathers. Rheema feels no such thing.

The confab takes place over glasses of hot tea and packs of cigarettes in a bare, stale room that serves as the lawyers' cafeteria. Two other women have joined Rheema and the two men. They're less flamboyant but just as directed as she. The case, they inform me, is a land dispute. Squatters against a developer. They're with the squatters, but things are not so good.

"We try, we try, we keep trying," one woman says.

Business behind us, Rheema and I sit despondent over our pistachio sundaes in a hotel café and drift into our own thoughts.

This serious side of Rheema wasn't so apparent the night we went carousing, the one before my meeting with the Patriarch. We'd gone dining and dancing with her boyfriend at a rooftop club overlooking the city where affluent Syrians go when they can't drive to Beirut for a lost weekend. For the first time in years, I was feeling absolutely, boundlessly free, and only the appointment with Pope Zakka in the next few hours kept me from dancing the dawn in.

"Do you believe in miracles?" I ask her as we play around with our ice cream.

"Why are you asking?" she responds in lawyerly style, question for question. Gold bracelets jangle on her wrist as she reaches for another cigarette.

I tell her about the visit with Abu George and his stigmata and visitation of saints, about Sister Salma with Mother Mary doing the dishes. I tell her about Pope Zakka, who asked after her, by the way, and about the coincidence of Hanna being Salma's daughter.

Rheema is an educated, strong-headed woman and I need her insight. I'm asking her to play devil's advocate.

She reaches for my hand across the table.

"Miracles?" she asks.

"Yes," I say. "Miracles."

"Why not?" she says. "Why not?"

CHAPTER 18

Time Traveler

The tomb of Muhyi al-Din Ibn al-Arabi centers a medieval quarter cobbled into the hillside of Damascus. A girlfriend, an architectural historian, once discouraged me against going there, claiming it was inhospitable. The eyes of the men, she told me, check out the eyes of the men, you'll understand.

I do. My glances at the melon carters, the bakers, the shopkeepers and pedestrians in the tortuous alleys that lead to the tomb bounce right back like reflections from a mirror. The eyes of the women are the same. They are the sharp eyes of people who'd think little of doing the Sunday *New York Times* crossword puzzle in ink. They do the math of metaphysics in their head, for fun, and they look right into you, checking to see if you, also, have worked the solution and caught the double pun. The streets are strangely quiet, but for the well-oiled turning of their minds.

Ibn al-Arabi, the late twelfth-century saint, was—or is—the cerebral Sufi nonpareil. Sheikh is an honorary title given to a wise leader, usually of a religious order or a tribe, and Ibn al-Arabi is hailed as the Sheikh of Sheikhs. Less known in the West than Jalal al-Din Rumi, the mystical love poet, whose adherents whirl themselves into an ecstatic state of holy union with The One, Ibn al-Arabi is the thinking person's Sufi. Although he practiced an ecstatic form of mysticism, he emphasized the serious side of Sufism and his writings are infamously impenetrable. His adherents do not whirl.

He's hard-core science, whereas others are liberal arts. His adherents claim that he broke physical barriers and time-traveled not only into the past but into the future, which is now. In other words, a form of him exists among us today projected from the past.

This may be a stretch, but, well, why not?

If I'm going to learn about the future as the old man on the Nile train had challenged, Ibn al-Arabi may offer some insight. His men haven't returned my calls (or even answered the phone, such is their complacence about time), so I've come to his tomb. Nabeel has insisted on escorting me, despite my having lost the voice of Christ on him.

Nabeel's Mighty Fine Escort Service is not entirely altruistic. Ibn al-Arabi, a product of Andalusia, that multicultural hot spot, has a strong pull on Christians. His writings graft Christian mysticism onto Eastern Islamic mysticism and left an impact on both. He studied under the famed Averroës in Spain and by the end of his life translated the works of Indian mystics, infusing them into an already potent mix. As a member of the then global village, he also racked up the frequent-flyer miles (and tax write-offs) as philosopher-advisor to courts from Morocco to Mecca, as well as Egypt and Seljuk Anatolia, outliving some, outrunning others. *Bezels of Wisdom,* written when he finally settled in Damascus, sets the Old and New Testament prophets (including Jesus) as bejeweled exemplars of God's wisdom.

Ibn al-Arabi's mosque, or meetinghouse, is itself a small jewel in a plain setting. A sober stone fountain laps in front of the main entrance. Hard-nosed pigeons refuse to scatter as we try to walk through them, forcing us to walk around. We follow a shaded path that leads to the tomb, remove our shoes outside the entrance, and stumble into a dark room, crowded with religious geegaws and lit by dim gaudy bulbs. Nabeel pulsates with excitement; we stand on the threshold of the Sufi Netherworld.

Immediately within the entrance, an erect body occupies a tall, straight-backed chair. The guardian of the tomb faces forward, arms poised on the carpeted armrests of the chair, riffling prayer beads in one hand, the first sign that he is alive. Stiff white prayer cap over a closely shaved face, mustache and clipped gray hair, eyes focused within, he monitors the air for any suggestion of movement. Tacked to the walls around him are framed verses, a small prayer rug, and a hand towel for ablutions. He nods at us to enter.

Despite the visual overload, the room is serene. An elderly man, a grandfather or virile late bloomer, holds the hand of a toddler in shorts and points out artifacts of the saint and his spiritual lineage in glass showcases. The walls are crammed with framed verses and finely carved candleholders, boxes, and symbols of office. So absorbed am I by the beautiful dusty chandeliers that hang unlit like faded stars from the ceiling, that I tread a young child underfoot. He doesn't notice; he's absorbed in fingering his reflection in a gigantic metal turban at the end of a beautifully carved stone tomb. This is not Ibn al-Arabi's grave, however, and Nabeel leads me to a green velvet curtain pushed halfway back.

Behind it, in the center of the room, a casement of glass seals Ibn al-Arabi's tomb like a greenhouse conserving a rare plant. Tombs of holy men and women in the region are believed to emit *baraka*, essential blessing, and whoever touches or visits one, shares that blessing and has prayers answered. Trees that grow out of tombs of saints, their roots tapping the body and soil, their limbs reaching upward with renewed life, are especially treasured. Following ancient cultic practices, these trees are often decorated, as are some tombs, with pieces of cloth or metallic tinsel as prayer trees. Years ago, a flamboyant British art historian told me these were forerunners of our Christmas trees, ornamented with charms and wishes.

Ibn al-Arabi doesn't need a tree to extend his *baraka*. As I press my face against the glass, I wonder if the shield is to protect the saint or the observers, whether like the energy of Assad Ali after prayer, the blessing released from the saint's tomb is so potent that only few can come into direct contact without being electrocuted. Other tombs I've visited were surrounded by a barrier of ornate metal grilles, but with glass you can still project yourself beyond it.

My mind wanders to something Assad Ali said about glass. How we learn in stages both to emit and receive. Let's look at water, he'd said, which we cannot see unless in context—reflected against the sky, for example. An opaque container, even one of colored glass, can hide the water it holds. But just as we can see water within a transparent glass, so also the spirit can be seen within a transparent vessel. Through mystical exercises, he said, the body becomes transparent to the extent it can show you the spiritual being within. A child who has not come of age to perceive depth, however, will see nothing.

I stare into the glass container at the saint's tomb, and see nothing. I figure if Ibn al-Arabi mastered time-travel, he's sure to be off somewhere other than lying prone in this stuffy greenhouse.

Nabeel and I finish studying the displays and the guardian signals for us to sit with him and meditate. He offers us the blessings of the saint, which we receive by sharing holy spring water from a metal cup. I sit on the worn old rugs to the guardian's side at a distance comfortable enough not to crane my neck, my knees folded under the long linen skirt that has become my holy uniform, my hair hidden beneath a white gauze scarf, my sandals outside the door. Nabeel folds himself into a rather wilted lotus position, center front, and my heart goes out to him. Finding God is an intellectual pursuit and he's tasting every fruit offered to him, careful not to eat any of the seeds.

As we settle in, two thirty-something women in long black robes and head coverings enter and begin praying at the tomb.

One caresses the glass wall and cries softly. She kisses the grate and moves to the side of the room where she sits cross-legged, holding her belly, rocking back and forth in prayer. Black puddles of mascara dribble down her cheeks. The other woman catches my intrusive stare, and returns it with a shy affirmation of that feminine bond: the desire for children.

I've seen the pained face of the childless woman before. In a mirror. I've recognized myself in the faces of all the women I've met this week in that same mirror: Lena, Myriam, Hunayna, Rheema—yes, especially Rheema—and even Salma, but none strikes a chord as the face of this dark stranger. I send her love, and the child or children I never had.

"They are praying for children?" I ask the guardian as an ice-breaker I reserve for religious men.

Saints in the Middle East are ecumenical, just as the desire for children is universal. In a continuation of ancient fertility cults, women, Muslim and Christian alike, often pray for children at the tombs of saints, regardless of faith or denomination. The keeper of the tomb, however, is not interested in baby talk.

"They are praying for wisdom," he replies tartly. "All come to the tomb of the saint seeking wisdom. And Knowledge of God."

Wisdom. Of course. But I could have sworn I recognized the faint tick of a biological clock.

So there can be no doubt, the guardian reads me Ibn al-Arabi's words from an inscription above the tomb. Rather, he doesn't read. He points toward it and recites.

He is blind.

"God has given me Knowledge that cannot be explained to others. He has taken me to the place of His throne and shown me things that cannot be explained through the physical, only the senses."

"Senses?" I ask Nabeel for a replay of his translation, while I copy it down in college-Arabic.

Ibn al-Arabi does not leap to mind when you mention the senses: That would be Rumi. Crack any of the milder translations of the Persian poet's work and you'll be seduced by the sensuality of his words. Delve deeper and you'll be sucked into his wild flights of depression and ecstasy, his abandoned, erotic, crazed love for God. No wonder we Westerners adore him. His is mad with sublime abandon. He'd give our Saint Teresa a run for her money any day.

Not so with Ibn al-Arabi. This globe-trotting mystic would leave even a Mensa queen with a migraine; he'll challenge you with hidden double-mirrored images of the inside of God's head. While Rumi is beating his perfumed chest, Ibn al-Arabi is off warping around with time and space, comparing notes with God. Ibn al-Arabi's "senses" were definitely not the ones Rumi was talking about.

The guardian's deceptive eyes focus in middle space as he considers how best to explain.

"Mawlana has said that Knowledge of God is given in three ways," he says, using again the honorary title of Our Master. "Knowledge of God comes through the Mind, the Heart, and the Senses."

I would definitely place Ibn al-Arabi in the Mind School, but then the old man proceeds to shake my Western perceptions.

"The Mind," he says, "is expressed in Nature as the stars, the sky and heaven. In Man, it is the Understanding."

The stars and heaven of Assad Ali's poem spring to mind.

Apart from this quick thought, the guardian and I are tracking. But when I volunteer that Ibn al-Arabi represents the Mind, he cuts me with a glare.

"Second, the Heart," he says, using the palm of his hand as a blackboard. "We receive Knowledge through the heart. It is expressed throughout the universe as Love."

"Rumi?" I ask quietly but determined not to be silenced.

He nods. Good. I'm back on the Dean's List.

"And the senses? Smell, touch, and so on?" I volunteer.

The guardian sits for a minute, his head cocked, listening to a distant sound. I'm trying to discern what has captured his attention and, hearing nothing, begin to drift. Perhaps he has forgotten our conversation.

Suddenly he says, "The senses experience God through the Wind."

In sharp reflex, as if hit by the wind itself, I cover my face with my hands and breathe in deeply. I breathe in and out for an indeterminable time, and when I lower my hands his gaze is on me.

"Yes, and through the breath," he says. "*Ruh*. The Spirit. Breath. Soul. Calm. Peace. This is the wind. And through all of these is Knowledge of God."

Ruh is a formidable word in Arabic, so short and yet so powerful. The word is so layered with complex meaning and is closely paired with others, that I'm not surprised Nabeel falters with the translation. *Ruh* also relates to the inbreathed spirit, that breath that gave life to Adam. In many Sufi orders, ritualized breathing practices are central to the communal Ceremony of Remembrance, the *dhikr*. And reed instruments, the flute and *ney*, for example, that transform the human breath into music, invisible yet sensed, are revered by mystics. Sufis also have this thing about fresh breath.

The complexities of the guardian's words could keep me here for a lifetime. Never have I heard the works of the Master expressed with such simplicity in such a short time, or in opposition to the logic I'd been taught.

The guardian's saying that Ibn al-Arabi, one of the most intellectual mystics, places the mind beneath, not above, the spirit and the heart. So also did the Grand Sheikh of Islam. The Coptic Bishop. The Syriac Patriarch. The Sufi poet. The shopkeepers, waiters and taxi drivers. They all say the same.

In this persistent value system, knowledge is first felt or sensed, then picked up by the heart. The mind is the last to get it. The concept fits like a tight shoe.

An old black telephone jangles off the wall next to the

guardian but he doesn't bother to pick up the receiver. It is the signal from the main mosque that prayers are about to begin, he informs us. The tomb is closing. He slides a huge brass key from a ring on his belt, ushers us back across the threshold, and locks the door.

As we cross the courtyard I ask him about Ibn al-Arabi's legacy. The library of the mosque is rich in thought. The multiple meanings of the ponderous words of the Sheikh of Sheikhs will take generations yet to tap. The guardian offers an alternative, however. The saint's legacy was not intellectual; it is his belief in peace and love among mankind, all mankind. And hospitality. The scholarly saint loved hospitality. Peace be unto him.

A thin stream of sharp-eyed men on their way to prayer trickles through the wide gates from the street, some in timeless long robes and white skullcaps, others in modern shirts and trousers. They're not exuding the hospitality Ibn al-Arabi extolled. The two women from the tomb have joined others in street dress and headscarves at a side door. For one of the few times in the Middle East, I am not invited to join or observe prayers.

To be fair, I've encountered the same exclusiveness in Catholic churches in America that do not permit the sacrament to non-Catholics. Once in a Latin-speaking chapel in Italy where I'd dropped in for some art history and prayer, an old lady forcibly tried to eject me when it became obvious I was not native to the ritual. After the guardian's short discourse on Ibn al-Arabi's love of hospitality, however, the lack of it among his adherents irritates me.

This is a serious religious enclave that does not welcome the frivolity of tourists, or frivolity from anyone, to be precise, so I'm doing all that I can to show respect. My headscarf is in place, my long skirt and blouse are more modest than many in the streets of Damascus. Still, one rigid, middle-aged adherent scowls at me as we approach each other near the street entrance.

I make a move to scowl back, but my heart nudges my hard head forward. I remember Lena taking my hand, and Abu George sharing his holy wine, and Salma opening her home. I think of the Patriarch sighing that peace is tired and old, and Assad Ali reminding me that our words manifest our hearts.

"*As-Salaamun aleykum,*" I say quietly as we come face to face in the gateway. "Peace be with you."

The adherent stops in his bristly tracks, studies me for a long second as if noticing me for the first time, then replies.

"And peace be with you, sister."

We bow slightly toward each other, and continue on our paths.

Nabeel pulls me through the gate into the street. He's watched me push the envelope of peace far enough for one day.

talking in circles

Mawlana asks you to summarize your time here in three words," Dr. Khayyam directs me. Assad Ali, the Syrian Sufi poet, beams like a solar panel communicating happy news from deep space. The almost-full moon pauses above the open window and draws a lunatic stairway to heaven, which I'm considering as an escape hatch.

Tomorrow, I leave Syria for Egypt, land of the Pharaohs, to continue my quest for the future. I'm suffering the mixed emotions of a student both leaving summer camp and facing a final exam. Assad Ali, as chief examiner, has mischief up his sleeves and I'm determined to meet his surprises.

I'm distracted from my three-word assignment by the drop-dead gorgeous man in a long white robe and turban next to Assad Ali. He's my spiritual blind date, the poet's first surprise. He sits appropriately under a framed calligraphy of the "Ninety-nine Beautiful Names of God." Tall, shaven-headed, bull-necked and with shoulders of a wrestler, he could bring traffic to a standstill by raising an eyebrow. His face captivates me; it is calm and serene.

He's driven all the way from Beirut to meet me. In his gold

Mercedes. Only I don't know about the gold Mercedes yet, which is a good thing, because I'm on the verge of becoming a very shallow woman.

My whole female being is jumping up and down trying to get my attention. Take a skinny dip in the gene pool, hon, it shouts, and for a moment I regret I've given away my childbearing card to the woman at the tomb.

I clear my throat.

"When I arrived in Syria," I reply, "I expected nothing, and expecting nothing, the unexpected took over."

My voice is weak and strained and conveys none of the sincerity it's meant to. In one week, my reality has changed.

"Yes, Doktora," Dr. Khayyam says after conferring with Assad Ali. "This is fine, but what are your three words?"

Assad Ali continues to beam. My confusion amuses him.

"Three words, please," he says.

I steal a glimpse at the visitor again and three distinct words come to mind.

God. Help. Me.

Like Assad Ali, he radiates to the point of transparency. He is the glass vessel of which the poet spoke, through which you can see the spirit within. I'm light-headed from peering into his depths.

To do justice to the master's question, I try to focus. The experience at Ibn al-Arabi's mosque is fresh in my mind, as are the faces of those who have guided me down unsuspected paths. So many windows looked through, doors opened, thresholds crossed. And reflections, reflections in faces, eyes and spirit.

"I have three images, three words," I finally reply. Actually, I have four as the words window and door meld together. "They don't make a sentence. The first is path. The second is door. The third, mirror."

I think I'm playing it safe, if not cheating a bit, with these three words as they are well-worn concepts in mystical circles. I know this intellectually, from books and classroom settings, not from experience or sitting knee to knee with a roomful of mystics. Unfortunately, I'm playing with the master's own deck of cards.

As Dr. Khayyam translates the words back to the poet, they come alive through context and I begin to pick up on their multiple meanings, or at least the first layer of their many meanings. They first appear in two dimensions, but like Lena's Fire Bird, they continue to take on dimension and become real. I can almost smell them, or sense them, and begin to float in them.

I haven't felt this stoned since my lost youth in Sydney. The guys across the alley were heavy into opiated hash, and on a good day with a high breeze, you could see green dragons.

I glance at the glass of fruit juice beside me, which I haven't touched, and then at the stranger, whose eyes are closed. There's some serious mind-melding going on here.

I wonder if the others are having the same experience, but lose the thought and float back into the words.

Strangest of all is the word mirror, which smells like damp earth after the rain. A mirror smells like water on parched red clay.

These are not my thoughts, I'm sure, but I surrender and keep floating on this strange sea.

Hmmph, I say and smile as I float through the word, mirror, in Arabic, stranger still as it's not my language. In Arabic, mirror, *ayni*, holds the meanings of a source of water, a spring or well, and a place of self-reflection. Where you see yourself. Where you drink. The source. I almost giggle with childlike wonder as I run my hand through the mirrored water and watch the reflection disperse.

My thoughts return to solid earth, and the two masters smile gently.

Narcissus, that master of self-reflection, could have no better Echo than these two men, whose life is The Word. Assad Ali, the Sufi poet. Beside him, Sheikh Chaaban, a Muslim Gnostic, leader of an ancient mystical line that, interwoven with Jewish Kabbalism, early Christian heresies, and Central Asian and Indian cults, identifies God through words and their mystical values. In his world, the external does not exist, the body is but a covering for the spirit. We exist as allegory.

We spend the entire evening into the morning untying the long, languid knot of these three words: path, door, and mirror. I try to hold back from Assad Ali, protecting myself from wherever he might take me. But he applies Newton's Third.

"Three words," he says, "but there is no description to this scene you've laid out. Now go back to your window, your door. Let us see what you are seeing inside."

The others bend forward, except for the Lebanese sheikh, who sits erect. His eyes are serenely closed.

I close mine.

I'm in a narrow cobbled street, Damascus perhaps, and shuttered windows at street level open onto a courtyard. There's movement inside I can't quite make out, yet drawn to it, I move to the huge door and peer in. There are candles and lanterns and people, talking and talking. There's a long table piled with food like an Italian wedding. I push on the huge door until it opens wide enough for me to slide in.

Inside the courtyard, the air moves over me in rivers of warm and cool. Birdsong encircles me, a fountain laps in the background. Flashes of color—flowers, the glint of sunlight on polished metal, a ceramic dish—hum around me. There is music in my belly and I know I will dance for my feet are already off the ground.

I don't tell the poet any of this. It's a little foolish and I'm starting to sober up from whatever just happened.

"And what do you see in this courtyard?" Assad Ali asks, despite my silence. I am no longer surprised that he sees my thoughts and take his knowledge for granted. Or as Adel Beshai in Cairo had described Saint Kyrillos: "He pulled thoughts from my head."

At the table in the courtyard there are faces, wonderful ordinary faces. And someone pulls up a chair for me to join them. I see wine and roast lamb and kibbeh. I see grapes and a woman passing them to a child. I see Abu George and Saint Elias topping up wineglasses, and Sister Salma and the Virgin Mary serving chicken and rice. Assad Ali is licking sugar syrup from his fingers while sweet Lena shares a story. The Fire Bird perches on her shoulder, wraps her golden feathers around her head like one of the Queen Mother's exotic hats, and sings.

"A mirror," I reply stubbornly. My brain has kicked in, and now I will lie to protect it. "I see the unexpected mirror."

Assad Ali taps a long finger against the arm of his chair. It is the only sign I recognize that he is frustrated.

"Then, sister," he says, "I wonder you did not see the bountiful table?"

I bow my head. My thoughts are transparent. He has seen my will to dance.

"Yes," I reply. "I did. I saw the table."

Assad Ali claps his hands. This is all he wanted to hear. I expect a look of reproof; there is none.

"Good!" he says. He immediately proceeds to quote a sura from the Qur'an about the bountiful table: verse 114 from chapter 5, The Table.

"O God, our Lord, send down upon us a Table out of heaven, that shall be for us a festival, the first and last of us, and a sign from Thee. And provide for us; Thou art the best of providers."

"This is the Last Supper," I say.

"Good," he says. "But from the Qur'an. Christ has invited us all to eat and celebrate at the bountiful table, regardless of background. The first and the last of us."

He's alluding to Saint Paul and inclusiveness, just as Pope Zakka had a few days earlier.

The poet sweeps his hand around the room to the other guests, many of whom I met the first night.

"The first and the last of us. Christian, Muslim, Armenian . . ."

He pauses at Nabeel and taps his finger in the air with mischief.

"Even a New Age-Buddhist-Hindu-Christian."

Nabeel blushes. The others laugh with affection.

"Christian, Muslim, Jew, our brothers and sisters across the world," he says. "There is bounty at this table of Christ."

"You are Muslim, and you quote from the Qur'an, not the Gospels," I say.

"Muslims are also Christian," he says, "and Christ is The Bountiful Table. The Word. Tonight, Prophet Muhammad is our host to The Word."

As master of ceremonies, Assad Ali claps his hands again.

"This talking is our preface to the night," he says and grins with pleasure. This hour-long preamble introduces the evening and the stranger who sits quietly next to him, radiating peace, wisdom, and holy pheromones.

"We have prepared a bountiful table for our sister tonight," the Sufi poet says. The others applaud softly. "And we have invited certain distinguished guests. Our friends, whom you have met. And some who could not come."

He mentions the name of a member of parliament, a leading Sufi, advisor to the president, who is held up on a late session, and who sends his regards.

"And our distinguished Mawlana Aref Chaaban, who has driven from Lebanon to meet you."

Assad Ali continues with an aside and the others begin to laugh before I catch the translation. All eyes are on me. It's at my expense.

"I confess I have taken advantage of our sister," he teases. "I have invited our beloved friend on the pretext of meeting you so I can share his company."

Ah. A spiritual *ménage à trois.*

The two old friends laugh with affection and hold each other's hands, each cupping the other's in his.

The Lebanese sheikh bows his eyes to the poet and then straightens. He loosens the white shawl across his chest to free his arm, which he raises slightly, palm up, to eye level.

He folds me into his lashes, like cream into a dessert.

Silence descends.

His voice is resonant and measured, like the steps of Dr. Mohammed in Cairo, and I glide along beside him waiting for Dr. Khayyam's translation.

"Our sister's words belong to a poem I have only begun to work on," he says.

He nods slightly toward me, and closes his eyes.

"*I look at You in every Word*," he begins.

I'm not sure I want to hear another word for the rest of my life.

He continues.

"*I see You in my Heart and Everywhere.*"

If I sigh, nobody notices. The entire room is rapt. Assad Ali exhales loudly on behalf of us all and the two masters begin to discuss the finer points of meaning, making cross-references to the Qur'an, to other poems, to the works of other mystics. They hold each word up to the light. One word turns into a minute, then forty. Bassam, Zeina, and Ermejian add their comments and questions. Nabeel sits quietly, his long neck craned, his eyes wide open, unblinking.

I follow along, left to my own devices, since Dr. Khayyam has abandoned me for the discussion. I weave in and out of conversation, free to roam, restricted only by my own limitations. What I understand is not what Bassam next to me or anyone else understands, but that is fine. Assad Ali has already told me that we each learn or perceive at different rates.

While the two poets compare the meaning of love, and the finer points of the initiated heart and the kindled fire, Dr. Khayyam turns to me.

"This love," he says with a grin. "He is talking of God, unfortunately."

"Unfortunately," I agree.

"*Blind are those who have not seen their own Existence. . . .*" The sheikh adds another line.

The poem continues to tread water as we discuss the properties of blindness and sight. Of life and primordial existence.

"*Blind are those who have not seen their own Existence,*
In their Being the Off-Spring of the Light of your Spirit. . ."

A spirited discussion of spring as well as offspring, of source and reflection, sun and radiation, takes us far into the moon-drenched night and toward morning.

My attention slides. While I'm rolling the cricks out of my neck, I'm thinking of the blind guardian at the tomb of Ibn al-Arabi and how he sensed the world. The conversation winds its way toward the relationship of man, technology and creation.

"Atlantis." I hear the word. "Atlantis."

The masters have me snagged. Dr. Khayyam lends me his extra ears like a set of earphones as the two men back up and summarize what I missed.

"We started by saying that the Creator of the Sun, which is a symbol of the Essence of Being," the Lebanese sheikh says. "The Path that our sister spoke of would represent the Essence as that ray represents the source of light, which is the Source, the Great Creator. Since, Allah be praised, is the Ego, my ego, my ascended ray has that profound yearning to possess the Ego."

"When a child sees his father at work," the Syrian Sufi elaborates on the thoughts of his counterpart, "the child tries to imitate his parent. As it is said, a child is like the father. In the same way that a child is known to imitate his father or parent, the creation of God who have gone astray and who have set themselves at a great distance from their essence—from the Creator—so they also have a tendency to imitate God. And so they try to worship the Creation—their imitation—and not the Creator."

I'm scurrying to keep up as Sheikh Chaaban continues to lead us over the horizon with his lines of poetry floating above us like a silken kite.

> *"So they went astray in floods of darkness,*
> *In surges of darkness . . ."*

Nods and murmurs of affirmation bob through the room like toy boats on waves.

"Mawlana refers to the continent of Atlantis," Assad Ali says, interpreting the sheikh's poetry.

Atlantis? This is where I reentered the conversation. I don't have time to pinch myself as they rush forward.

"The Atlantans created more than imitations," the Sufi poet says. "They created their own fanciful imaginings, their fancies. And even in spiritual powers . . . some of them used these spiritual powers not for the essential purpose, but for their own purposes, to meet their own desires. In Atlantis they started to create their own state of fancies, and they used these fancies for purposes they are not meant to."

Atlantis?

The two masters and the guests talk about Atlantis not as far-fetched science fiction but as another allegory. These men are from a line of thought as ancient as the Atlantis story and like the miracles of Abu George and Sister Salma, the subject is part of their reality. They talk about Atlantis, that lost civilization in the Sea of Consciousness, as easily as Patriarch Zakka talked about outer space. As the Syriac Pope said, Why not?

Sheikh Chaaban interrupts my thoughts.

"Right from the beginning," he says, "God has promised his true believers Paradise, which attributes are known to everyone."

"Now, returning to this comment about Atlantis," Assad Ali continues the flow, "they created their own technology to provide themselves and their followers with whatever comfort and peace possible, an allegory of that Paradise promised by God to his true believers."

Atlantis was man's attempt to build Paradise without God? I flash on the image of Las Vegas built far from water's edge.

"The fate of Atlantis is the inevitable fate of those who misinterpret the work of the Creator," he says. "The more the people are concerned with quantities, the more distant they will be from the qualities of their senses."

"Yes, the blind . . . ," Nabeel says.

"They go astray in floods of darkness . . . ," Sitt Zeina repeats.

At two in the morning we stop briefly. For dinner.

Assad Ali stands, full of energy, as if we had not been engaged in conversation for hours. My whole being is spinning gently into equilibrium.

"The Bountiful Table awaits," the poet announces dramatically and ushers us into the dining room. In the center is a round table as large as the room is small, weighted down with platters of lamb and chicken, braised, grilled and stewed, of vegetable dishes and rice, of sweet honey-dripped pastries and fruit.

We pull mismatched chairs into tight spaces that build new intimacy. Silence descends for a minute as we begin to eat, but only for a minute, before conversation bubbles up again.

Assad Ali, who is staying unnaturally quiet in order to let others get a word in, is being ribbed by Bassam. After a few minutes the poet can no longer contain himself and starts calling out, Beer, beer, to the laughter and delight of the table. I start laughing, too, caught up in the sheer joy and animation of the Sufi master, without knowing the point of his story. His humor is contagious.

Dr. Khayyam explains: "That was a joke by Mawlana," he says. "He said someone was being scoured by whip and the torturer said, I will stop if you say the word Bir—not the drink, but in Arabic, the well, the water, the source. The man said nothing. Some people passed by and said, 'Why don't you say, Bir?' He said, 'I avoid this. If I'm going to say Bir then I will start to say too many other things. If I start talking, I have the thirst to talk too much. So either a long answer or no answer at all.' "

"When the heart is full," Bassam adds, "it overflows with the name of God. When the heart is full by the name of God it overflows with that name. This is why I'm repeating, Allah, Allah, all day."

The shy schoolteacher is tapping his breast and smiling widely.

I begin to laugh and a small rock dislodges from my heart. For so long now, I've been living at the bottom of my own well, squeezing water from the mud and lost objects that clutter it. The fire in the Turkish village filled the well with ash and added to the muck. I begin to laugh and tears roll down my cheeks.

Assad Ali is wiping laughter from his own cheeks.

"In the same way as the spring acts when it is full," he says, "it explodes through the ground and overflows. Soon, the well cannot contain it."

"God is the Him," the sheikh adds softly. "The Absolute Beauty and the Absolute Love."

The room settles as we absorb his words.

"Tomorrow, our sister returns to Egypt," Assad Ali says, turning the conversation to me. Between mouthfuls, there are murmurs—stay longer, don't leave yet, we will miss you—and I acknowledge them with some sadness.

"Perhaps if I don't solve my puzzle by morning," I reply, "I'll have to stay."

Sitt Zeina and her husband look up. Bassam puts aside his bread. Nabeel stops chewing. Even Assad Ali raises an eyebrow.

A puzzle?

I tell them the story of how, fourteen years ago, I met the dying old religious man on the Nile train. How I made a promise to him in response to a challenge he gave me in the form of a simple word game.

"Return to Egypt, and you will see the future," I say. "This is what he said."

The two mystics are waiting for the punch line.

"So I returned to Egypt," I say, "and asked about the future . . . and tried to find the old man . . . but haven't found either."

"His exact words?" asks Assad Ali. A slight grin is beginning to crack. "Return to Egypt and you will find the future?"

"*See* the future," I reply.

The two mystics glance at each other, and begin to laugh vigorously. Their abandoned silverware rattles on the table and I frown at it as if I have the power to make it—and them—be quiet.

"This is too simple," Dr. Khayyam intercedes. He is being more charitable and trying not to join in the merriment.

The two men compose their grins.

"You visited today with Muhyi al-Din, al-Arabi, the Greatest of Masters," Assad Ali says.

I nod.

"Then you have your answer."

"I visited his tomb, yes," I say. But trying to clarify, I add, "But not with him."

Dr. Khayyam shakes his head, signaling that I'm not getting it.

The Lebanese sheikh raises his finger for me to listen closely.

"Your puzzle is solved, sister," he says. "You have only to exist in it."

I remain unconvinced.

"You are thinking too much, sister," Bassam says to me. "Too much."

"And what is the name of this mysterious man?" Assad Ali asks.

"Nuweiba," I say. "Bishop Nuweiba."

The two Sufis look at each other and begin to laugh again.

"Yes, yes," Assad Ali finally says. "That would be so."

I look at Dr. Khayyam, who is also chuckling.

"His name, in short, means the springs in the desert."

There are too many coincidences. I smile halfheartedly.

The Spring. Eye. Source and Mirror.

We clear the table and go into a huddle around it. I earlier asked the two masters for a message for the planet, and although it flows from the evening's conversation, more good-hearted discussion and debate continues to turn the water wheel. And because the bountiful table is inclusive, the message, guided and inspired by the two masters, includes the voices of all who eat here: Nabeel, Sitt Zeina and her husband, Bassam, and several others whose names escape me at this late hour.

Exhaustion settles over us as we finish our discussion. The light is changing. Dawn drifts through the curtains. We drink hot tea against the chill morning air and to soften our stiffening spines. We stretch and move around, talking in muted tones.

Assad Ali and Sheikh Chaaban refine the final words together. The sheikh dictates the message in his sonorous voice as Dr. Khayyam translates and I squint and write half-blindly.

So this is the message. It is in seven parts, because seven is a beneficent number, and is in the form of a circle.

I wish that the human kind will remember
1. *the spring from which they came,*
2. *the first recipient of the first breath of initiation,*
3. *the multitudinous overflowings or descendants of that spring,*
4. *to be sincere and loyal to the purity of that water,*
5. *to be assured that they shall be happy by maintaining that purity,*
6. *to remember the most important point, that is, to gain the immortal self and not the mortal world,*
7. *to be aware that the salvation of humanity is through Peace and Love derived from God.*

"This is like a circle," Assad Ali says as he draws on the table-cloth with his long fingers. "We started up and finish up in a circle. Freedom from selfishness and toward infinite love—the notion of peace is bothering everyone—so we wish to enter it here. In this way, we have related each point and all to God."

I add Assad Ali's circles to Bishop Musa's and Adel Beshai's. More will soon be added.

Assad Ali escorts me through his garden at dawn. A cool breeze slides off the mountain and the Sufi poet pulls his white cloak closer around him. A cock crows in the distance.

With us is the Lebanese sheikh, his robes fluttering around him. Dr. Khayyam follows closely behind as does Nabeel and several of the group. We wear the fresh euphoria of having camped in the wilderness, under the stars.

"Oh night," I say, repeating Assad Ali's poetry, "how do you embrace people and things?"

There is a personal question that presses me and I take this last minute alone with Assad Ali to ask it.

"Mawlana, we talk about peace," I say, "but how does one find this peace?"

"Ah, The One, He *is* Peace," Assad Ali replies. "But you are asking how or where do *you* find peace, yes?"

"Yes," I acknowledge. He insists on keeping me honest.

"Then it is clear." He waves his hand dismissively. "We have already told you, have we not?"

Dr. Khayyam has joined us and the poet looks to him for confirmation.

The Lebanese sheikh also agrees, and we stand in silence under the fruiting peach tree. Together with not seeing the solution to my own puzzle, I feel I have disappointed them.

"It is simple," the sheikh says in his soft hypnotic voice. "You must return to your family."

"My family?" I ask.

The answer stings my pride. These fabulous mystics are steeped in ancient traditions of wisdom. They're supposed to give me an enigma to mull over the rest of my life—"Peace can only be reached through tasting the golden walnut," for example,—not some dismissive practical advice: "Go back to the farm, girl."

After our highfalutin' conversation, there has to be more than this. An indignant internal voice protests.

I want to know how to stop people from destroying the planet. I'm searching for a grand answer on the scale of my perceived destiny. Or at least something dramatic. Operatic. I want at least my private Coca-Cola ad, to teach the world to sing in perfect harmony, not to shout over the mad cacophony of my siblings—or my mother. Oh God, my mother.

But that voice I hear in my head is the voice of a week ago. It is no longer mine.

Tears of frustration prick my eyes. The mystics have set an impossible task. Rather a hermitage in the desert than a weekend with my family. After the last extended stay with them in Australia, I put a blanket over my head on the plane and cried all the way across the Pacific. Twenty bloody hours, and it wasn't enough. I'm still crying.

"Yes," the sheikh expands his statement. "Peace radiates outward, a circle from within you. From God to you. From you, your family. Your neighborhood. To the world. Then peace radiates back to you, inward."

"But, my family?" I turn to Assad Ali. I'm willing to work a deal and start with the larger circle, with a village in India or the entire Turkish Land Mafia, and then work backward to the smaller circle of my family.

Assad Ali refuses to indulge my thoughts and continues to chasten me.

"Yes, if you do not first have peace with your family, you cannot bring peace to the world," he says. "After this you will be ready to help heal the world. Many leaders find this too late."

He embraces me at the gate.

"Good-bye, sister," he says with affection, and adds the Islamic salutation, "May you go with Peace."

As the three men confer in their farewells, tall, gawky Nabeel walks with me down the steep stone stairs into the street. We hug a brief good-bye. We are both shivering and damp with dew and I feel his bones through his clammy shirt.

"Go with your heart," I say.

"Your senses," he replies.

Dr. Khayyam chuckles as he joins me alone in the street. The Lebanese sheikh has been assigned to drive me home.

"We are saying that I will accompany the two beauties," Dr. Khayyam says.

He is still laughing as he walks with me across the cobbles where the sheikh holds open the doors to his gold Mercedes sedan.

"We are saying a sort of joke with Mawlana," Dr. Khayyam continues in the car, and the sheikh joins in his mirth. "That what if our beloved sheikh is in an accident taking you home alone? The headlines of all newspapers tomorrow will say: 'Religious Leader Found Dead With Foreign Blonde.' Ayyyy. A big scandal."

I laugh too, but quietly. It is a delicious image, but the headline wouldn't capture those last ecstatic minutes from my perspective. Driving into the Damascus dawn in a gold Mercedes with a drop-dead gorgeous Sufi mystic composing love poetry . . . to God. Two out of three isn't bad.

The sheikh slowly repeats his poetry as he drives with one hand through the wakening city.

I look at You in every Word,
I see You in my Heart and everywhere,
Blind are those who have not seen their own Existence . . .
Blind are those who have not seen their own Existence,
In their Being the Off-Spring . . .

I'm sorry, Ms. Friedan, but I almost swoon. The pulsating engine of a golden Mercedes is no contest for a defiant biological clock, but in the name of all educated women of the planet I struggle to rein in my thoughts and tune in again to the Sufi's poetry.

So they went astray in floods of darkness,
In surges of darkness . . .

Oh damn, if we floor it, we could be in Beirut by noon.

The two men walk me to the door of my hotel. The street sweepers watch, mouths agape, as the gentleman, the sheikh and the blonde hug and laugh full throttle on the sidewalk at sunrise. We're happy to be alive.

Dr. Khayyam kisses me on both cheeks three times.

"Go with Peace," he says quietly.

I am washed by inexplicable sadness, and swallow hard as we hug good-bye.

Sheikh Chaaban places the tips of his long fingers on my forehead. His hands smell of leather from the steering wheel and orange blossoms.

"Remember that you exist," he says.

"Yes," I reply, still not understanding.

The night clerk is sipping his morning coffee. He hands over my key and a package delivered last night.

Inside is my sight returned, my new glasses.

Upstairs, the door to my room is slightly ajar.

My stolen passport lays propped on my pillow. Beside it is a piece of bittersweet chocolate.

It's time to leave.

PART THREE

Egypt

CHAPTER 20

Them There Eyes

The Sinai buses cluster together at the farthest end of Cairo's bustling depot, outside the gates, as far as you can get from the shining tour buses that now dominate the yard. These are the buses to the back-of-beyond, the bandaged limping veterans whose bladders leak oil and who belch black gas. There's no first class on these old wrecks; those who travel with them usually have no class at all.

The bus to Saint Catherine's stands alone. She's a postwar charmer, sandblasted and sun-bleached until little more than an abandoned cicada shell remains. Her suspension and air-conditioning (and driver) are on their last legs, and she hasn't taken a bath since Rommel. Her seats are grooved and humped, the velour covering, evidence of her glory days, stained and matted by sweat and spittle. I'm too tired to be repulsed. By the end of the day, we will be wedded.

My return from Syria has been anticlimactic. Nothing, not one grain of sand has moved since I left. I'm stymied in trying to meet Matta al-Maskin, the Coptic living saint in the desert. Yesterday I finally reached his assistant and he agreed, after talking with the monk, that we could talk. I'm elated. I'm dancing in circles, doing the macarena.

And then I call my ride. My security clearance won't be ready in time and without it I cannot visit the monastery. Leyla explains it's for my own protection: Terrorist threats against tourists are on the rise. My dance slows to a waltz.

I call the Coptic monastery again. The brother is also disappointed. How do we solve this glitch in physical space, I ask? If only I could space travel like Ibn al-Arabi in Syria, or even it's said, Matta, himself. Fax myself, I suggest, half joking. The brother and I hit on a perfect solution for the Age of Technology: We fax paper instead. A list of questions the holy man will answer and get back to me.

Also, since I returned I've been trying to reach the Greek Orthodox monks of the Sinai to set up an interview. The mystics isolated from the world in Saint Catherine's Monastery. I envision them lost in a world of solitude and silence, too occupied by meditation to answer the phone when I've called.

Only three days left.

That leaves me with the unfinished business of the Future. How to find the Catholic Bishop of the Nile? Assad Ali and the Gnostic mystic think I've already found the answer, but I'm still puzzled. I can taste it, but my mind doesn't identify this unnamed taste. I call the cathedral in Asyout again. The line this time is busy.

As I slow waltz around the hotel room—I've convinced Leyla that a hotel works better with my late hours—a string gently tugs me. The only way to reach the Archbishop, one of the famed mystics in the Sinai, is to go there myself, knock on the monastery door, and see if the monks will let me in. So my feet are telling me as they drag me forward. I check the timetable for Saint Catherine's. There's a bus in less than an hour.

St. Catherine's Monastery is one of Seven Wonders of the Christian World. Its walls are loaded with fabulous icons. The library is stuffed with precious books and crammed with history.

Greek Orthodoxy, like the Catholic Church of Rome, was a latecomer to Christianity. By the seventh century when the

Byzantine Emperor Justinian converted to Christianity, the Coptic and Syrian Orthodox Churches had been around for six hundred years and the Nicean Creed was something to lose your head over. Just down the road, Muhammad, the Prophet of a new religion called Islam, had just been born.

As part of a cunning vision statement, Justinian established the monastery of Saint Catherine's on holy real estate, Gebel Musa or Mount Moses, where the Patriarch received the Ten Commandments. Before his epiphany, however, the Greeks were responsible for some brutal waves of persecutions in the region. The schisms remain today, faint but deep scar tissue on the Body of Christ. Catholicism would add another fracture.

While the body of the Church may be somewhat battered, respect for its holy men crosses religious lines into Islam, which shares Abraham as patriarch and the biblical saints and prophets as guides. Fourteen hundred years ago, not long after the Emperor founded the monastery, Prophet Muhammad sent a message declaring not only peace, but protection, for these wise men of the Book. The monastery therefore remained untouched when the Arab generals conquered Egypt and Syria along the path to their own world empire. The written declaration still hangs on its walls today.

But that's not all that draws me. If you're looking for someone who combines science with faith, Catherine's your man. My relationship with her is personal.

Growing up, most kids have a monster that's used to scare the living hell out of them when they don't do what their parents want. Some boogeyman or other. I had Saint Catherine. I learned about her by accident, literally. One Bonfire Night I got too close to a fizzled Catherine Wheel that unexpectedly sprang to life, spitting fire and sparks into my face, burning off my eyelashes, brows and a decent patch of hair. Saint Catherine, a curiously strong-willed Egyptian female, a scientist and philosopher who refused to renounce Christianity, died tied to a tumbling wheel set ablaze. She met a fiery end for her beliefs and learning.

"Keep your head in the bloody books, young lady, and you'll end up just like her," my stepfather used to say. He was against wasting resources on the education of the girl species. His threat became my challenge and I turned my own inner Catherine Wheels with the determination of a bloody martyr.

Hours into the desert, across the Suez, the bus grinds to a halt. Another desolate roadside stop. Cairo's far behind us; the monastery hours ahead.

The Bedouin village woman who crashed beside me outside Cairo snorts awake, gathers her heft of packages wrapped in newspaper, tied with recycled string, bundled in plastic bags, and duck-walks them onto dry land. A wide-assed man in the half-mustache of the lower-rung Egyptian bureaucrat eagerly moves forward to take her place. His eyes are focused on the object of his desire. Not me. Above the seat is the only working air-conditioner duct on the bus and he's willing to override the social taboo against sitting next to an unrelated woman just to get close to it.

We nod and settle ourselves back down into the sweaty hollows of the once-plush seats to ignore both each other and our respective body odors for the next few hours. Despite the dribble of air above us, my cotton skirt is a sopping rag of sweat, which quickly evaporates into a warm, engulfing miasma.

Miasma. A beautiful word. I remember it from a description by a ninth-century Arab historian describing the foul air of Egypt. Perfect for malaria, he claimed, but any mosquito that can get it up right now has my admiration. My mind is disintegrating.

A fresh infusion of passengers at a rare fork in the road promises to shake our stupor. The back half of the bus is taken over by a group of army boys returning from leave to their desert barracks, determined to squeeze out every last drop from their limited freedom. Some are barely teenagers. They're dressed in mismatched military gear; they're bedraggled, unshaven, and grinning from ear to ear.

They light up never-ending rounds of evil-smelling cigarettes and start a hand-clapping, foot-stomping, village sing-a-long. One of them pounds out a bum-wagging tune on a small, skin drum, accompanied by his mates on the metal rims of the backseats. *Boom-takka. Boom-takka.*

The air conditioner struggles to keep up with it all and the windows rattle like false teeth at a country jig. The bus bumps and grinds her way along the desert road, proving there's life in the old girl yet. The driver shifts his lethargy from one hip to the other, checks out the action in the rearview mirror, and sighs.

I notice then the young village woman in the adjacent seat. In her black gauze veil decorated with gold and ruby spangles, she is the focus of commotion and has stolen the hearts of all the men on board. With good reason.

It is difficult to describe such transparent beauty, one that draws strength from the admiration around it. She glows. Draws strength, again. And glows.

Her head and body are covered by the long black gown of the local Bedouin which, rather than concealing, serves her as both mask and magician's foil. By mesmerizing sleight of hand, she rearranges her spangled veil, sliding slivers of brown-gold skin, her face and neck, in and out of view. Her eyes, exposed through a two-inch horizontal slit, glint like golden mirrors. She squeezes light from the sun, sucks it in and, for a moment, eclipses it. She watches for effect, draws strength and glows again.

It's all done with mirrors, I'm sure, but I watch to catch the trick.

She continues to add artifice to art. The bridge of a straight nose. Black eyebrows painted into perfect arches. Honeyed eyes outlined with kohl. I catch the rhythm of these eyes as the magician peers out from behind her veil, opens them wide, then closes them slowly with the suggestion of a smile.

From my vantage, however, I am disturbed by her full, wide hands, almost masculine in their strength. Almost as if the Mona Lisa's had been crudely rendered from blocks of heavy wood. But perhaps these strong hands are what her admirers find attractive;

that she can milk goats, carry wood, and pull tent ropes to perfect tautness.

The mobile theater before me now hums with overacting. Brave army boys venture down the aisle one by one or in pairs, holding hands, scouting the terrain. On the stage, the young beauty lowers her lashes and erases them from being. The boys retreat with manly giggles and jousts as they continue to vie for her attention. Others view the spectacle, chewing pumpkin seeds, making sucking noises through their teeth. The old woman next to the starlet clucks with temperate disapproval.

Meanwhile, farther back in the bus, a young soldier leans forward, silent, not breathing, allowing her beauty and his desire to suck the air out of him. The drummer continues his chant. *Boom-takka. Boom-takka-boom.*

I'm sure I've bought tickets for the wrong show.

Directly in front of her another veiled woman observes keenly. There are just enough years between them to pass as sisters, but I'm certain she's her mother. She raises her own carved brows at the antics, whether in hope of a suitor for her daughter or disapproval is hard to tell. The seat beside her becomes free at the next stop, and her daughter slides in. The army boys give them both their full attention and some forget to sing.

But for age and decoration, the two women are identical in their long, embroidered black dresses and sheer, decorated veils. Side by side, their eyes and eyebrows flicker back and forth in silent code. Their heads come together to exchange half-phrases, to laugh at some private joke. Between them, with that knowing chuckle, they are a thousand years old, ageless in their conspiracy.

As they talk, the older beauty pushes back her veil as a housewife would a curtain from a window, works an unfiltered cigarette into her mouth (still modestly shielded from view) and lights up with that sigh of relief and pleasure universal to old-hack smokers. The army boys become quiet as she exhales.

Smoke and mirrors. These women are working magic with smoke and mirrors.

The army boys de-bus at their barracks and stand by the road to wave good-bye to the women they will possess in dreams tonight. Farther down the rutted desert highway the Bedouin women are deposited near their own camp and the bus feels empty. Passengers, each more shriveled as the day grinds on, get off and on at unmapped landmarks—a twisted tree stripped to arm height for firewood, a certain rock, a path into a barbwired horizon.

We who remain sink into blank silence, conserving even our thoughts. Only the infrequent puff from the driver's cigarette assures me he isn't decomposing.

A stop sign and a traffic circle in the middle of nowhere. A few oleander bushes. A soldier guarding the great empty beyond. Signs to somewhere. Nothing moving.

I am looking through a dust-filmed window into a grand emptiness. We've passed though landscapes of gargantuan boulders, each more fantastic than the last. I've arrived on the moon without leaving home.

Passengers swim their way out of stale dreams and begin to scratch and rustle.

A mid-aged man leans over the back of my seat. The crease in his shirt is crisp and impossibly fresh. His hair is neatly combed and parted. He smells of lemon cologne.

"You must get off here," he says in English. "You are going to the monastery, no? Then you must get off here."

I'm not sure where the monastery is, or even if I will be able to stay there. I have no reservations. I made this bus by minutes. I ask the driver about the monastery. No, he tells me, lady, you will not get off here. I will take you to the tourist hotel. He revs the bus and moves on before I can make a decision. I shrug at the nice man and return to my seat.

Behind me, three Indonesian university students are suddenly alert. They have heard the word "monastery." We are the only for-eigners on board and between us we've memorized the first five pages of the dictionary of Modern Arabic. My antiquated grad school Arabic has rolled over dead.

The bus halts in the middle of a wide dirt road—the town square, there's no other traffic—disgorges the passengers and takes off with the Indonesians in a cloud of dust. The driver's whisking them off to a no-star hotel.

The town of St. Catherine's is a best-forgotten, three-dog dust bowl. It is a scene from a sci-fi flick without the sci. Ratty hotels and pensiones cluster around the end-of-the-line bus stop. There is nowhere to go from here, but back again.

At sunset the air is redolent with greasy lamb kebabs and hashish. A Bedouin in a red-checkered headscarf and army surplus crosses the road, dwarfed behind a touring Visigoth in purple reflecting shades and Nikes. A runted yellow dog sniffs at their footprints. I'm looking around for Princess Leia. Or Priscilla, Queen of the Desert.

"Excuse my inconvenience to you," the nice man from the bus says. "You are not wanting to stay here. You are wanting the monastery. I look at you on the bus and say to myself, this nice lady, she is wanting the monastery. Am I not correct?"

I look around at the village. A hangover in the Outback is less painful than this place.

"You are correct," I reply. "I am wanting the monastery."

I sense the presence of the bishop from the Nile train. I don't need to look around. I know I'm being led into the future.

The man from the bus is the air control manager at Sinai airport, and offers the services of his driver, who his assistant has gone to call. We pass the time with civilized small talk about the weather. I feel like I've survived the Bataan Death March to end up at a cocktail party. Australians are raised on surreal desert experiences, so I go with it.

"Yes," he says. "Two days ago I bring in a charter of American tourists here to the monastery. They came from the resort . . ."

The old bus grinds to a dusty halt beside us. On board are the three Indonesian students.

The driver negotiates to take me with them to the monastery and pockets a small fee for correcting his earlier mistake. He drops us in a cloud of red dust back at the intersection, a mile or so down a dirt road from the monastery, and we trudge forward into the silent night, holy night.

The legendary Mount Moses, or Gebel Musa, rises before us. Here, before time and Technicolor, God gave the venerable patriarch the Ten Commandments, the laws that continue to guide the majority of the planet's population. We are dwarfed by nature and imagination. Mountain and darkness begin to absorb us. Bedouin dogs telegraph our passage.

We reach the monastery lodge at the foot of the mountain in silence.

"You are correct," I repeat to myself as I try to stretch out on sun-bleached sheets after a shower. "I am wanting the monastery."

But how did the man on the bus know? I don't expect an answer. My journey is being guided by the knowing of strangers.

After supper, the supervisor of the monastery lodge asks how long I will be staying. I don't tell him I've come on impulse. That my schedule had finally shuffled itself into impasse and I sensed nothing would happen if I stayed in Cairo.

Nor do I tell him that I knew I had to come to St. Catherine's. To talk to the Father of the Desert. To climb Mount Moses under the full moon of the solstice.

I could tell him that some force almost propelled me onto the bus. Yes, I could have resisted it, but I've learned the peace that comes with following this kind of message, this intuition. I am supposed to be here. Perhaps as Dr. Mohammed, my Sufi patron in Cairo, said, until he sees me, he won't see me. I can't explain more. I am learning to listen to intuition.

Instead, I tell the supervisor, "Until the noon bus tomorrow," I say. And then I ask what time the monastery opens in the morning.

"It is closed," he replies. "No tourists on Sunday."

Not possible, I think.

"I'm not a tourist," I say. "I've come to talk to His Holiness, the archbishop."

He asks what time is my appointment.

There's no point bluffing. I make a face.

"I don't have one," I say.

He makes a face.

"I had to come," I say.

I lay a finger on my heart as Lena and the tea boy had done to me in trying to explain the unexplainable.

"It came from my heart," I say.

The supervisor nods. He understands. He leads me to the darkened souvenir store, to a telephone, and turns on the single bare lightbulb. He calls the monastery, a little ways up the hill in the darkness. A conversation follows in Greek.

I'm sure he's telling them he has another nut case on his hands.

A refrigerator of bottled water and sodas hums in the back of the shop. Racks of postcards, handicrafts are strung across the wall with embroidered bags and gallabiyas, icons and mementos. I'm a voyeur in the half-darkness and remember the basement of the Smithsonian, where this journey began. Long ago. Yesterday.

The conversation continues in Greek and I gather from the rhythm of repetitions of phrases and of pauses that the phone on the other end is being passed from hand to hand.

I think of the old bishop on the Nile train who dared me to come back to Egypt and see the future. I'm still waiting to find it. I decide that if there's no message waiting in Cairo when I return, I'll jump a train into the security zone to Asyout and try to find him.

Finally, the supervisor nudges me from my inventory and hands me the receiver.

"Tell him why you are here," he says, and nods at the mouthpiece. "You may speak in English."

"Ullo? Yes," the voice says.

I ask the voice on the other end if it would be possible to talk to the archbishop. About the lessons of history. About the state of the human soul. Could he relay the message for me?

Silence.

I pray the person on the other end will relay my request.

"I am the archbishop," the voice replies.

We agree to meet in the morning after I've climbed the mountain.

Outside my room, a man slides out of the moon shadow.

Mohammed, a Bedouin in blue jeans, asks if I need a guide to climb the mountain in the morning.

I pause to consider. At dinner, the German pilgrims next to me at the communal table explained that you just follow the crowd. A novel idea, but I'm open to new experience and, so, reject his offer.

I'm tired out of my mind. Can't sleep. Mosquitoes fossick around the unhealed layers of bites I've collected over the past weeks: Aegean, Cairene, Nilotic, and now the Sinai. Every bone feels shattered. My spine is locked into a permanent knot from sleeping upright in planes, trains and buses, and resists my attempts to straighten it. I'm a damn sorry specimen.

Outside my window, in the haunting full moon of the summer solstice, looms Mount Moses, huge and ominous. Perhaps I was too hasty in rejecting the offer of a guide. I float in and out of consciousness, one weary eye tied to the alarm clock.

At 2:30 it's time to climb the path to the moon.

At the path's end lies sunrise.

climbing mount moses

At 2:30 the brain is idling in its deepest sleep cycle. To climb three hours up an unknown mountain's peak in the chill desert air is to pass in and out of reality. I step into the darkness not sure if I'm awake or dreaming. I'm sleepwalking into the surreal.

Mohammed, the Bedouin guide, is still there, sitting in the dark outside my room, waiting, more wise than I. We mumble good morning. Negotiate a price. And I seal the bargain by confidently walking off in the wrong direction.

Not far from the monastery, grotesque camels groan and twist their prehistoric moon-shadowed heads toward me, feeding my fantasies. Close by, taciturn camel drivers huddled around a campfire, their faces distorted by crackling flames, offer to rent me a ride, special price. I don't trust anything with legs longer than mine, and decline.

Mohammed and I pick our way among the confusion of pilgrims and start across the plain toward the cliff face. I muffle my jacket collar around my ears and bury my blue knuckles in the sleeves.

Disembodied faces and feet flicker in the flashlight, then disappear like lightning bugs. Voices float through the shadows.

"Dark side of the moon," a voice exclaims. Male voice. American. Hushed. Deep in wonderment.

"Huh?" his companion replies. Her face jumps out of the dark, her eyes fixed on the beam of flashlight that guides her feet along the cliff edge.

Mohammed and I skirt past the young American couple. We are now far enough ahead of them to slacken our pace, but their voices continue to trail us in the dark. The path curves back upon itself and, although we're a fair distance ahead, they're just feet below us.

"Look, we're on the dark side of the moon," the young man repeats to himself. His voice drifts up to us. We are ghosts listening in.

Mohammed and I rest in shadows as the full moon passes behind the peak of Gebel Musa, the Mountain of Moses. From this wild terrain, the known world seems bottomless, still to be invented. Yet here, where bare volcanic ranges thrust up along the great tectonic rift, law was given to mankind.

We stand at a symbolic point where light was divided from darkness, where laws were passed down to us to guide us in decisions of right and wrong, justice and injustice.

These laws distinguish us from animals, some say. But in this rush to the mountaintop we also celebrate our belonging to a Universal Herd. Hours from now, in the most primitive of moments, we will watch while day and night meet, touch fingers, exchange life, and return again, in their celestial wisdom. Tonight is the summer solstice. Earth is at her farthest point from the sun, and light prevails. Tonight, the water wheel groans into equilibrium. We are born and pushed forward.

"Yes," I reply quietly to the disembodied voice. "We're on the dark side of the moon."

I understand his awe. We've entered the liminal.

Like the moon, Mount Moses is one of those places we return to in our imagination and self-questioning. It is a reference point. An inner companion. Moses. The Burning Bush. The Ten Commandments. We have made it holy.

The guide sits on a rock beside me and smokes a cigarette while I catch my breath. Below us a trail of bobbing torches marks the thread of several hundred pilgrims from the monastery. They phosphoresce like the infinite curve of a midnight wave. In another two hours of climbing we should reach the peak, where together we'll wait for the dawn.

Mohammed lopes ahead. He's small and wiry and built like a mountain goat. He's twenty-six, he tells me, but looks fifteen.

The Bedouin of St. Catherine's hold themselves apart from other tribes of the region. They are fiercely proud of their ancestry as offspring of local tribal women and the soldiers Justinian sent from Rumania and Alexandria to guard the monastery. Recently they surprised a group of Rumanian tourists by embracing them as long-lost blood brothers.

The mountain is also holy to the Bedouin, as Mohammed will soon show me.

We scamper past knots of early pilgrims on this trail to the sky, weaving in and out of a repeated, breathless phrase: the wish of a good morning.

"Buon giorno."

"Sabah al-hayr."

"Guten Morgen."

"Hai."

"#@%)*."

"Günaydin."

"Good morning."

The altitude, the moonlight, and lack of perspective continue to play tricks.

A group of Brazilian women in high heels and short shorts totters up the chilly, twisting incline in front of us. I wonder if I'm hallucinating or if High-Heeled Mountain Climbing is a new division of the Olympics.

My heart is now being squeezed out of my ears and I'm light-headed. Range after range of stark, moon-tinted mountains lie behind us. I am now familiar enough with darkness to make out my feet, tufts of low-lying brush, individual rocks over which we leap in shortcut. The city lessons on walking slowly have fallen behind. The wildness of the desert mountains propels us both forward.

We are racing to the sky.

Higher up, a chill wind whips around each bend. I am drenched with freezing sweat. I offer my bottle of water to Mohammed between cuts of breath.

"No. No," he says and waves my offer aside. "Too much water makes you weak. That's why the Bedouin is strong. We drink little water."

Our Arabic, his and mine, is simple. We have no need to communicate high concepts. There will be no exams at the end of the day.

He explains that from childhood, Bedouin learn to live on the smallest amounts of water so they can survive in the desert. I think briefly about selective evolution as I gulp water and Mohammed lights another cigarette. To each his own poison.

"Tell me," I ask at another stop beneath the peak, "what do you think Egypt will look like in the future?"

Egypt is the Mother of Civilization. *Umm ad-Dunya,* as the Arabs call her. More than the Pyramids and the Nile, this land was the incubator for our faiths and beliefs. Once, she was the America of her known world. She was a scientific and cultural innovator, a political power to be reckoned with. At the end of my stay I'm still wondering how, having survived so long, she will continue to age and what she can teach us.

Mohammed and I rest against a boulder in relative silence for a few minutes while he considers my question. We're familiar with each other's rhythm by now—Mohammed smokes, I suck down water—and look out at the desert far below.

Around us, pilgrims are sliding off their camels for the final stretch on foot, three hundred stairs carved into the rocks that lead to the summit. They linger in clusters on the rocks and Bedouin rugs around two tacked-together concession huts and stare into nothingness. The camel's rhythm has lulled them into sleepfulness and now they struggle to rouse their energy for the final push to the mountaintop.

In each of the concession stands, a youth sells sodas, packaged cookies, hot tea and chocolate in the raking light of a single bare bulb fueled by a rattling generator. There is hushed quietness even in the transactions. We are all half-dreaming.

On another boulder, Bedouin kids drink cola and chew on factory-made cookies, the hearty breakfast of the desert young. They're gearing up for their trade in geodes, rocks they find in the mountains, crack open and sell to tourists as mementos. I wonder what Moses would say.

"Egypt?" Mohammed asks.

"Yes," I say. "In the future, what will she look like?"

He's quiet. He is giving it his full attention. I wait.

"Like Cairo," he says slowly. "She will be like Cairo. I went to Cairo once, for three days. I couldn't sleep. Too many people. Too many cars. *Beep. Beep.* All night. *Beep. Beep.*"

He pauses again.

"In the time to come," he says, "all the world will be like Cairo. Nobody will sleep."

We reach the peak well before sunrise, but we're not the first. Twenty or so Koreans have gathered on the tallest, wind-pounded rock outside a small stone chapel dedicated to Moses. A middle-aged man in a suit faces them and reads aloud in Korean, with decided passion, from a soft, leather-bound Bible. He reads, extends his hand and sweeps it across the mountain to the fading moon.

The only word I understand is "Moses." Moses. They are in thrall.

A few yards from the chapel another jerry-rigged kiosk brews hot tea and chocolate. Mohammed walks in and salutes the owner, a thin, local Bedouin in headdress and blue jeans. He waves aside the offer of tea, stretches out on a rough, wooden platform, pulls a coarse blanket over his head, and goes to sleep. I continue to explore.

A pack of young Australians in sleeping bags is camped out on a sheltered bluff behind the kiosk. Some have obviously not slept. They sit propped up against boulders, staring bleary-eyed into space with that euphoric "wow" look on their tanned, open faces. They are having their mountaintop experience; who can think of sleeping?

Two, on the other hand, are oblivious to the world, or to the fact that they have fallen asleep sitting on a narrow ledge of the mountain peak, cocooned in their sleeping bags. Their bodies lean toward oblivion, then nod and jerk back to stasis, like two giant chrysalides. A sudden breeze, a shout, a clap of the hands could set them afloat. I tiptoe around possible disaster.

Silence is broken by the arrival of the Universal Herd. Several tall, young Cairene men in tracksuits arrive yipping toward the head of the ascending pack, but after the Germans. They are robust and vitamin-supplemented, and loud. The Australian cocoons on the cliff edge begin to stir, nodding into the void.

"What do you mean, be quiet?" one Cairene shouts to another barely two feet away, who tries to shush him by indicating the sleeping campers. "They came here to watch the sun rise, not to sleep."

The kiosk is now doing a brisk predawn business in hot chocolate and blankets. Mohammed is dead to the world behind the counter. He has seen the sunrise on Mount Moses all his life.

On the bluff beneath us, a Greek Orthodox monk in dusty black robes emerges from a cave in the cliff side. The gathering Universal Herd leans forward to watch the morning antics of a live monk in captivity. Here is Religious Man in a zoo.

The monk ambles out onto a stone ledge that serves as a terrace and looks toward the horizon. His shoulders are stooped and his disheveled gray hair is pulled back into a lank, unwashed ponytail. He is going bald on top. He stretches and scratches, and only then looks up at the assembled crowd above him. He frowns.

The two Australian chrysalides have woken, unzipped their sleeping bags. Their tousled heads nod toward him.

The monk's assistant, a young man in jeans, crouches and brews tea over a butagas stove while the elder visits the chapel.

During his absence, the Universal Herd continues to gather. Danish pilgrims compare camera equipment with an American who has set up his tripod into the pending sunrise. Muslim Indonesians. Catholic Italians. A quiet family of Jewish Turks arrives in dribbles and finds a perch among the French and Israelis who have staked out a vantage point. The Brazilian Olympic high-heeled, mountain-climbing team finally arrives with self-fanfare and begins to ooh and aah. The Cairenes start flirting with the Brazilians. The Koreans are now reciting prayers.

The monk returns to his ledge and turns his attention to the crowd above him. He shakes a fist at a young man who has climbed over the iron railing that guards the chapel, and at another who has let a candy wrapper fall into his sanctuary. The transgressors apologize like good convent children and we all hang our heads in shame.

The hermit now turns his back to the Herd, pulls up a wooden stool, and watches the sun begin its ascent over the mountains. In one hand is a glass of hot tea. In the other, a cassette player is raised to his ear like a longtime bettor at the racetrack. He's listening to a Byzantine chant on tape. For him, we no longer exist. He's lost in his own Communion.

I stand on my toes and lean forward, trying to separate myself from the crowd. For the first time on my journey I feel that I am among strangers. Real strangers. I'm not at home with these people who look away from my eyes, not into them. A cold finger runs along my breastbone and I clench with rebellion.

No! I almost shout down into the valley. No! I don't want to go home. I don't want to be one of these people.

And a small voice says: But you are one.

I close my eyes to bite back the tears.

My time has come to rejoin the Universal Herd. To return to my family. To seek my circles of belonging. To find peace.

On the cliff beside me a ripple of excitement and camaraderie brushes our skin. The sky is changing face.

I meet the eyes of strangers. We laugh, nervously at first.

A hand is extended. A back is touched lightly. Friends and strangers embrace each other.

The Universal Herd. We've made it this far together. The Ten Commandments, Moses, the laws of humanity were set in stone here. We have all disobeyed them, but for an instant we are all believers. It is a universal moment. God knows, it is a moment for celebration.

Something unseen is pulling us together.

We are here, everyone is saying.

We did it.

We are here.

Together.

The mountain ranges blossom in front of us like a faint, Japanese ink painting, each layer more existential than the last. The Australians stretch out their tanned legs by leaping from rock to rock to take variations of group photos, one of thousands they will take home. The Koreans are singing hymns, tears rolling down their cheeks. The Brits stare with their mouths wide open.

In the center of the Herd one of the young Egyptians elbows aside a French couple to pose with the red sun rising behind him, just so, in the palm of his hand. He has seen this pose in a wall painting of a Pharaoh's tomb and wants himself similarly immortalized as a young god, ruler of the universe.

The sun forms herself before our eyes, drawing beauty as she gives it. She draws it. Grows larger. And draws beauty again.

The Egyptian youth then leaps onto a rock and flaps his wings like a giant bird. The sun rests, a golden egg, beneath him. His face is in shadow, but ours are lit gold.

The faces of the two Turkish children glow and I catch my breath. They are Lena. The tea boy. But they're not.

I look once more toward the golden egg, the sun, its reflection that lights us.

The Fire Bird. The Phoenix.

And then I see.

We are the Golden Egg. We are the circle of flawed but good-hearted people who, each day, will the Fire Bird, her peace and blessing, into life. We are the Fire Bird.

The Fire Bird continues her ascent and we stare at her until we are blinded.

Moon has been absorbed by sun. Our planet again responds to the Fire Bird's song. Light and dark continue their ageless dance.

The spell is broken and the Universal Herd begins to prepare for its descent to earth.

The Indonesian university students hug each other while the Koreans sway back and forth and sing another round of hymns. The English retirees apply sunblock, taking special care around their socks and sandals. The Danes meanwhile light up some hashish and are inhaling with their eyes closed.

A few souls linger in the hush.

I rouse Mohammed. We drink a final glass of hot tea while he smokes a morning cigarette and wait for the return of silence before we head down the mountain to the monastery. My appointment with the archbishop is in less than two hours.

I am elated, energetic, and alive. Mohammed senses a race.

As we set off, a competition ensues between the monk and the Bedouin boys. The kiosk boys turn their tape players on high and play sonorous verses from the Qur'an. They are claiming the air for Allah. Beneath us, on the ledge, the monk has cranked up the tinny volume of his cassette player until the voices vibrate with incomprehension. He raises the machine and its Byzantine hymns to the sky. For each, the sun has risen.

We travel landward by another route, passing through a tight, fantastic gorge. The sounds of competing religions above us have faded, but before us hundreds of small pyramids of stacked rocks balance on stark boulders like pagan sacrifices. Or primitive boundary markers. Fluttering from scores of these shrines are small, sun-bleached Israeli flags. Swatches of blue-and-white peek from between the field of cairns.

I pause. The weight of politics has brought me down to earth. I'm trying to hold on to the moment on top of the mountain and I stretch my hand back toward it.

Mohammed shrugs his shoulders at the sight of the flags, and pushes forward on his own mission. I linger another second, then follow.

"Here," Mohammed, says and suddenly stops.

He's quiet and serious.

I'm puzzled.

We've halted our airborne descent on a rather nondescript boulder. Below us, the Sinai stretches toward the unknowable.

"Here," Mohammed says.

He crouches, pointing at a bowl-shaped indentation in the rock, not much larger than his fist. This is the footprint of the Prophet Saleh's camel, he informs me. Here, before us in the rock.

Saleh is the protective saint of the Bedouin.

"This is where his camel flew with him into heaven," Mohammed whispers.

I kneel beside him on the rock.

"*This.*"

He points to the imprint in the rock.

"*This.* Not that." With his eyes he indicates the valley of Israeli flags, the mountaintop with the Christian monk, the sound of the Qur'an. "*This* is why the mountain is holy."

CHAPTER 22

Desert in the Heart

His Eminence Archbishop Damianos dominates the rowdy corner of a small second-story room of Saint Catherine's like a favorite uncle at a family reunion. His gray-plush beard frames a face from which all angles have been worn smooth. Regardless of the form, the nature of stone remains stone, his eyes say as he takes me in from behind his tinted glasses. We have entered one of those conversations without words.

I am still radiating from the five-hour hike of Mount Moses and the three mugs of strong black coffee upon rapid descent. My interview finery remains rolled up in my satchel and I wear instead an African-print sarong, a white T-shirt under a denim shirt, and sand shoes. I have decided ahead of time that this man will not be impressed by appearances.

In the West we refer to Damianos as a Father of the Desert, one of a long line of venerable Christian mystics of the Greek Orthodox Church and Eastern Rite. The local Bedouin have another name for him. Grandfather. Wise and Holy Man. They come to him to mediate their disputes and arguments. His word is final.

Sunday morning mass has just finished and the archbishop is surrounded by a dozen or so priests and hearty souls, European men and women, young and old, the parishioners of the desert enclave. They're eating frozen ice-cream cake trucked in from civilization and downing thimbles of brandy. We could be in suburban Athens, not the far reaches of the Sinai, except that here in the back of beyond there is a hunger for the sound of human voice.

I've seen this hunger in the faces of Peace Corps volunteers from the early days who were sent off to a foreign land without a partner. Alone, on their first assignments in a foreign culture, separated from the sound of their own voice, not yet able to communicate in the local tongue, their senses were bombarded by new smells, images, and noises that they couldn't organize according to words and sounds that once gave meaning. Run-Spot-Run became gibberish, hummed to yourself at night to ward off mosquitoes and loneliness. With useless tongues, infantalized to fools, who was helping whom, they asked. Many turned inside out.

I wonder if the animals in Eden knew who they were until they heard their names spoken by Adam. I am a gazelle, one would say, or a fox, and become conscious of its gazelleness and the other's foxiness. I am a woman, Yvonne, I would say, born in the faraway land of Australia. Wherever I travel, people rename me, modifying my birth name into one that has meaning for them and their context. Eve, Havva, First Woman, Universal Mother, Ivana. Would I know who I was if nobody named me?

At Saint Catherine's everyone is talking at once in Greek, not a conversation so much as an exchange of self-confirming words. They are squeezing words out of each other with their eyes. Some are expressing themselves by swapping gossip. Others by getting details. Archbishop Damianos is talking with all of them, all at once.

Damianos navigates the room without moving from his core of peace. He lipreads one conversation while his ears take in another in the far corner and his mouth responds to yet another beside him. I watch his quick touch as he answers questions from his parishioners and priests with a cluck of the tongue, a grin, an opening of the palms that says, "Let's be reasonable, shall we?"

I wait for the parishioners to leave. Curtains levitate, cloth wings pushed upward by the hot desert wind. The plastic table-cloth slaps against the tape recorder and I pin it down with empty coffee cups. The last of the morning cool has burned off and I'm thankful for any movement of air. Hell will come with the midafternoon stillness. Outside, the stone columns and colon-nades of the monastery declare man's whimsical attempt to civi-lize God's mountain and I glimpse them as curtains rise and fall on a painted stage.

Beside the archbishop, a weathered, sun-dried old priest eats his melting cake and drains a liqueur glass. He could be fifty, he could be five score and ten. He has stood silent, a statue in the desert, for an unknowable age, only his eyes moving, submitting his flesh to the loss of time and sin.

I wonder the reason for his penance. A few of the monks here are supposed to be bad boys, the incorrigible, the priests gone astray from the Greek Orthodox Church, the wanderers into false doctrine. These are the ones that even Mount Athos has given up on. A stint in the desert is sure to straighten them out. Many are acknowledged mystics.

The old priest looks away quickly as his eyes begin to burn into me. Everyone in the room has those eyes. It has to do with searching for the invisible on the horizon. It has to do with the silence.

I sip Arabic coffee and contemplate the many shades of black as I wait my turn. This morning I climbed the mountain and wit-nessed the point of darkness where night meets day and begins to recede. That is one shade of black. There is also the translucent black of the spangled veils worn by the Bedouin women on the bus, a black that displays more than it conceals. And the sun-bleached black of the ancient's robe before me, faded to a wan brown and worn thin.

In front of me hovers the outline of darkness in the face of a ponytailed priest, who stands, arms crossed, rocking back and forth. His beard is edged to the severity of a knife blade against his skin, and he wears his leather-belted, black robe as if spliced into it. His eyes are so dark and deep-set, they appear crossed. I am uncomfortable under their unmoving pinpoint until I realize that in his eyes I don't exist. He stares into and beyond me.

Another young priest strides into the small room and heads bungee away from, then toward, this force of energy. He's irritated not with the dust that streaks the dark fabric that flaps all around him, but that he has to wear garments, any garment, at all. He is clearly flying.

And there is also a certain blackness that lies against pale flesh and seems to draw life from it. This is the color of the hooded robes of the extenuated Texan who sits next to me, to the right of Archbishop Damianos. His long, transparent hands, which only Munch could have painted, fold themselves within the deep black sleeves and disappear. His voice comes soft and slow from behind a scraggly brown beard. He is the translator who adds structure to the archbishop's wandering English.

The young American priest appears almost alien, from another planet. I realize that is exactly where we are. A space colony in a moonscape, scoured of vegetation and human life, isolated from the rush of the planet. We are as far away, as removed as we can be, without leaving Earth. From here, the perspective is truly unique. This is the ultimate retreat.

Archbishop Damianos is from a line of holy men who contemplate the soul of the planet. For what seems like eternity, they have gazed at the ancient stars to find the face of God. Now satellites crisscross their perfect night sky. Today's monks continue in the study of dusty texts and in meditation of the otherworldly landscape, where Moses received the Ten Commandments, our moral guidebook. I half-covet their lack of distractions. No television or computers. Only one telephone in the whole joint. Or so it seemed last night when I tried to reach the archbishop.

Now that I am sitting opposite the Holy Father of the Desert,

I'm thinking how unreal it all seems, how divorced these men are from the realities of the outside world, eating ice-cream cake behind high walls while only feet away the Universal Herd swarms around them. German tourists, the Brazilian Olympic high-heeled-hiking team in short shorts, the Koreans, Australians, Brits who have come from around the planet to climb Mount Moses, check out the icons, have a religious experience. Behind the stone walls of the fortress, however, these men are isolated from the wars, poverty, violence, even daily stresses. They have retreated from the mess.

In so doing perhaps they have traded one bloody hardship post for another. Isolation is not always a pretty picture. Most of us don't deal with it comfortably. We may dream about The Big Alone— that self-fulfilling journey. But honestly, would you want to wake up to this every morning? To all this . . . space?

The archbishop seems to have read my mind.

He smiles.

"The desert belongs to God and we are here for the love of God," he says. "This isolation is by love."

"What do you do with all your aloneness?" I ask him.

He laughs. He makes the transition in conversation from his remaining parishioners. After our informal introduction on the phone last night, he dismisses the need for formality now.

"I am busy answering questions from visitors," he says, "with little time to enjoy it. I have solitude, but not time."

The modern lament reaches to the monastery.

"This isolation . . . ," he says.

I lean forward. The wind has sucked his words out of the room and I'm trying to catch them.

"You know," he says, "we can also make a desert in the heart."

He has my attention.

"A desert in the heart?" I ask, making sure I heard him correctly, trying to understand why anyone would want to create a desolate, barren void within her. I think of the noise and pressures of modern life. Of the noise and lack of sleep that Mohammed the Bedouin guide referred to.

A vast wasteland? Or time and space to hear the wee, small voice of God?

Space becomes the common ground for opposing perspectives. Space.

As I gaze out at the moonscape of the desert mountains, I'm thinking about space. Not the space that we all need, but out there, that dark canvas, the Universe, against which we project our thoughts. Deep, outer space.

Archbishop Damianos seems game for anything. I ask him about space, as I had Patriarch Zakka in Damascus.

"I wonder," I say, "out here, under the night skies, do you think about life in space?"

He laughs and resettles his glasses on his nose. He's delighted. Finally, a question he hasn't been asked before. He repeats it in Greek for the priests who remain in the room.

"Perhaps," he says and shrugs. "Perhaps there is. You know, it is God who makes creation. Therefore if we are very close to God, we can have knowledge as in Paradise. We can solve all things. However, we will know everything only after our death or after the Second Coming."

The others in the room lean forward, and a rumble of amens signals approval. The sun-dried old priest tops up his brandy.

"We should not be surprised if God keeps surprises for us," he continues. "Why not? Everything is possible, including these new galaxies."

Why not?

He shrugs again and explains what he considers obvious. As with the unexpected response of the Grand Sheikh of Islam toward cloning, I am surprised. Where are those hellfire and brimstone lectures I'm accustomed to in the United States, the ones that shout that Man is the center of the Universe? That equate aliens with Armageddon? I'm feeling cheated.

"Why should God not give some of the good elements to others?" Damianos says. By "others" he means aliens, and not those guys south of the border. He gives me one of those granddad smiles that says I know you're hoarding the candy God gave you. Your hands are full as it is—why would you want more knowledge? And what would you do with it?

"Our knowledge here is so small, so small," he says. "I think that we exist as a small atom, with small knowledge."

Because of their majestic isolation, bounded by stark nature, the monks also have a unique perspective of the planet. Life on the margin allows them to pull back and to think in longer, broader terms.

"Is this what history teaches us?" I ask. "Our small knowledge?"

"Throughout history," he replies, "dogma has been mistaken for knowledge."

Throughout history there have been fights between Eastern and Western Christianity—between Occidental and Oriental, between Catholicism and Protestantism. Over dogma.

"Even today, we are born into the Catholic Church or the Protestant Church," Damianos points out, "the Anglican Church, or the Orthodox Church. So there will be always religious points of difference between Christians. It is really a very sensitive issue, but we still have a good chance. Through love in Christ."

"How so?" I ask.

"You believe," he says, "like the Orthodox, that you have a theoretical basis and you accept it. But it is has to be more than theory. Teaching is all right, but it must also be practical. Practice. On its own, teaching is nothing. We don't accept this."

"And the Ten Commandments," I ask. "In practice, the laws of Moses, are the ancient teachings still relevant?"

"The Commandments were excellent guides," he says, "but not enough."

He leans forward and pulls my idle notepad toward him.

"Here," he says.

He draws a circle. It is the circle of the Coptic Bishop of Youth and Adel Beshai. Of Assad Ali. The circle of Lena's Fire Bird and the golden egg of good-hearted people.

I look up quickly. My circle has come full turn.

He places an X in the middle of the rough circle.

"Here," he says. "Christ is at the center."

He taps the pen to the circle again.

"I start from here," he says. "I may believe I have the most straight theoretical way to the center, but if I remain on the periphery, it is nothing. I must move closer to the center."

"What if our beliefs differ?" I ask him. "What if you are not Christian?"

"Yes," he says and taps another spot on the circle. "Then you are at another point. But maybe we have some zigzagging with our beliefs."

Zigzagging? Although Archbishop Damianos is speaking in English, his Texan translator is befuddled at how to translate his English into English. This becomes a joint effort.

"That our beliefs may overlap or even intersect?" I ask him.

"Yes," he replies, surprised that we didn't get it the first time. "But if we stay on the periphery, and don't try, we can't have any form of union. We cannot touch."

He explains that each person, according to his or her own religion or religious belief, should move as close to the center as possible. The center is the world of the spirit.

As you move toward the center, he instructs, you experience the spiritual life. Book-learning and theory are not enough. Commandments and laws are helpful, sure. But the paradox of the spiritual life, is that range precedes depth.

"It is enough for the heart to have a full perspective," he says. "A spiritual perspective. Spiritual experience will be rewarded in Paradise."

"And on earth?" I ask.

Without a spiritual life, you cannot build a moral society, the archbishop believes.

"If you don't believe in spirituality, there is only materialism," he says. "Everyone is under the pressure of materialism. What is materialism? It is nothing. After everything is finished, what have you?"

"Nothing," I say.

He shrugs.

"Nothing."

"There are spiritual leaders," I say, "even secular leaders, who pursue wealth and material pleasure."

He returns my grin with a roar of a laugh.

"I can say some, not many," he says and raises an eyebrow. "Some leaders, etcetera, they teach but they don't believe strong."

Christianity, now a minority within the Middle East, is decreasing proportionately in the world. And, although the Greek Orthodox Church is one of the largest of the Eastern line, Orthodoxy is a minority within even the Christian world. I ask the archbishop how the Greek Orthodox Church defines its identity under these pressures to survive and what beliefs keep them going.

"We believe our mission for all the world is not to increase the number of Orthodox in the world," he says, "but to provide a good example for all people. By praying more, by being more mystical, more spiritual. That is the meaning of Orthodox."

The Greek Orthodox, he explains, never proselytize.

"If I live by example," he says, "it remains for the soul of the individual to accept heaven, the light, the way of the *correct* Christianity."

Ooo, la la! The *correct* Christianity?

"Is there such a thing as a *correct* Christianity?" I ask.

"Well," he says, a grin spreading across his face. He is unabashed in his bias. "The Orthodox is not the more correct Christianity, in reality. But, in theory, we believe, it is true."

I can tell that alone, at night, under the perfection of the desert sky, the archbishop has grappled with the Catholic view of the world. He suggests that all churches are mixed in their doctrine, but that the faults of the Catholic Church have risen out of syncretism. They have added local beliefs to their original belief system. Again, they became caught up in dogma.

He refers specifically to the Catholic imperative to increase the size of the Church through birthrate and conversion. At first this policy was a consideration even for the Orthodox Church.

"But then," he says, "for us, a deeper spiritual life is better than numbers."

He leans forward. I move closer. So does the Texas brother, his translator, who smiles with affectionate familiarity at where his elder's conversation is about to take us. We could be sitting over coffee in some Aegean village. The archbishop opens his eyes wide as if to share new details of a well-known scandal.

"The pope," he says, in half-whisper, "the pope saw the millennium more as a political relation, a very good occasion for Rome. More as public relations for the Church."

Archbishop Damianos waves his hands in dramatic exaggeration.

"There are 800 million Catholics," he says. "We make 900 million now."

I'm stunned. His irreverence? His attempt at a Polish accent? His feigned disbelief? He speaks without malice, as your uncle would, regaling you with the latest fool scheme your dad's caught up in.

I try not to laugh. Brother Texas enjoys the wake of a passing grin.

"No. We don't agree with that now," the archbishop concludes, straightening his face and wagging a finger at his unseen colleague. "He makes the best of it, of course. But for us, the best is not to make a census of countries."

He becomes serious and the good-natured ribbing stops. There is also the delicate matter of politics.

"We are obliged, of course, sometimes to make a little politics by discretion," he says. "Such still is necessary to facilitate spiritual matters."

This appears the crux of his difference with his colleague in Rome.

"Religious matters are not to become an instrument for the political or economic," he says. "It is the opposite."

Social divisions, and social problems such as drug abuse, poverty and AIDS can be traced to the entanglement of dogma in our modern life, he explains.

"Social problems are also theological problems," he says.

"Destruction of the environment?" I ask. "Is this a theological problem?"

"It is a symptom of the chaos in which we now live," he says. "We naturally suffer from our own actions. For example, atomic energy is common now. Nuclear warheads can be made from it. All right, this is dangerous. Even the testing of these weapons leaves nuclear particles in the atmosphere. We must stop it."

The archbishop believes that we now have the ability to destroy the earth more than any other time in history, that the Second Coming will be a result of our mistakes involving technology—not of technology alone, but of technology without spirituality.

"God gives us liberty," he says. "But because we claim to be God, then we make ourselves into Holy Men."

If scientists are not men with spirituality, he warns, then the present advances in science are dangerous. Whatever benefits humanity, we should keep. If a particular technology has the potential for catastrophe in human life, however, then we must stop it.

"To control life," he says, "to have, for example, men like copies. Like cloning. Okay, we know we can do this, but we also know this is not okay. Then we should give glory to God for what we have discovered, then stop it."

He emphasizes that what we think we create or invent, we only discover. That is, it already existed in God's knowledge. I'm pondering the Syrian discussion about Atlantis but can't find a break in which to wedge the topic.

"We believe that what we discover is a miracle," he is saying. "That it has come out of our own hat. We make ourselves into gods. We make ourselves divine through our own efforts, not through the spirit."

Throughout our conversation, Damianos has fielded brief questions from his priests, kissed good-bye to several parishioners and taken a short phone call. The room is almost empty. Bearded heads pop around the door with increased frequency. He signals to them to be patient.

An attendant stands beside him and shifts back and forth. I finally understand that they are waiting for him. Prayers, perhaps? Our runaway conversation is being corralled.

I look at him for confirmation. The archbishop nods his head and shrugs his shoulders at the same time. Yes, he regrets our time has come to an end, but what can he do? he says in body language, and begins to rise.

"I am their servant," he says.

I continue to ask him questions as I reluctantly begin to stand.

"Your Eminence," I ask, skewing toward formality. "What message would you give to other spiritual leaders?" I've told him about the people I've already spoken with, and those I hope to see.

Ah?

He readjusts his glasses and sits again. We all sit.

"Egoism. Spiritual leaders today suffer from egoism," he says bluntly.

"We act from our heads," he says, "not our hearts."

I burrow farther into my chair and he narrows his eyes.

"Our hearts are the chairs for our spirit," he says. "Our heads are the chairs for the ego."

He is referring to the issue he raised earlier. The value of spiritual experience.

Like his colleague the Sheikh of Islam, the archbishop also advocates cooperation and the need for understanding. He points to the circle he has drawn on my notepad and to the need for us all to move toward the center from wherever we are on or within that circle.

"We are all creations," he says, "and we are all a point of creation. The Orthodox follows, but in a different way."

"And the Christian Church?" I ask.

"Christianity has lost its spirituality," he says and points to the center of the circle. "We need to return to spirituality."

He adds, almost wistfully, that because the leadership of the Church has lost its spirituality, its members "divinize themselves without knowing Christ." Knowledge without spiritual understanding or leadership is dangerous.

"And history?" I ask. "What does it teach us?"

"If we are looking to the past to find truth," he says, "we are not going to find it."

Truth, like faith, has been changed over the centuries by the minds of men.

"Christians," he says, "have given truth a mentality until they invent things."

Truth has become buried in dogma. The head not the heart now rules society and religion. The chair now sits on the sitter.

I leave the holy men to their prayers and obligations. They are out the door before I reach the courtyard.

"What a life," I'm thinking as I round the final protected corner of the monastery and step through the gate into the bare, dusty world. "Peace and quiet. And the still, small voice of God."

The silence is broken.

Unbridled laughter rolls from beneath a huge eucalyptus tree outside the monastery. The archbishop and his men are hitching up their robes and climbing into the cabins and backs of several pickup trucks parked in the shade. Black robes flapping, holding tightly onto their tall headdresses, the Men in Black head off for a yahooing joyride in the desert. This is what they've been waiting for.

After all, they're only human.

CHAPTER 23

Letter from the Future

The two o'clock train snakes as slowly as possible out of Cairo and follows the muddy Nile south toward Asyout. Fourteen years ago I traveled this same track, tracing the steps of a turn-of-the century archaeologist. On that journey an old wise man, Bishop Nuweiba, the Catholic Coptic Bishop of Upper Egypt, ended up as my seat companion and exacted the promise that I would return.

Return to Egypt, he said, and you will see the future. It's time to bring my Egypt trip full circle. Time to fulfill my oath to the bishop. This is my last chance. My flight out of Egypt is tomorrow night.

Fourteen years ago. That's twice times seven, the width of two childhoods. Fourteen is the entry into adolescence, into the adventure and uncertainty of youth. The number seems symbolic somehow. The Egypt I last visited was the land of an old and dying man whose memory I'm still chasing. The Egypt I returned to is characterized by youth. It has the smell of optimism, and aftershave, about it.

The Thursday afternoon (that is, the weekend) special train to the south is fresh and clean, and air-conditioned, unlike the sweltering bone-shaker I had taken in the mid-eighties. The first-class car is sold out. Second-class is crowded with the New Egyptian, predominantly male, all young—engineers, sales managers, bank clerks, college students—returning to their villages, their hometowns, for long weekends.

A twenty-something Egyptian male throws himself into the vacant aisle seat beside me. He scuffles around in his blue canvas briefcase, shuffling computer-generated pie charts within eyesight. I sense he's trying to impress me. His letterhead indicates he's a district rep for Coca-Cola. I'm disappointed. I want to talk to a wise elder in long robes, not a young Pharaoh with a pager attached to the waist of his jeans.

For a few seconds while we settle in, our eyes are inches apart. His are like steaming, black coffee. Lots of sugar. I find myself unexpectedly stirred. I watch the flutter of his lashes, as his eyes quickly brush over my face and return to my own unswerving ones. We arm wrestle with eye contact for a few seconds. In the past weeks I've become so used to people looking within my eyes that lowering them now seems like an artifice.

I sink farther into my seat, burrowing into the small desert I'm tending in my heart. The skin burns taut around my eyes. Every inner corner is tender from the external exhaustion of an internal journey. But it's not just the unceasing heat and fatigue that's getting to me, nor the overdoses of strong tea and sugar I've been living on. The voices of my Egyptian friends pester me and their tension has infected me. What on earth am I trying to prove by racing into the military security zone of Asyout, they tried to persuade me before I left. A foreign woman traveling alone into an area of political unrest? In hindsight, with the massacre of tourists by religious extremists that same month in Luxor, I now acknowledge their concern. Reluctantly.

This final journey is more than residual strong-headedness on my part. Like a student before final exams, I'm leaving the most important assignment until the last minute. I have twenty-four hours to get back to Cairo for my flight. Twenty-four hours to get in and out of Asyout's security zone before the local authorities become curious. Who am I fooling? There's no way I can blend in. Besides, with the places I've been digging around lately, I'm sure my movements are being tagged. He could even be the little charmer whose hip rests beside mine.

My neighbor and I nod briefly, calling it a stalemate. We turn our backs on each other like an old married couple and set about trying to ignore each other for the next six hours while knowing that we'll end up talking.

I settle in to the hypnotic pulse of the train and reassure myself of my invulnerability by watching the world from my dusty window.

On the ragged outskirts of Cairo, we slide into the last station before taking off into the desert. Young children are flying colorful, wild-tailed kites from crowded tenement buildings that spill over onto the track. Within a few meters of the air-conditioned carriage, a child, with the brown stick legs of a praying mantis, crouches on a crumbling cement wall. He seems oblivious to the train as it slowly grinds past him and to the litter and debris that surrounds him. He has lost himself in the kite that flutters free above him. He pulls the string toward him and embroiders the sky with fantastic figures.

He holds tightly to the wings. He sways as it sways, flies and soars on the other end of the line, forgetting that he holds this fanciful imagining in his hand, that it is he who stands, bare feet planted on earth, who controls the flight, not the reverse. No less wise than the ancient mystics, he has discovered the miracle of flight and it takes him to currents above the airless, packed city.

Computers, Internet, television, these are the kites of today's young elite and middle-class Egyptians. They are the dream machines to which they hold tightly to lift themselves above the reality around them. Since arriving here, I have been forced to think much about this new culture that has become the face of Egypt. By forfeit, with its high birthrate and reduced infant mortality, the land of the ancients is rapidly becoming the land of the adolescent, brimming with expectations and energy.

Like the boy with his kite, Egypt balances on an uncertain wall of tradition that threatens to collapse under the impact of American culture. Some Egyptians believe that the restraints of tradition prevent them from flying. Others, on the contrary, that tradition offers them a safe mooring from which to explore a new world. Icarus never had so many decisions.

In Cairo, globalized youth culture has already made itself felt, and you don't have to venture far from your package tour to find it. Western rock music, or local versions of it, seems as prevalent now in the streets as the sound of the call to prayer. McDonald's has surpassed falafel as the food of choice, just as Coca-Cola outpaces fresh-pressed orange juice. Students are increasingly accessing the Qur'an on computer, *Baywatch* by satellite television, and the ideas of the world by Internet.

In returning to the land of the past, I had not expected to be blatantly challenged by this modern culture. I was less prepared for the open attitude of the wise people I was led to both in Egypt and Syria. For the "Why not?" that met my questions. Perhaps it was a conspiracy, after all. But then it was a conspiracy of good people.

If this is the future, it is strangely familiar, yet foreign. And oddly jarring. Like tricks of memory, the worlds of the old and the new, reality and fantasy, which are not mutually exclusive, have begun to fold back on themselves. I am no longer teacher but student, past and present have melted into one.

I remember how, after not seeing one of my sisters for many years, she had met me at the airport in Sydney. We hadn't seen each other in so long, I barely recognized her. We had both grown taller, wider, more creased. Beside her were two young children, my niece and nephew, a redheaded, freckled pair of hellions who looked much as we had at that age. Instinctively I reached for them before I did my sister. They were part of a past with which I was familiar. They were recognizable, and as trusting and innocent as anyone in our bloodline could be. My adult sister and I were the strangers. Her children became the familiar bridge to the past.

In my Nile train to the south, I also am moving between two worlds. Bishop Nuweiba promised me insight into the future if I promised to return here. I sense his presence and that he is taking me from the safety of the past to a place from which I cannot return. The future is now the present, and simply by returning here—or continuing to live—I have become part of that future of which he hinted. That was the conundrum he had presented to me in his challenge. Stay alive, and the future becomes today.

The enigma of the river that Heraclitus posed has a second stage. He had believed that transition was the only possible real state, that permanence was an illusion. Both Egypt and I have continued to move forward but, like true love in Marvell's poem, I can't yet decide if we are parallel lines, or if we intersect. In their own way, Adel Beshai, Bishop Musa, the caretaker at Ibn al-Arabi's tomb, Archbishop Damianos and Assad Ali have all told me this.

By staying alive, by promising the wise old man not to self-destruct, I have lived to see the future. Now. This today. The hope of a future kept me from sliding into the darkness of the Turkish fire. His challenging eyes that had peered over the cliff at death, that promise extracted, put an unexpected face on that hope. The will to live.

I close my eyes and remind myself to breathe. And I am soon rocked into sleep.

At Beni-Suweyf, a village stop south of weary Cairo, I wake somewhat refreshed and begin to wonder why the countryside appears greener, more lush and alive than on my first journey here. For sure, white cranes still stride with cocky assurance between *fellahin* who still till the rows of dark alluvial. A slow smile wanders across my face as I record the images in my mind as if I were a video camera.

Young women still flutter in their vivid neons of midsummer, the oranges, purples, and pinks that rival the loud-mouthed jacaranda trees. As before, matrons are swathed in long black gowns, their severity mocked by lace scarves and breezy veils.

Naked, slick-skinned young boys still throw themselves into the gushing irrigation canals, after pulling off their cotton gallabiyas over their heads in unself-conscious eagerness.

As the train continues south, we pass precise, divided fields, each the size, I estimate, of twenty slow paces. Each is dressed by mounds of black fertile soil to capture the regulated inundation of the Nile canal as it gushes around the stalks of cotton and stalwart corn. Okra waits to be picked in the morning when it is the tender size of a thumbnail. Ground vetch puts on a sensuous display for the water buffalo and donkeys. Bananas and dusty mangoes soak up the last rays before they are carried off to the juice stands of Cairo.

For a moment I am carried back to the vast sugarcane fields of Queensland and the days of my own childhood. I can almost smell the damp earth, the rush of ozone before a storm.

The train carries me through an airbrushed postcard world and, contrary to my academic training, I am delighted. My heart is leading my head for a change. For all its skill at conjuring up the past, however, I finally have to admit that this is not the fabled land where time stands still. Even in the villages, youth races against time and tradition. I reluctantly turn my attention to the hum of activity inside the train and discover I'm part of a delicate slice of life being carried forward into the future.

Many of the young professionals in the carriage are only a generation or a decade away from the farmers in the fields, the shopkeepers in the bustling marketplaces, the women scrubbing clothes in the agricultural ditches. In the streets of their hometowns, their proud parents still wear the traditional long gowns, the gallabiya, which the young men will slip into after shedding their Bart Simpson T-shirts and ready-to-wear suits at the front door. They, too, presently journey between two worlds.

For the first few hours we have all snored in shared and open-mouthed exhaustion, a sound broken only by the hawkers who board the train at each station to ply their wares: cold juice, chunks of raw sugar, verses from the Qur'an, plastic bags of combs and needles, thread and mirrors, fresh flat bread, cookies, eggs hard-boiled to a life-threatening shade of purple, and falafel sandwiches. The delicacies fail to rouse the weary and we shoo the sellers away like bothersome flies.

Awake now, I check for any eyes that linger too long on me. Security police, potential terrorists, men looking for a marriageable Green Card; it's easy to let one's imagination run wild.

The guy next to me has also stirred. He is not the first I have met since beginning today's journey down the Nile. An intense young college graduate who sat himself next to me at the train station in Cairo tried to convince me that there was still something I could do to save a small part of the universe. He offered a romantic sail down the Nile on a *faluka*, an Egyptian sailboat, in return for marriage and a Green Card. Not a bad deal, but I am way past the concept of marriage as an act of charity.

I promised to distribute his phone number at every chance, however. For any women interested in helping an articulate and ambitious young Egyptian, I still have it on a crumpled piece of paper. Or better yet, go sit on the bench outside the ticket office on Platform 5 of Cairo Railroad Station, and wait. You won't be disappointed, or alone, for long.

The nap has taken the edge off my exhaustion and I'm feeling more amenable to speaking with my neighbor. After sharing the same sleeping and breathing space for several hours on the train, conversation seems the only polite thing to do. He is as much humored by my bastardized Arabic as I am by his broken English. The universal urge to communicate overcomes our inadequacies.

His name, Gamal, appropriately means Beautiful. His last name is Muslim and his business card is as bilingual as his youthful dream, to migrate to America. Land of sex, CNN and computer software.

I study his eager young face as he talks, and he smiles as if my eyes hide a movie camera. He has the softened profile of a well-nurtured and well-loved Egyptian son and, as he speaks, he turns it for me to record. You know his mother adores him and that his father loves him beyond life. And you know that when he has his own children, they too will be as cared for, and as loved as he. His brown eyes are alive with intelligence and questions, so many questions, and I am a willing audience. A generation ago, his warm, young face would have been marred by brown, diseased teeth. His are perfect, a monument to Egypt's improved health care system.

When this young champion begins to speak of market share and spreadsheets, however, I lose myself in the pomegranate sunset. With each minute I'm aware of edging closer to my promised rendezvous with the old bishop. In anticipation, I ride off on my imaginary donkey through the palm groves to some mythical place where computers, cell phones, and fax machines cannot reach me. This conversation is the last I would have expected, or wanted, to have in the outback of Egypt. Again, I check myself. I have come seeking the future in Egypt, and upon meeting it, still seek refuge in the past. Perhaps that's what we all do.

The train finally approaches Asyout, our destination, and the tea seller rattles through the carriage one last time, just as he had fourteen years ago. We have arrived at that crook in the soft, brown elbow of the Nile. The passengers have roused themselves. Some are playing a version of gin rummy. A few have exchanged business cards but nobody seems to be networking. That has all been left behind in the city. Here, everyone knows everyone else.

My own limited history has finally brought me back to this dusty town, one of my own circles of belonging. Now, to find the old wise man.

My uneasiness has returned. My new friend, Gamal, is sticking to my side, and I'm not sure I should be comforted. Which is he— secret police, potential terrorist, or Green Card gigolo? His beguiling innocence may all be an act. So be it.

As I step off the train, nothing is familiar. For the first time I acknowledge that coming here may have been a mistake. A knot has tightened in my chest where my heart is supposed to be, and I close my eyes to recompose my thoughts.

Fourteen years ago, I had arrived in the blinding heat of day, hugging the shadow of the Coptic Catholic Bishop of Asyout, the venerable Johanna Nuweiba. Now the town is dark and silent. The dark, ghostly silence of a desert town haunted by the unknown. Unlike before, there is no bevy of welcoming priests to meet us and sweep us away in their good humor. The bustling daytime vegetable market with the ear-piercing shouts of its vendors has closed for the night. Like Alice, I have walked through to the other side of the mirror where there is no reflection to reassure me.

Instead, the young sales rep and I slowly pick our way over construction debris that litters the road. The clopping of a donkey cart echoes off the narrow side alleys as we thread our way forward. A few snatches of music or television dramas snag us from open windows, but we see no faces, hear no human conversations in real time. Life has all been prerecorded.

I try to concentrate on getting my bearings, but they're clouded by memory. Finally, I turn to Gamal.

"Do you know where the cathedral is?" I ask.

"Which one?" he replies. "The blue one, or the other?"

To complicate things, I now learn there are two Coptic cathedrals. One blue, the Catholic. The other white, the Coptic Orthodox. The distinction is important. In this isolated part of southern Egypt, the Orthodox and Catholic Copts do not get along despite their both being endangered species.

I pause. I'm sure about the Catholic part, but I don't remember the cathedral being blue. In my mind it was yellow, an aged but vivid yellow. A wave of doubt unsettles me.

"The blue," I decide with conviction. I need to dispel this uncertainty.

Gamal is watching me closely.

Yes, the blue cathedral is close to his house, he tells me. He knows it well.

Voices and music drift from the distance, from somewhere around the corner, and we head toward the source. It is the local youth hostel, the YMCA, where I will spend the night.

"The blue church?" he asks quietly. "That is where you are going to meet your friend, then? The old priest."

On the train, I had sketched for him my appointment with fate.

"The old bishop, yes," I say.

We continue to walk in silence. The air is heavy with night jasmine. Gamal begins to slow his pace. I've been waiting for this moment. Gamal is going to do or say something I won't like. What's his game? I believe I'm ready for anything.

"But, your friend," he finally says. "He is dead. For a long time, your friend is dead."

Dead? Impossible. He can't be dead. I reason to myself: The cathedral was yellow, not blue. Therefore Nuweiba can't be dead.

I hear Gamal saying something about fate, but I am too busy wrestling with logic to reply. I still have to see for myself.

My young companion carries my beaten-up satchel to the door of the youth hostel and departs after a warm handshake and an invitation to meet his family. As much as I've enjoyed his company, I'm tired of such good cheer. I need to be alone, to stretch out my head, massage the knots in my soul.

Now, in the cool of midnight, I sit on the edge of a furrowed bed in the YMCA. Beside me sits the ghost of the old bishop, and he holds my hand. His palm is warm and soft. It is a hand without calluses, the hand of a scholar who has spent his life turning pages.

I'm washed by sadness. I know he's dead. I've known all along, but have continued to deny it. How could I have otherwise convinced myself to go to so much trouble, just to chase a ghost and a promise? Now I know I could. The knowledge does not lessen the emptiness, however. Against the odds, I have wished him to be alive. Selfishly, I still want to see the light in those rheumy eyes of his go on just one more time and for him to nod his approval.

Thank you, is what I'd want to say to him if he were alive. Thank you for bringing me on this journey. I say it anyway.

Thank you for seeding my heart with the challenge to live.

Tomorrow, when I trace my steps to the cathedral, I will find out for certain that the old holy man who led me on this journey is dead. He has also been forgotten by the young parishioners who prefer a more pragmatic, or modern, style. His successor will tell me, when I finally track him down on his way to Rome, that Bishop Nuweiba belonged to the past. That the parish has to live for the future. For the young people.

I will hardly recognize the old cathedral when I find it after first going to the wrong one. The old bishop's library of cracked, leather-bound books has been replaced by a youth counseling center. In the corner is a computer. The musty, parchment-colored walls of the chapel now echo through coats of fresh white paint. The dining hall where the lively monks had shared their lunch with an earlier version of me now seems small and claustrophobic. The unshaven young priest who opens the doors in the morning scratches himself and yawns. He's been up all night shooting baskets at the recreation center.

But that's tomorrow. The future.

Meanwhile, this is where the dead bishop has brought me, and I struggle to understand if this is what he wanted to show me.

Here, fourteen years later, is the future he has led me to. A youth hostel.

Thursday night, the beginning of Egypt's one-day weekend, and the Y is hopping. Sleep is difficult among so much excitement. Basketballs pop along the outdoor court, families drink sodas and eat ice cream in the expansive gardens while toddlers bubble around them. Everyone is noisy but well behaved; only the hibiscus and bougainvillea dare to shriek under the floodlights.

Over the loudspeaker an Arab balladeer laments so good-naturedly about lost love that you can't take him seriously. Short-order cooks are tossing the spicy Egyptian version of burgers—lamb, not beef. The smells, the noises, everything is vaguely familiar. Except for the accents, I could be in an American suburb.

On the open-air terrace beneath my window, twenty or more kids are glued to a television set. At midnight they're squeezing every minute out of the holiday. Their large eyes remind me of my own nephews and nieces in another desert country. They start singing something I recognize and I begin to hum along. *Wim-a-way. Wim-a-way.* The children are watching a video of *The Lion King* in English. Africa is just over the horizon, and yet for most Egyptians, it could be a world away.

Egypt and the children in this compound have more pressing concerns. Armed guards and security men swivel their heads like radars as they walk. Guard dogs patrol the area but not for stray lions. They are on the alert for possible attacks from Islamist militants who strive to keep Egypt off balance and threaten her dream of pluralism.

After a hot shower I'm a new person. I wash down the remnant of a squashed croissant and half a packet of dry biscuits, taken from the hotel in Cairo earlier this morning, with some lukewarm bottled water. I remember the concerns of my friends and check the locks to the door. They don't work. But what the hell, what can I do?

I roll over in the stiff, clean white sheets and forget what was so important a minute ago. The dead bishop, Lena and the tea boy, the Lion King and the Cyber-Copt, they all dance soft-shoe through my dreams.

PART FOUR

Turkey

CHAPTER 24

postscript on a postcard

My suitcase from Egypt lies unopened on the stone floor where I dumped it last night. I pull clean shorts from the storage chest, shaking them free for scorpions that may have nested over the past year, and release the acrid smell of afterburn. I grab a swimsuit off the hook, but leave my camera on the chair. I want to use my eyes, unfiltered.

A year after the fire, fresh scrub pokes through the charred skin of the Turkish village. Workmen chisel new marble thresholds for the old stone houses. The one-eyed cowherd steers his stubborn charges away from the tender pine seedlings and up into the meadows by the ancient ruins. Down the mountain, the sea is still turquoise and its timeless springs are frigid against my skin as I hold my breath and dive for marble pebbles along the floor.

Late afternoon, I walk to the square of the delta village under the still suspicious eyes of the old villagers. Among them are some who last year wished me and my friends dead. Conversation stops as I enter the dingy general store that serves as the post office and gossip factory. My yellow dog stands guard outside the door. I am the foreign woman with the domesticated jackal.

"Peace," I say to the old man behind the wooden counter. His eyes dart around the room.

Black-toothed smiles feint against the nicotine-stained walls. A couple of the old foxes clear their throats. A young herder shuffles in his sandals. He guards cattle on the salt flats and, until the fire last year, hailed me as Sister.

"Peace," I repeat.

The storekeeper looks down at the counter, his cracked fingers, then up at the faces of the men, then at me.

"Peace," he replies. "Peace. Salaam."

I hand him a postcard to mail to my long-silent mother. I love you, it says. Writing these three words was more difficult than walking into this room. Tomorrow I'll write the same three words to my brother. And my sister.

I buy a loaf of fresh bread, which I will share tonight with my dog. On impulse, looking at the shelf above the storekeeper's head, I also buy a pack of cigarettes. I don't smoke.

I unwrap the pack, pulling the cellophane and the foil into a circle. I tap the bottom of the pack as I've seen the locals do and flick the unfiltered cigarettes forward.

And hand the storekeeper one. And the old villager next to him.

And then I hand him the packet.

He roots around the wooden cash drawer and hands me a candy.

In the silence of the watchful room, I place the furry confection on my tongue. My belly, my soul, fills with the perfume of incense.

acknowledgments

I am indebted to friends and colleagues who read and commented upon multiple drafts and incarnations of the manuscript. Donna Giannoulos, Danielle LaPorte, Jerome Glenn, Brenda Bickett, Meena Sharify-Funk, Bruce Curtis, and Marianne Lonergren immediately leap to mind. My special thanks to two writing partners whose friendship I came to rely on: Robin Brown and her alter ego, Amira, whose probing questions, humor and insight kept me honest; and Margaret Venske, who kept me thinking off the page.

Several writers provided support and inspiration at critical stages of the book: David Ignatius, who unwittingly got me started; Ellie Seagraves, whose life is example; Linda Shalwon Kettner, who understands white space; James Barratt, who reminded me of what I am not; Patrick Prentice, who helped me hear my own voice; and James Grady, who kept a bead on the whole process.

A host of visionaries guided the project along its path: Prof. Şerif Mardin, a friend who believed; Prof. Abdul Aziz Said, who primed the journey with wisdom; Drs. Sellama Shaker and Ghaleb Abdurrahman, who opened their home and hearts; Dr. Mohammed Shaalan, who unlocked doors; Pir Vilayet Khan, who teaches peace by living; and Sandra Martin, whose own vision is peerless.

I would also like to thank several people who worked behind the scenes and brought order to a grueling schedule that defied time and logic: travel expert and friend Ibrahim Mansour; Nabeel, Nuha, Dalia, and Amad; Drs. Farouq El-Haitamy, Ahmed Sitki Dajani, Omar Mahjoub, Abdul Hai, and Shareen El-Mufti; Dr. Akhram Kemal Wilson and Father Yohanne; Ahmed Abdel-Khalik, Dr. Lutfi Asadi, and Daad Mousa.

In a class of his own is Patrick Huyghe of Paraview Press, to whom I am sincerely grateful for his keen eye, his love of words, and his encouragement.

Above all, I wish to thank my husband, Rich Bechtel, whose love is a constant and safe harbor.

I have tried to remain as true as possible to the honesty, human dignity and humor with which each of the wise individuals in this book shared their vision. Their words and insights are offered with respect and high regard. Any error in interpretation or fact is my own and unintentional.

index